The Gardener's
Guide to Growing

PENSTEMONS

The Gardener's
Guide to Growing
PENSTEMONS

David Way & Peter James

David & Charles
Newton Abbot

TIMBER PRESS
Portland, Oregon

PICTURE ACKNOWLEDGEMENTS
Karl Adamson 7, 21, 48–9, 64, 77, 92, 97, 100–101, 109, 116–17, 136–7;
Duncan Coombs 39, 124; Peter James 14, 16, 22, 23, 29, 32, 33, 53, 66, 68, 70, 72, 76, 78, 84,
86, 87, 88, 89, 94, 127; Anke Way 35; David Way 2, 3, 9, 26, 31;
Justyn Willsmore 1, 17, 25, 30, 36–7, 102, 103, 105, 106, 114, 121, 123, 129, 132, 135.

Illustrations on pages 11, 12, 13, 15, 41, 42, 45 by Coral Mula.

Note on flowering times of cultivars
In general, the hybrid nature of penstemon cultivars provides characteristic long-flowering
qualities. Under northern European conditions they flower for 3–4 months from early
summer, in milder climates up to twice as long from late spring to late autumn, and in most
favourable climates some cultivars have been known to flower almost continuously.

First published in the UK in 1998 by David & Charles Publishers,
Brunel House, Newton Abbot, Devon
ISBN 0 7153 0550 6

First published in North America in 1998 by Timber Press Inc.,
133 SW Second Avenue, Suite 450, Portland, Oregon 97204, USA
ISBN 0 88192 424 5

Front jacket inset: P. 'Agnes Laing'; *back jacket inset P.* 'Sour Grapes' (Type 1); *page 1* Mixed
penstemon border in David Way's garden; *page 2 P.* 'Cherry Ripe' set off against *Sedum
spectabile* behind; *page 3 P.* 'Pennington Gem'.

Typeset by ACE and printed in Italy by Lego SpA

CONTENTS

FOREWORD

I was delighted to be invited to contribute a foreword to a book on the genus *Penstemon*. During some 50 years of growing alpine plants I have always grown a few penstemons, because their beauty is irresistible. My enthusiasm for the species was greatly enhanced when I had the opportunity of seeing them growing in the Rocky Mountains, in the Wenatchees of Oregon and in the hills and plains of Nevada and Utah. With the acquisition of a bigger garden my interest broadened to cover the larger species, and the garden hybrids, although I did not take these seriously as potentially permanent ornamentals until the recent Royal Horticultural Society trials at Wisley, fully described in *The Garden*.

The deeper one's interest in a genus develops, the greater becomes the need for a readily available source of information on it. It is difficult to think of any other genus of comparable size and complexity that does not have its own monograph, or at least a gardener's guide on the subject. Enthusiasts have an invaluable source of information in the bulletins of the American Penstemon Society, and various brief articles in the bulletins of the Alpine Garden Society, culminating in the publication of more extensive accounts by Geoffrey Charlesworth in 1994 which added considerably to our knowledge, but until now no comprehensive work covering the whole genus has been available. The size and complexity of the genus and the number and state of confusion of the hybrids and cultivars has evidently daunted the most stout-hearted in the past, and the present authors must be commended not only for undertaking such a task but for covering the whole subject so exhaustively.

Peter James has been studying penstemon cultivars and species and their classification for some years, and in addition to extensive research into the genus and its history he has had the practical experience of growing a very large collection in his garden in Kent. David Way has long been an enthusiastic grower, with a special interest in the garden hybrids, and he has studied in depth their cultivation and, with Peter, their complicated nomenclature problems, both in the available literature and in many European gardens, as well as in his own and other gardens in the UK. The authors' combined expertise has produced a remarkably comprehensive work which gives a full account of the botany and history of the genus, and of its cultivation and ornamental uses in the UK, the USA and around the world, with sections on propagation and pests and diseases followed by descriptions of all the species and hybrids. My first reaction to reading in the introduction that all species and cultivars were covered was one of doubt, as it sounded a near-impossible task, but my doubts evaporated when I studied the text. Wisely the authors have described most fully the plants most likely to be cultivated, and have written much shorter accounts of the species which are unobtainable or ungrowable. This book should prove an indispensable guide to a fascinating genus.

Dr Jack Elliott V.M.H.

Plate I. A selection of Group 3A cultivars in which the influence of *P. isophyllus* is apparent.

PLATE I

All flowers are shown at approximately ½ size

P. isophyllus

P. 'Connie's Pink'

P. 'Torquay Gem'

P. 'Windsor Red'

P. 'Cherry Ripe'

P. 'Taoensis'

P. 'Cherry '

INTRODUCTION

To be asked to write what, it seems, is the first-ever monograph on penstemons is both a privilege and a challenge. It is a privilege to be given the chance to write a book on a subject we love; it is a challenge because neither of us would claim to be a leading authority on a genus which is by any standard complex and which has thrown many 'experts' into error and confusion, virtually from the day that John Mitchell published the first account of a penstemon in 1748. It does, however, mean that we have no position to defend nor reputation to lose, which perhaps in the circumstances is an advantage.

The danger with this book was that it could have become two books in one – one about the species familiar to North Americans and the other about the European Hybrids familiar to Europeans. This is not all that surprising since, although it was not always so, the species now have a general reputation of being 'difficult' in Europe and the European Hybrids, derived as they are from Mexican species, cannot take the North American winter, except in the very mildest areas. We shall not pretend that this is not a real problem, but our hope is to show that the divide can be bridged given an understanding of the cultural requirements of specific groups of penstemon, and that, as a result, gardeners in both continents may be able to enjoy growing a wider range of varieties than they might previously have hoped for. We have taken various practical steps to overcome this dichotomy of interests, the principal one being that, where a garden variety is readily identifiable with a single species, we have included it in the account of that species.

European Hybrid is a term we reserve to describe the hybrids based on Mexican species. In so doing we crave, for the sake of simplicity, two indulgences of American readers: first, to allow as European Hybrids at least two varieties of Californian origin, and, secondly, to allow as Mexican two probable parent species discovered in Texas before that state joined the Union.

The European Hybrids suffer from a lack of historical information. Considering that there has been a book on practically every aspect of gardening under the sun, and sometimes several, it is mystifying that no specialist book on these hybrids has ever been published. This has caused us to delve at some length into what literature there is, and to study a fascinating range of old catalogues which fortunately still survive. We have learned much, and have been able to solve some puzzles about the history and background of these hybrids, but problems still abound, as much concerning some of the modern varieties as those from earlier times. It is clear to us that much more remains to be discovered, and that such findings as we have recorded here should be treated as provisional.

HOW TO USE THIS BOOK

In the case of the species, because of the difficulties and disappointments caused by wrongly identified material in our gardens – a problem now reaching epidemic proportions in Europe – we have made identification our first priority. To do this we have followed the basic taxonomic breakdown of the genus. In order to keep the account free of repetitious detail we describe the common features at each level of classification (for example all Serrulati have serrated leaves) then take that as read when describing lower levels. Some back-checking may therefore be necessary. Similarly, we have adopted various measures to keep the descriptions of the

European Hybrids as concise as possible, and we emphasize that to use the 'A–Z' chapter effectively for purposes of identification it is essential first to read the preamble to that chapter.

We have covered all known species, since, due to the efforts of a number of knowledgeable native seed collectors, the range available to gardeners increases year on year. Where we do draw the line on detail, as this is a Gardener's Guide, is in giving only brief accounts of rarer species, many of which are extremely localized and difficult to grow and may never come into cultivation except in specialized collections. In addition, we mention taxonomic subspecies and varieties only where these have garden importance. We are mindful that many American aficionados are as interested in penstemons in the wild as in the garden, but for those who are primarily naturalists we feel that our omissions are more than made up for by the excellent state and regional Floras which between them cover every part of North America in great detail.

Mindful of the needs of southern hemisphere readers, and that the American seasons do not exactly match those in Europe, we have tried to use general terms to indicate time of year and to avoid the use of calendar months. Our gardening experience, however, is wholly rooted in Europe, and there may be times when this shows through in our comments, in which case non-European gardeners may need to adapt them to their own particular conditions.

It is unusual for a gardening book to touch on such matters as flower structure or evolutionary theory, but our chosen genus has so much of interest in such fields that we feel it would be a pity to overlook them. We hope that these botanical passages will not be found too heavy, but at the same time we make no apology for treating our readers as inquisitive in their pursuit of what is arguably mankind's greatest hobby.

William Thompson, founder of the famous English seed firm now known as Thompson & Morgan, wrote in 1855 that 'were we so unfortunate as to be compelled to limit our collection of plants to two genera, we think we should, without hesitation, select for one of these the Penstemons, and for the other, the Salvias'. At the time he would have known of perhaps only 20 species and a handful of hybrids. With the much greater variety now available to us such enthusiasm can turn into 'penstomania', a disease to which some of us succumb

P. 'Schoenholzeri' (syn. 'Firebird') in a mixed planting. This extremely robust European Hybrid has become popular all over the world. It was bred in Switzerland and dates from 1939.

quite happily. So what precisely is their special appeal? As always, different people will give different answers, but three words will usually categorize what they have to say: abundance, colour and charm. Abundance, because the sheer profusion of flower in most penstemons, and the length of flowering season in many, makes them outstanding garden subjects; colour, because their range of colours and strange markings is perhaps only bettered by the orchids; and charm because the form and variety of their flowers, and their airy disposition on the plant, impart a sense of both grace and interest, as appealing to the heart as to the intellect.

Let us therefore without further preamble commence our exploration of this fascinating genus.

1

THE BOTANY OF
PENSTEMONS

The genus *Penstemon* is native to North and
Central America. It belongs to the large family
of Scrophulariaceae, an awkward but worthy
name derived from the use of some members of
the family in the treatment of the glandular disease
known in past times as scrofula. This family contains
over 100 genera, including many of garden interest,
perhaps the best-known being snapdragons (*Antir-
rhinum*) and foxgloves (*Digitalis*). In this age of
microscopes and biochemistry it is most accurately
told apart from other families by features that are
invisible to the naked eye, but gardeners can still rely on
the family resemblances which guided the early
botanists:

1 A flower of five petals which is a tube for part of its
   length, but then separates into an upper lip of two
   lobes and a lower lip of three.
2 Leaves which are arranged in opposite pairs
   up the stem, each pair being at right angles to the
   pairs above and below it. The leaves themselves are
   what botanists call simple, that is, not divided into
   leaflets.
3 A flower which possesses four fertile stamens and a
   four-chambered seed capsule. The four stamens are
   arranged in two pairs, one behind the other. The
   fifth stamen and seed-chamber, which are normally
   to be expected in a five-lobed flower, are missing.

Within these basic rules, the individual genera of
Scrophulariaceae produce many variations of habit,
flower and foliage, and *Penstemon* is one of the most var-
ied of all. As a rough guide, it is useful to think of
a penstemon as something between a foxglove and a
snapdragon, since at one extreme some penstemon
flowers are bulbous and open-mouthed like foxgloves,
while at the other there are some with narrow tubes and
closed mouths like snapdragons. But the comparison
soon breaks down, because penstemons have one
important feature that distinguishes them – they do
have a fifth stamen. It appears as a prominent, albeit
infertile, filament lying along the lower centre lobe. It
is infertile because it lacks anthers, that is, the sacs in
which the pollen is produced.

Any infertile stamen is called a staminode. Staminodes are very common in garden flowers since
in most double flowers the doubling is the result of
breeding that has caused stamens to become petal-like
and as a result be sterile. Though they are less common
in the wild, over 40 genera have them, albeit usually
small and insignificant. Seven genera with staminodes
are placed in the Scrophulariaceae, together making a
group known as the Tribe Chelonae. Of this tribe, only
in *Penstemon* is the staminode prominent, and this
together with some less noticeable features distinguishes it from its neighbours. The top part of Fig. 10 in
Appendix VIII illustrates how these features can be
used to separate the seven genera.

Since having a staminode is so distinct a difference,
why is Chelonae not a separate family? The simple
answer is that the early taxonomists took the view that
the similarities between the seven genera and their
fellow members of Scrophulariaceae were more similar
than the differences were different. It was a matter of
judgement, but we must always remember that, originally, taxonomy was simply about distinguishing and
indexing plants in the most convenient way –
Linnaeus, for example, always held his system of
classification to be artificial, his religious beliefs
not requiring any scientific theorizing about what lay

a) Staminodes, showing degrees of hairiness and shapes of tip.

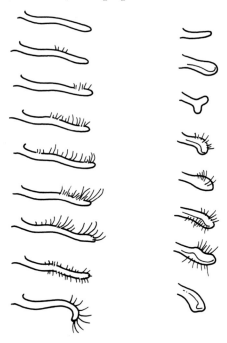

b) Anther sacs distinguish the subgenera.

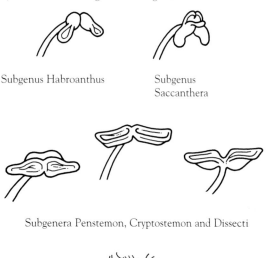

Subgenus Habroanthus

Subgenus
Saccanthera

Subgenera Penstemon, Cryptostemon and Dissecti

Subgenus Dasanthera

Fig. 1. Staminodes, staminode tips and anthers (after
Robin Lodewick).

behind the similarities and differences between species.
Only in comparatively recent times has there been
pressure to reflect evolutionary relationships in our
schemes of classification, and to do this usually means
resorting to the microscopic and biochemical studies
mentioned earlier. In this particular case they bear out
the judgement of the early taxonomists, as indeed they
do for about 90 per cent of cases. It is the other 10
per cent that cause the changes of nomenclature so
detested by gardeners.

Which then raises another question – why should
a small difference in biochemistry be considered as
important as a big difference in structure such as
having or not having a staminode? This had long
been a dilemma for botanists since, with the advent of
even the early microscopes, the number of species
had proliferated as small but constant differences of
structure were revealed between plants previously
considered identical. How big did the difference have
to be to constitute a new species? Then, almost as a
way of shelving the problem, it was proposed that
all differences, large or small, should be considered
equally significant. It proved to be an inspired idea,

since the later study of genetics has indeed shown that
a single genetic mutation may result in a big change, or
a small change, or no change at all.

We can put this to the practical test if we are prepared
to look at enough penstemons. From time to time an
individual flower will show a staminode with anther-
like features: it may only be a small bump or protrusion
at the tip of the staminode, or it may be a functional
stamen with one or both anther sacs fully developed.
In other cases, perhaps more frequently, the staminode
will be much reduced or apparently totally absent.
(These aberrations are most often found on the top-
most flower on the stem.) In such cases, the rest of the
flowers, and the plant itself, is usually quite unaffected,
suggesting that a relatively small genetic 'sport' has
caused these quite big alterations.

The large variation of forms within *Penstemon* can be
summarized as follows.

HABIT

In general habit, there are herbaceous types from 10cm
(4in) high up to 3m (10ft), as well as shrubs and
sub-shrubs, but no trees. Some herbaceous species form

strong persistent rosettes, others lose their rosettes as the season progresses, others again make small tufts with no rosette. Many of the alpine shrubs form persistent mats of twigs less than 15cm (6in) above the ground, from which the flowering stems may, for a few weeks only, reach considerably higher. The European Hybrids are derived from Mexican species which are shrubs or sub-shrubs having a branched woody super-structure, and the hybrids can also develop a shrubby character if left undisturbed *in situ*.

LEAVES

Leaf forms are always simple, but with great diversity of size, shape, colour and texture. Serrated edges are common, in a variety of tooth patterns. The desert species normally have thick leathery leaves, often bluish or greyish in tone – typical of succulent, or xeric, plants. There is much variety and in a single species three or four different shapes and sizes of leaf may be found, often on the same plant. There is only one wild species with variegated leaves, and only one cultivar. All but one species is evergreen.

INFLORESCENCES

Inflorescences – the totality of the flowering stem and its flowers – assume various forms, from open panicles at one extreme to quite tight, clover-like mopheads at the other.

SEPALS

The sepals – the small green 'leaves' around the base of the flower – can also vary in a single species, but are useful in distinguishing some species where they are particularly long or short. In a few species they are typically papery, or 'scarious'.

PETALS

The tubular form of the corolla, extending into two lobes above and three below, is invariable but the flower can vary in length or width from 8mm (¼in) in some of the alpines up to 5cm (2in) or more in the larger hybrids. The length of tube relative to the length of lobes varies considerably between species, as does the 'set' of the lobes, which is to say the angle they make relative to the tube. Through all the variations there is an essential distinction between the bulbous, open-throated flowers pollinated by bees, wasps and

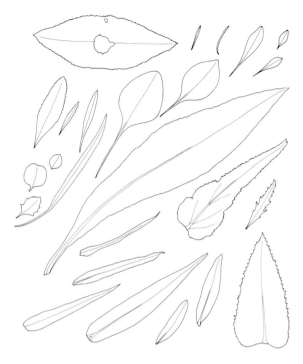

Fig 2. The variation in leaf size and shape among the species and hybrids is very wide, as illustrated by this selection (scale ⅛ life size).

other insects, and those which are long and thin with narrow throats which are humming bird-pollinated. The former tend to be in blue, purple or violet, and the latter in red or strong pink. Pale pink, yellow and white species also exist, and flowers in these colours may also occur in species which are normally red or blue – see Appendix III for a full list.

The throat is usually white, but many species have coloured streaks, usually known as guidelines since they are thought to attract pollinators towards the nectar sacs at the base of the tube. These guidelines are actually veins in the petals picked out in colour. Up to five veins on each petal may be pigmented, but normally they only occur on the lower three lobes. The veins divide and rejoin in complex fashion at the mouth of the tube so that, depending upon how heavy the colouring is, a variety of blotches, suffusions and networks may occur (see Fig. 4). The particular pattern in any one species is fairly constant, while in the European Hybrids it is often a major distinguishing feature.

STAMENS AND STAMINODES

There are invariably four stamens, with anther sacs varying from under 1mm in length to 3mm. In several species the stamens protrude beyond the mouth of the tube, and this is usually a good recognition feature.

The staminode varies between species in colour, length and shape at the tip. In most species, the amount, colour and distribution of hairs on the staminode is fairly constant. These features are helpful in identifying certain groups of species.

OVARIES

The ovary, which becomes the seed capsule, is at the base of the tube, and is served by a single thread-like style which receives the pollen. The style is usually white, and sits in the roof of the flower among the stamens, where it is ideally placed to receive pollen from visiting insects or humming birds. The seeds of some species are distinctive in size, shape and colour, and can be used to assist identification.

PUBESCENCE

Hairs abound on penstemons, and can be found on all structures including flowers, even the stamens. A few species are noticeably hairless, or nearly so. For any one species the pattern of hairiness is usually quite specific.

VARIABILITY

In all, a penstemon species tends to be constant in habit, type of inflorescence, flower shape and distribution of hairs. Leaf characteristics are a valuable diagnostic aid in spite of the tendency to variation in many species – the essential point is always to examine 'typical' plants rather than the obvious exceptions, although it may be difficult to judge this if only limited material is available for identification.

The large amount of variation in penstemons suggest that they have restless genes, and that in turn leads to the suspicion that we are dealing with quite a young genus, one that has not yet really settled down. Some evolutionists indeed feel that *Penstemon* is still evolving quite rapidly, bearing in mind that in evolutionary terms 50,000 years to produce a distinct new species would be rapid. The main evidence is that hybridization between some species in the wild shows all the necessary conditions to produce new species, without as yet having done so.

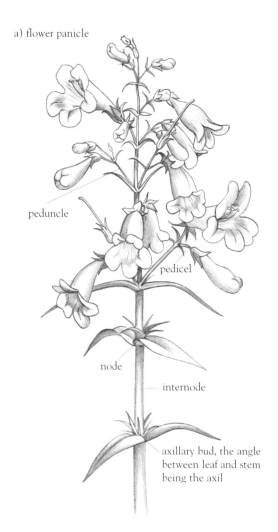

a) flower panicle

peduncle

pedicel

node

internode

axillary bud, the angle between leaf and stem being the axil

b) side view of flower

five sepals forming a calyx

(basis of flower length measurement)

c) front view of flower

two upper lobes

mouth

throat

three lower lobes

(basis of flower width measurement)

Fig. 3. The structure of a flowering stem

A real oddity! A flower of *P.* 'Old Candy Pink' with two fully formed staminodes. This aberration is connected, literally, with the extra petal to be seen in the upper lip. The staminode, although it lies on the centre lower lobe for most of its length, actually arises from the join between the two upper lobes, so if there is an extra upper lobe it can give rise to an extra staminode.

There is much debate about the evolution of the flowering plants in general, but the consensus is that Scrophulariaceae is a young family. This conclusion is based on the fact that it shows more points of difference from more primitive non-flowering plants such as ferns than do most other families. Precise dating is not easy but if flowering plants have been well established for 60–70 million years, the first Scrophulariaceae might have emerged about 20 million years ago.

That *Penstemon* is a young genus in its young family may be inferred from another evolutionary principle known as Centres of Diversity. This simply says that where you find most species of any group that is where

it probably evolved, and although it is a concept not without some difficulties, it is widely accepted as a good guide. The Centre of Diversity for *Penstemon* is the state of Utah in the USA, and it actually makes a good demonstration of the principle at work, since there are about 70 species in Utah, 35–50 in the bordering states and 10–25 in the next ring of states, finally tailing off into single figures in Alaska, eastern USA and southern Mexico.

But for Scrophulariaceae as a family the Centre of Diversity is eastern Asia, and several of the Asian genera are also found in the USA. Thus a picture emerges of the early members of the family spreading across the land bridge to the USA from Asia during favourable climatic conditions, and *Penstemon* then evolving later from some species that reached the southern USA. Successive Ice Ages would have encouraged the distribution of *Penstemon* species southwards, and then repopulation northwards as the ice retreated.

Seeking out new ground in this way would be quite in character for penstemons since they are very much plants for harsh growing conditions, often being among the first to recolonize bare or disturbed ground. Some appear to live on bare rock or scree, others in pure sand, yet others in hard boulder clays. Many are invariably subjected to dry, even totally rainless summers. The secret of their success seems to lie in the speed with which the seed can put roots down deep in the search for water and a little decent soil: it is quite common to find seedlings at the four-leaf stage – under 1cm (½in) high – with a root system 30cm (12in) long and dense enough to serve, say, a full-grown petunia. There are exceptions to the dry terrain rule, particularly those species in central Mexico, the eastern USA, and the Pacific coastal belt from Alaska to Washington State, all areas where moderate summer rainfall can be expected. Some species even have a preference for moist conditions. These, and other penstemons preferring or tolerating 'non-standard' growing conditions of other kinds, are listed in Appendix IV.

Fig. 4 (opposite). Throat markings in penstemons (based on original sketches by Doreen James).

a) Many species and cultivars have totally unmarked throats.

b) In some cultivars only the faintest of blotches and broken lines appear; nevertheless, it appears to be a constant feature.

c) In varieties with faint but unbroken guidelines, the guidelines usually fade out a short way into the tube.

d) Where guidelines are strong they can stay quite distinct and almost always line the whole tube. The area of pencilling in some varieties is confined to the lower lobe and the inner halves of the two adjacent lobes.

e) Other varieties have distinct guidelines that extend over all three lower lobes, and in some cases the markings may also be found in the roof of the throat. A distinguishing feature can be whether or not the centre line of each lobe is coloured as far as the lobe margin, as here.

f) Some cultivars are distinguished by a coalescing of the lines into bands of colour at the mouth, the colouring being darker than that of the tube and lobes. The bands often take the shape of separate crescents on each lower lobe.

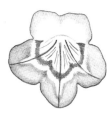

g) The bands of colour on each lobe can join up to give a distinctive 'necklace' effect. A white strip between the throat colour and the lobe colour is often present.

h) The presence of strong pencilling does not always give rise to banding, but there will usually be 'reticulation' where the guidelines branch and join each other in a network at the mouth.

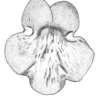

i) In some varieties the colour of the guidelines becomes very suffused and blends with the colouring of the lobes. Sometimes the only white to be seen is small patches in the angle between each pair of lobes.

j) The angles between the lobes may be the focus for patches of colour in otherwise quite lightly pencilled throats.

k) In one group of cultivars the throat markings are very heavy and extend in lines and bands almost to the lobe margins.

l) In a few cultivars the markings at the mouth are so heavy and clearly defined as to form geometrical shapes.

2

A HISTORY OF THE
GENUS *PENSTEMON*

The Native Americans used penstemon roots to alleviate toothache long before the arrival of the Pilgrim Fathers, so it would be wrong to credit the discovery of penstemons to any white man. However, the first scientific record of *Penstemon* as a genus was made by Dr John Mitchell (1711–68) in 1748, in an appendix to a treatise on the principles of botany and zoology. This appendix contained several new genera that Mitchell had found in his native Virginia. No species name was coined, but an impeccable description leaves no doubt that the species was

P. eriantherus with five stamens (see page 13). The flower is also more symmetrical than usual (see page 89).

P. laevigatus, a close relative of the much better-known *P. digitalis*. He was puzzled by the 'style-like filament' which we now call the staminode, and his description asked the question, '*Cui usi?*' – to what purpose?

Mitchell was one of those remarkable 18th-century polymaths. A classical training in Scotland led to a masters degree at 18 and a medical qualification at 20, which he used to practise back in Virginia. Botany and zoology were his main interests and he collected avidly, as well as developing concepts of taxonomy which were in advance of those of Linnaeus and of evolution which looked forward to Darwin; he also pursued his medical career, contributing to the improved treatment of yellow fever. Later his energies were devoted to practical matters like cartography, political economics and what we would now call chemical engineering. In 1745 ill-health led to a move to England where, on recovery, he played an important part in overseeing some of the construction work on the original Kew Gardens glasshouses, and in the organization of Kew's plant collection in the late 1750s. Earlier, in 1748, he had been elected to the Royal Society.

John Mitchell should be better remembered, and were it not for an early taxonomic accident he might be. Linnaeus accepted nine of Mitchell's new genera into his *Species Plantarum* of 1753, but because of the '1753 rule' – which decrees that no publication prior to that date is valid – these are attributed to Linnaeus, not Mitchell. However, Linnaeus did not agree that *Penstemon* was a genus: he accepted the find as a new species, but assigned it without hesitation to the existing genus *Chelone*. In deference to Mitchell he named it *Chelone pentstemon*, making the slight alteration of spelling in the belief that the name was intended to refer to the strange fifth stamen – *pente* in Greek meaning five, as in pentagon or pentangle. This spawned even further modifications by later authors, of which only *Pentastemon* is worth mentioning as being, we are told, slightly better Greek – if 'fifth stamen' is what Mitchell meant to convey.

In fact, when Mitchell's account was reprinted in 1769, *Penstemon*, together with its description, appeared unchanged. This may have been an editorial oversight, but it seems very unlikely that Mitchell would not have known of Linnaeus' 'correction' as Mitchell supported Linnaeus, and the correspondence between them was cordial. This 1769 description has all the credentials of a valid publication – in contrast to the invalid publication of 1748, notwithstanding the fact that precisely the same words were used – except that *Penstemon* had by then been described by Casimir Schmidel in 1762, in a book of plant illustrations. Schmidel's publication was universally given precedence, and is still widely accepted to this day. To be fair, although drawing on Mitchell, Schmidel's description was in great detail and clearly based on his own examination of *P. laevigatus*.

In this century, two American taxonomists, Francis Pennell in 1935 and Frank Crosswhite in 1967, took a fresh look at Schmidel's work and concluded that he used *Penstemon* only as an example to demonstrate the undesirability of lengthy descriptions without accompanying pictures. Much as we can all sympathize with that view, the difficulty is that the Schmidel record fails on two criteria laid down by the rules for valid publication: it did not have a taxonomic purpose, and the author did not accept *Penstemon* as a genus – 'so-called by the English' was how he put it. Precedence was therefore established for *Penstemon* Mitchell 1769 over *Penstemon* Schmidel 1762, although somewhat by default it has to be said.

To some people such labyrinthine episodes discredit the claim of taxonomy to be a science, but, without going that far, most non-taxonomists will surely wonder how, in the face of a simple fact – Mitchell's publication of 1748 – the rules can result in, if not nonsense, then at least non-sense.

The *Penstemon* v. *Pentstemon* debate has also lingered on. Under the influence of Linnaeus *Pentstemon* dominated the literature until this century on both sides of

P. hartwegii 'Albus' – a striking and reliably pure white penstemon under all weather conditions. A 'P. gentianoides albus' with matching description is known from the 1840s at a time when these two species were confused. If present-day stock is descended from this introduction it would make it the oldest known cultivar, but *P. hartwegii* is very 'sporty' and could have 'thrown' an albino variety more than once in 150 years.

the Atlantic, but the move back to *Penstemon* then started in the USA, based on the simple argument that this is what John Mitchell had written, twice: it did not have to 'mean' anything. This view took time to cross the Atlantic, but by 1960 *Penstemon* was in almost universal use. The 'fifth stamen' explanation of the name persists to this day, yet, having accepted that *Penstemon* is correct, this cannot be – *pen-* is not a prefix meaning five. It was not until 1966 that the American taxonomist Dr Lloyd Shinners, also a keen classicist, suggested that the correct derivation was from the Greek *paene*, meaning almost, which yields the prefix *pen-*, found also in Latin, as in peninsula and penultimate. Without going into details, Mitchell's description fits the feeling of 'almost a stamen' rather better, at which point we take the view that where reasonable explanation exists then unprovable error should not be presumed.

NEW DISCOVERIES

By 1753 a second penstemon, *P. hirsutus*, had been identified, and was likewise placed by Linnaeus in *Chelone*. Almost immediately afterwards began a series of political events that brought war and turmoil for several decades to what is now the USA. The situation did not encourage plant collection, but a keen interest in Central and South American flora developed meantime, so that the next new penstemons to be identified were Mexican – *P. campanulatus* in 1791 and *P. barbatus* in 1794 – but both still as *Chelone*. In all, *Chelone* was used in nearly 20 publications up to 1828, although some of these were predated by publications of the same species under *Penstemon* – for example *P. eriantherus* in 1814, 11 years before the synonymous *Chelone cristata* in 1825.

Mexican exploration continued apace in the first half of the 19th century, with important finds such as *P. gentianoides* by 1817, *P. kunthii* (1830), *P. hartwegii* (1836), *P. cobaea* (1837) and *P. murrayanus* (1838), these last two being from Texas before it became part of USA. Meanwhile, systematic exploration of the USA was begun in earnest with such enterprises as the Lewis and Clark expedition of 1804 across the northern USA from Illinois to Oregon, though nothing pertaining to penstemons was revealed until a much more modest excursion into the Missouri river basin in 1811 by the Scotsman John Fraser in company with a leading American botanist, John Nuttall. Subsequently, in 1813, John Fraser offered seed for sale from his London address, and this constitutes the first commercial dealing in penstemons that we have so far traced. He listed what we now know as *P. albidus*, *P. angustifolius*, *P. glaber* and *P. grandiflorus*. Further exploration of the plains and eastern species proceeded apace, with Nuttall as the principal authority, while during the 1820s the west coast states yielded 18 still valid finds to the famous Scottish collector David Douglas.

Just looking at the number of recognized species by date indicates the explosion of activity in the period from 1810 to 1850 – the four known by 1810 rose to 16

by 1820, 33 by 1830, 50 by 1840, and 63 by 1850. (These figures include some species now removed to other genera.) The take-up of these new finds into European gardens was a little slower than might be expected. The next catalogue known to us, that of 1835 by Flanagan & Nutting of London, lists only nine penstemons, including the intriguing *Penstemon hybridum*, plus '*Chelone barbata* in variety', both signs that nurserymen were beginning to take an interest in the commercial possibilities of selected, or even deliberately bred, forms.

The central states of the USA took longer to open up, but the absorption of California and the southern desert states into the USA provided the spur to intensive exploration by organized expeditions, as well as some by the occasional freelance. Although the main aims of these expeditions were economic, botanists were taken along and more and more species were identified. John Torrey, for example, accompanied both the Mexican Boundary survey of 1857–9, and before that, with Asa Gray, the team searching for a railroad route to the Pacific Ocean. Conditions were difficult and dangerous because of war, disease, terrain and, not least, lawlessness – a man could be killed for his donkey, a fate which it is thought befell the Scots collector James Jeffreys in Arizona. In the period between 1850 and 1900, almost 100 new names were added – counting only those which are still considered valid. These were principally from the Rockies and the Great Basin, plus a few in later years from Mexico.

This increase in known species was reflected in increased gardening attention in Europe, notwithstanding the very considerable competition from the spectacular success of the European Hybrids which appeared in large numbers during the same period. William Thompson had close links with the USA – America's leading botanist of the time, Asa Gray, was a friend – and clearly kept up with events there. In his catalogues of the period there were seldom fewer than 25 species on offer, often of forms only recently found. He was particularly strong on the western species, and had a good contact in the West. This may have been Charles Orcutt, who was selling seed by mail order in California before 1885, or a Colonel James Lloyd Lafayette Warren, who, in a rather short-lived career as a seedsman, was offering *P. gentianoides* as early as 1853. The relatively settled and prosperous Californian community, not to mention the good coastal climate, nurtured an active nursery business, and 250 nurseries have been identified as operating in the state prior to 1900. Those that offered penstemons concentrated mainly on Californian species, many of which are handsome and easily procured from the wild; and on the hybrid varieties, but whether these were of local or European origin is not clear.

Although taxonomic interest was maintained in Europe, the focus of effort had moved to USA by 1900, and has very largely stayed there to this day, with, sadly, a rather slow and patchy transfer of information to the Old World. Louis Krautter (1880–1909), Edward Greene (1843–1915), and Francis Pennell (1886–1952) were the principal early workers, to be followed by Arthur Cronquist (1919–), Frank Crosswhite (1940–), Arthur Holmgren (1912–), Noel Holmgren (1937–), Richard Straw (1926–), Elisabeth Neese (1934–) and David Keck (1903–96).

Much as the work of these authorities is to be admired, it is sad to relate that it resulted in both the ill-fated Douglas and poor Jeffreys losing their 'penstemonial' memorials, since both *P. douglasii* and *P. jeffreyanus* were found to be invalid names. This is just to mention two examples for, indeed, name changes and erroneous identification, already a problem by 1840, got progressively worse as the genus grew in numbers of species, and its botanical complexity became evident. (In Appendix II we list for reference some 200 examples of synonyms and errors applying to the commoner species.) To overcome this difficulty needed a unifying hand, and this was largely provided by Keck, who in a series of papers published between 1932 and 1957 comprehensively reviewed the classification and nomenclature of the US species; and by Straw, who redefined the 'Mexicans' a little later. There has also been a reclassification of certain species into and out of other genera – *Chionophila, Leiostemon, Nothochelone* and *Keckiella* – in order to achieve a tighter definition of *Penstemon* in terms of botanical characteristics. This process was taken to what is to be hoped its final stage in 1967 when *P. frutescens*, a native of Japan and Eastern Russia, was removed to a new genus called *Pennellianthus*, thereby, incidentally, rendering *Penstemon* an entirely New World genus.

In the middle of this effort, in 1946, a group of friends came together to start the American Penstemon Society with the aim of furthering gardening as well as botanic interest in *Penstemon* and researching the genus in every way possible. In taxonomy, the first president of the APS, Ralph Bennett (1897?–1978), worked with David Keck to produce a booklet entitled *Penstemon Nomenclature* in 1960, updated in 1987 by Kenneth and Robin Lodewick. This booklet contains all known taxonomic references to *Penstemon* and its related genera, and traces the relationships between currently valid names and their now invalid predecessors.

More thorough exploration during this century of the vast and inhospitable Great Basin has yielded yet more new species, some only recently, to bring the total to 272 – including a couple that are doubtful or probably extinct. Every state of the mainland USA, including Alaska, can boast at least one penstemon species. They are also represented in every province of Canada from Ontario westward, in Mexico except for the Yucatan peninsula, and by a single species in northern Guatemala. Together with subspecies, varieties and so forth the total number of botanical forms comes to around 400. More are no doubt to come.

In this book we have relied on *Penstemon Nomenclature* very closely. Much of the genus is now stable in its taxonomy, but some traditionally contentious areas remain, and are still hotly debated. This is mainly because taxonomists are divided into 'lumpers' and 'splitters', the former liking species to be large in scope covering if necessary several varieties by sub-classification, and the latter preferring to give species status on the basis of relatively minor variations. With penstemons the 'splitters' have definitely held sway, and there are those who feel they may have gone a little too far at times. Be that as it may, we feel that penstemons need a good long rest from unnecessary nomenclature changes, and since the Keck/Straw classification has a coherence based on systematic and thorough analysis of the whole genus, it is to be hoped that any further changes will be advanced on evidence and experiment rather than on personal opinion – to echo a view of taxonomy which John Mitchell, no less, expressed back in 1748.

3

THE HISTORY OF THE EUROPEAN HYBRIDS

Gardeners, like most people, either like history or detest it. To the latter group it is enough that the plants of today are what they are, and if better varieties come along then out go the old ones, consigned to oblivion and the compost heap. Whether or not the plant is correctly named is not a matter for concern, nor whether it is a recent variety or one that has been with us for 100 years. It is a perfectly reasonable approach to take, and in this busy and time-pressed age, one that is perfectly understandable in amateur gardeners – although less so in professional nurserymen. For the other group – to which we unashamedly belong – the history of plants has a definite interest, whether as a guide to cultivation or breeding, or for the simple satisfaction of finding out and knowing a plant's background – history for history's sake, it might be said.

With penstemons there is an added dimension as, with no previous comprehensive survey of the European Hybrids to guide us, a definite detective element colours the subject. Consider for example the following facts gleaned from different sources:

- The 1835 seed catalogue of Flanagan & Nutting lists what it calls 'Penstemon Hybridum' without, unfortunately, any description whatsoever;
- An article in the *Gardener's Chronicle* of 1842, quoting Paxton, introduces the new variety *P. gentianoides* var. *splendens*, emphasizing strongly that it was from wild-collected seed and 'not obtained by English art, through the medium of culture and hybridisation';
- The current *Hortus III* states the European Hybrids to be derived from variants of *P. hartwegii*, or crosses of *P. hartwegii* × *P. cobaea*.

Given these facts from reliable sources it might be supposed that hybridization using the two species mentioned had commenced in Britain before 1835, but a little more delving yields the following:

- Seed of *P. hartwegii* does not reach Europe – Belgium, it would seem – until 1836, sent by a young French naturalist, Henri Galleoti. It was labelled *P. gentianoides* – which it could not have been, since Galleoti did not reach 'gentianoides country' until the following year;
- Seed of *P. cobaea* reaches England from a Mr Drummond of Texas slightly earlier in 1835;
- In 1855 William Thompson publishes a short account of new penstemon hybrids, in which he states them to be derived from *P. hartwegii* or *P. hartwegii* × *P. gentianoides*, and mentions M. Alfred Pellier of Lille (near the French/Belgian border) as the leading breeder involved.

This paints an altogether different picture: first, the 'P. Hybridum' of 1835 is not connected to the mainstream development with *P. hartwegii*; second, *P. cobaea* did not figure in the early breeding work in spite of its availability; and third, the work began in continental Europe rather than the UK. Corroboration for these conclusions comes from a number of sources, for example the 1861 trials held by the Royal Horticultural Society contained many examples of continental origin, several traceable to the nursery of Victor Lemoine of Nancy (France); and the *Floral*

Plate II. *P. kunthii* and *P. campanulatus* hybridize freely in the wild and in gardens. The unlabelled examples in this plate were all 'volunteers' in Peter James's garden in 1997. Compare with the named cultivars in Plate VIII (pages 100–1).

PLATE II

All flowers are shown at approximately ½ size

P. kunthii

P. campanulatus

Two Downie, Laird & Laing introductions from the German *Illustrirte Garten Zeitung* of 1871. On the left 'Purple King' and on the right 'Mrs Arthur Sterry'.

Magazine of 1870 congratulates Messrs Downie, Laird & Laing (of Edinburgh & London) for producing an improved range of hybrids 'quite equal to the best of the continentals and in constitution probably superior'.

And so on. From such snippets we can begin to understand what happened in those early years. Without going further into the minutiae of the evidence, we can surmise that development originally was quite slow. In the 1840s only a handful of varieties are recorded, mainly as red forms of *P. gentianoides*. In view of the confusion between *P. gentianoides* and *P. hartwegii* at that time (see page 78) we can be fairly sure that these were all forms of *P. hartwegii*. The same can be said of the white variety *P. gentianoides albus*, introduced in the same decade – it appeared in the 1861 trials under the telling description, 'creamy white, long tubed' which virtually precludes it being *P. gentianoides* (see illustration page 17) However, at least one cultivar, *P.* 'Clowesii', was in circulation by 1850. From its description, it seems to have been a large-flowered hybrid, 40mm (1½in) wide but only 45cm (1½ft) high.

EARLY BREEDERS

Alfred Pellier was probably breeding penstemons by 1850, and other French growers were known to be active by 1860 – Gerbaux, Rendatler, Rougier-Chauvière, and last but not least Victor Lemoine, probably the most prolific plant breeder of all time. Meanwhile the true dark purple *P. gentianoides* had become better known, but was considered inferior to *P. hartwegii* in garden value. Pellier's *P. gentianoides atro-coeruleum* was widely cultivated by 1855, and is recorded as *P. gentianoides × hartwegii* by William Thompson, who rated it a considerable improvement on the species. In all we can count about 20 hybrid forms known by name by that date. The craze also reached Germany in the early 1850s, and by 1857 Wm. Pfitzer of Stuttgart was listing 24 varieties, some of which seem to be species masquerading under exuberant latinizations, but some were undoubtedly hybrids. For comparison, Lemoine's 1860 catalogue listed 29 – 19 of his own raising, 7 by his fellow countrymen, and 2 varieties credited to John Salter. John Salter had nurseries near London and Paris, and thus probably provided an important link for penstemon trade between France and Britain.

But what of the 'P. Hybridum' of 1835? Did it die out, or did it survive, and what could it have been derived from? *P. gentianoides* is a possibility, although it is not yet clear whether this was in cultivation in Europe at that time and in any case it is not very 'sporty'. A much stronger possibility is that it was from the *P. campanulatus/P. kunthii* complex, since seed of these species obtained from the wild would almost certainly have been well-hybridized. Small-flowered varieties appeared in the 1861 trials alongside their medium- and large-flowered cousins, but it is William Thompson who once more gives us the best clue, referring to the species *P. atro-purpureum*, *P. roseus* and *P. campanulatum* as apparently being related. *P. atro-purpureum* also appears in the 1835 catalogue, together with *P. pulchellum*, and since those names then stood for *P. kunthii* and *P. campanulatus* respectively, all the elements are in place to explain 'P. Hybridum'. It would be stretching the evidence to assume a direct breeding line between 'P. Hybridum' and the small-flowered varieties entered in the 1861 trials: but it strongly suggests that the hybridizing properties of these two species were known to penstemon breeders from an early date and that, as will unfold, is of considerable importance. (See Plates II and VIII).

The 1861 trials provided much information of interest, thanks to good albeit brief descriptions, and to the replacement of those unhelpful latinizations by, often, the names of friends or celebrities of the time. These can provide useful clues, for example when Lemoine christens a new variety 'A. Pellier' we can assume contact and regard between the two men. Among the 78 entries in the trials were some natural species such as *P. serrulatus* and *P. spectabilis*, plus the small-flowered hybrids already mentioned, nevertheless over 60 were categorized as medium- or large-flowered – many more than were apparently known just a few years previously.

Clearly the breeders had been active, in the UK as well as on the Continent, for, besides John Salter, we now find mention of Downie, Laird & Laing being well-established by 1860, offering many varieties of both British and French origin. This firm became even more important in the next ten years, when big improvements in penstemon hybrids clearly took place, publications of the day listing such qualities as larger and more open flowers; colours which were brighter, more uniform and of better substance; bigger and tighter flower spikes; and lower, more compact habit. Such features fitted well the taste and fashion of the times, and they also strongly suggest the introduction of new blood into the breeding line. Is this when *P. cobaea* made its entrance? We cannot be sure, but the general thrust of these advances is in line with the character of that species, and not many years later it begins to be mentioned for the first time as a parent of the hybrids. Some authors also cited *P. murrayanus* as a possible parent, and this is quite plausible: it was a much-favoured species at the time; its unusual colours would have recommended it to hybridizers; and some hybrids to this day carry the green anthers which otherwise are unique to it and the related but rarer *P. rotundifolius*.

Whether this breakthrough came about by chance or by design is not clear. Lemoine indicates that at least some of his introductions were the result of deliberate crosses, but there is no doubt that the enormous variation that occurs in seed-raised progeny was responsible for many more. Nowadays the latter method accounts for most new varieties, since fewer and fewer

P. 'Agnes Laing', another Downie, Laird & Laing introduction from 1869 and the oldest surviving cultivar known, stock having been in the hands of the same family since that date.

nurserymen have the time to practise 'the English art', but we must never underestimate the skills of the old-timers in their ability to predict how a particular cross might turn out – 'art' it is indeed, since instinct and feel play as much part as knowledge and science.

If the French breeders were the first with these new varieties then the British growers were not far behind. Downie, Laird & Laing seem to have been the leaders – at least 20 varieties are known to have been raised in the 1860s by this firm, of which one, 'Agnes Laing' (1869), was recently rediscovered in a Kentish garden (see illustration above). They made a few more introductions in the 1870s, but Laing left the partnership in 1874 and thereafter Downie & Laird pursued other interests. Their place, however, was taken by another

Scottish firm, John Forbes of Hawick, which from 1870 until its demise in 1968 was to become the largest penstemon grower in the world, having eclipsed even Lemoine by the late 1880s.

If there was rivalry, however, it seems to have been of the friendly kind, since each marketed the other's introductions under their original names – not a universal practice even in those days. Many nurseries followed Forbes' lead in offering lists of named varieties, but never to the same extent. In the process someone coined the name *P. gloxinioides* for these new hybrids, but this is of course a totally invalid name, and one that moreover has unfortunately been applied by some to describe any hybrid penstemon, whether 'gloxinia-like' or not.

For the last 20 years of the 19th century it was a matter of more of the same – although bigger, brighter, better if we are to believe the catalogues – but no further breakthroughs seem to have occurred. The statistics sum up the period well enough. In 1884 Forbes, for example, offered 180 named varieties, including 18 new ones. In 1895 the figures were 168 and 26. Of those in the 1884 list only 7 appeared in 1895, while from the 1895 list 36 survived until 1900, and 25 until 1905. Although these figures suggest a slight improvement in the appeal and persistence of the later varieties, nevertheless the turnover was high – a variety was doing well to stay in the catalogue for more than five years. Forbes offered 550 varieties in all before 1900, while Lemoine actually raised nearly 470 before his death in 1911.

DUPLICATION OR VARIATION?

All of this of course raises the question as to whether all these new names were nothing more than that – new names for existing varieties. Faced by such a question, horticultural opinion usually polarizes into two camps – those who say that there must have been duplication, hence duplicity, because there simply is not that much variation available, and those who say that the old nurserymen did not deliberately deceive, for if they did they would soon have been blacklisted by their comparatively limited and knowledgeable clientele backed up by their usually formidable head gardeners. For this was the era of the gentleman gardener, whose demands for the new, exotic and, some would say, gaudy were apparently insatiable.

Every age and every profession has its sharp operators, and horticulture is no exception. The coining of new names for old varieties to revive market interest is particularly unfortunate, while passing off someone else's creation under a new name without attribution is scarcely less so. But in our view the chief fault in this case is with the penstemon itself, for the European Hybrids throw up such a wealth of varieties from seed that some inadvertent duplication is bound to occur between nurseries isolated by geography and ownership. All the RHS trials records after 1861 commented on the difficulty of telling some varieties apart, and we see the same thing happening nowadays, so it is no wonder that some duplication happened in an age of greater breeding activity and slower communications.

On the other hand it would require considerable hubris to offer in a single catalogue over 20 varieties with the same basic description – 'red flowers, white throats, red markings in throat' – if they were fundamentally all the same. Yet Forbes did that for many years, with frequent name changes, and Forbes thrived, so differences there must have been – perhaps in flower shape and size, perhaps in desirable non-floral qualities of habit and foliage. The introduction of increasing doses of *P. cobaea* to get bigger and better flowers would certainly require steps to overcome adverse effects on foliage – not to mention reduced persistence, and there we undoubtedly have one reason for the rapid turnover of names: hard winters such as that of 1878/9 were usually followed by doleful articles in the horticultural magazines regarding the serious losses to penstemon stocks.

Gradually doubts emerged about the persistence of these large-flowered varieties, and for many authorities they became relegated to the annual or half-hardy categories. Nevertheless a mixed seed strain of large-flowered types received high praise from the RHS judges in 1906, and thereafter appeared a number of named varieties which have survived to this day and can offer a reasonable degree of persistence in all but the hardest winters – at least in the south and west of England. The severe winters of 1947/8 and 1962/3, however, must have taken their toll, and contributed to the decline of popularity in penstemons. Forbes appears to have felt the pinch, offering a virtually unchanged list of a mere 45 or so varieties from 1952, the year of its last introductions, until the firm closed in 1968.

The great variation in seed from large-flowered hybrids is one reason why little success has been had with the development of single-colour seed strains in this group, not that there is much incentive to do so since mixed-colour strains, it seems, sell better. The notable exception is the German *P.* 'Scharlachkoenigin' (syn. 'Scarlet Queen'), which was introduced from Germany in 1932. With the medium-flowered hybrids there was more success, from Sutton's of Reading, England in particular, otherwise seed strains seem to have been mainly based on developments from *P. barbatus*, *P. glaber*, or hybrids of these and similar species.

THE DEMANDS OF FASHION

Until the First World War the needs of formal bedding had largely dictated the way in which penstemons were developed – indeed, they became so popular during the 19th century that it was not unknown for whole borders, even whole areas of a garden, to be devoted solely to them. But, in the 1890s, a change of fashion was beginning to grip the British gardening world, influenced by the writings of William Robinson, Gertrude Jekyll, E. A. Bowles and their supporters. Their emphasis on the herbaceous border as a unified blend of colour, with informal romantic lines, did not admit the vivid colours that typified the large-flowered penstemon scene.

Something else was needed and the impetus duly came, this time from England. This was the emergence of a medium-flowered range of bedding penstemons with bushier growth, better foliage, tidier habit and greater persistence. The key variety in this development was one from James Backhouse of York called *P.* 'Newbury Gem', which appeared around 1900. 'Newbury Gem' is known to have been 'sporty' since it gave rise to red, scarlet, cerise, pink and white variants, and to seed strains based on these colour forms which were reported to be quite reliable. Not much later – before 1910 – *P.* 'Myddelton Gem', a favourite of E. A. Bowles after whose house it was named, was raised by Wallace & Co. of Colchester, Essex. At the same time the Southgate (north London) breeder J. Bradshaw raised *P.* 'Southgate Gem' from a cross of *P.* 'Newbury Gem' × *P. hartwegii*. *P.* 'White Bedder' and *P.* 'Hewell Pink Bedder' were to follow shortly afterwards, introduced by Forbes in 1912 and 1915 respectively.

P. 'Southgate Gem' – a hybrid dating from around 1910.

'Southgate Gem' proved extremely popular, particularly in Europe, where it remains well represented in the catalogues to this day. It has a pure, bright but refined scarlet colour, a good upright habit and pleasing foliage, and it is not too large – all the virtues in fact except guaranteed persistence. This defect attracted the attention of the Swiss breeder Hermann Wartmann of St Gallen, who set out to breed a better constitution into 'Southgate Gem'. In 1918 he produced the famous *P.* 'Andenken an Friedrich Hahn' (syn. 'Garnet') from a cross of 'Southgate Gem' and, it is reported, *P. hirsutus*. This seems at first sight an unlikely, even outlandish, cross, but if improved persistence was the objective then *P. hirsutus* was a good choice, and that species might also have left its mark in two other ways – a slight closing of the throat compared to 'Southgate Gem' and the distinct plum tinge in the flower colour, hence the trade name 'Garnet', adopted to improve its appeal in English-speaking markets.

P. 'Osprey', an outstanding hybrid.

Some 20 years later, in 1939, the Swiss grower Paul Schoenholzer released the variety *P.* 'Schoenholzeri', from a cross of *P.* 'Andenken an Friedrich Hahn' × *P.* 'Southgate Gem'. The stated aim was to remove the plum tinge from the colour without sacrificing constitution, and in this the cross was brilliantly succesful. Again for trade reasons, the name was changed in the UK and the USA to *P.* 'Firebird'.

We are fortunate that the actual breeding record for two such popular varieties has come down to us – through a number of lucky chances, it has to be said – with the surprise finding that the entire gene content comes from one cultivar and two species. The same cannot be said for the plethora of Gems, Bedders, and similar types with medium flowers which were to appear between the two world wars – *P.* 'Stapleford Gem', *P.* 'Pennington Gem', *P.* 'Purple Bedder', *P.* 'Modesty', and many others. They have some characteristics in common, such as leaves reminiscent of *P. gentianoides*, but there is no evidence at all to link them into a common ancestry. Similarly *P.* 'Newbury Gem' itself is of unknown parentage, although from its foliage and flower shape the presence of *P. hartwegii/kunthii/campanulatus*, but without *P. cobaea/gentianoides*, is a distinct possibility. If allowed a moment's speculation, we might look back at those medium-flowered hybrids in the 1861 trials and imagine a link, but all we can say at present is that apparently similar varieties continued to emerge during the late Victorian period in Britain and that they carried names like 'Gem', 'Mrs R. Clark', 'Rosy Gem', 'Elegans' and 'Scarlet Gem', with more than a hint that 'Gem' in the name became a code to indicate a bedding variety.

MODERN TIMES

What this account has tried to show is that our modern penstemons have been derived from not one but a number of different breeding lines beginning from different species combinations. There is also evidence that these lines are mostly interfertile, so that many intermediate forms can be recognized. Partial confirmation of this view comes from the great French nurseryman Louis de Vilmorin in his *Les Fleurs de Pleine Terre*. His account of penstemons in the 1909 edition makes a clear distinction between varieties of *P. hartwegii* and hybrids of *P. hartwegii*. In the first category comes *P. hartwegii coccineus*, the scarlet form of the species first encountered in the 1840s, and two blue forms both carrying the synonym *P. gentianoides caeruleus*, and clearly of that species – one in bluish violet, and one deeper purple, both with clear throat markings. In the hybrid section he notes a large number of named cultivars notable for their diversity of colour, and distinguishes two particular sub-groups – one with very large open-throated flowers, virtually symmetrical, like gloxinias, the other similar but with erect form, both as to habit and the upward facing of the flowers. This last group, to judge from Vilmorin's illustration, is no longer with us. Finally, under

P. campanulatus he lists '*var. hybride* (syn. *P. pulchellus hybridus* Hort.)' a blanket category for all the numerous varieties of *P. campanulatus*, these exhibiting the same range of colours as the hybrids of *P. hartwegii*.

To bring the story up to date, four developments deserve mention. First, the apparently quite recent appearance of a group of elegant clonal varieties with long, narrow trumpets, strongly suggestive of the presence of *P. isophyllus* in the lineage (see Plate I). That species is known to be present in one of the group, *P.* 'Connie's Pink', otherwise nothing has yet been definitely revealed. Seed strains of 'isophyllus hybrids' and 'new isophyllus hybrids' were entered in the 1930 RHS trials, giving, surprisingly for a red species, 'mostly bluish shades'. However, a plant labelled *P. isophyllus* 'Lilac Mist' of, probably, pre-1930 vintage was recently found in an old collection, though it has not yet been seen in flower to confirm whether it is as the name suggests. There is great promise in this group, and it would help if some of the mystery could be replaced by facts.

Secondly, the various small-flowered hybrids similar in form to *P. campanulatus* 'Evelyn' are proving to be among the most popular of all penstemons with gardeners because their restful colouring gives the understated effect that so many seek, plus they are thoroughly reliable. 'Evelyn' itself dates from before 1935, but there is little doubt, as we have already explained, that this small-flowered group has been with us in one form or another since at least 1835. They were less prized in Victorian times – 'colours washy', 'of no great merit' were typical judgements – nevertheless they seem to have hung on, and Vilmorin for one rated them highly. The basis of these modern hybrids is almost certainly the *P. campanulatus/kunthii* complex with, in some cases, a little *P. hartwegii* in the genes as well – see plates II and VIII.

Thirdly, all penstemon-lovers owe a debt to the late Ron Sidwell of Evesham in the UK, who took to developing penstemon varieties around 1960, just as they were going out of fashion. His technique was to refine a line by growing seed from selected plants over a number of seasons until he was happy with the outcome. The result was a series of outstanding hybrids in form, colour and persistence, all of which were given the names of birds – *P.* 'Blackbird', *P.* 'Raven', *P.* 'Osprey', *P.* 'Whitethroat' and *P.* 'Flamingo'.

Fourthly, we should acknowledge the work that is currently in progress. Planned breeding became the prerogative of the Americans after 1945, and this is dealt with in more detail in Chapter 7, but recently they have been joined by a small number of full-time breeders in Europe who are working to parameters based on the demands of the high-volume gardening market, that is to say mainly the small-flowered range suitable for pot culture. The results in terms of control of the breeding line are impressive, and the hope is that in time these skills can be more widely applied to other groups of penstemon that may have more limited appeal. Meanwhile, many nurserymen with an eye for a good seedling are at work in less planned fashion, but this is still the source for some very interesting new varieties. When one looks at an old catalogue and sees the range of colour combinations on offer it is clear that many of these are no longer with us, even discounting the nurseryman's hyperbole without which the gardening world would be a less colourful place. Any effort that may result in the reintroduction of some of them should always be welcomed.

4

CULTIVATION

Although penstemons are regarded as one of the native glories of North America, it is Western Europe, and the British Isles in particular, that can be regarded as the seat of penstemon cultivation. In Europe both species and hybrids have been grown as garden plants for over 150 years, time enough for them to have developed a reputation for not being very hardy. Like many generalizations this hides more information than it reveals. Gardeners in countries with low winter temperatures tend to be very influenced in their choice of plants by a concept of hardiness based on the minimum temperature a particular plant is likely to withstand. But tolerance of frost and resistance to low winter temperatures should not be considered as overriding other factors affecting successful cultivation. To the gardener, hardiness in the sense of low temperature tolerance is only one factor in longevity. Penstemon survival is influenced by, in addition to winter temperature, a range of factors including rainfall (amount and timing), drainage, desiccating winds, genetic constitution and physiological condition. Persistence is a term that integrates the influence of all these factors on penstemon survival, and we prefer to use it rather than referring to hardiness.

TYPICAL LIFESPANS

Long experience of cultivating penstemons in the British Isles has led to the recognition of groups with different degrees of persistence. Two species suitable for planting in a border, *P. digitalis* and *P. hirsutus*, stand out as good survivors, lasting 5–10 years or more. Other species which regularly survive at least half as long are *P. procerus*, *P. serrulatus* and *P. pinifolius*. Where the

right conditions exist *P. cardwellii* and *P. barrettiae* have been known to survive under cultivation for 15 and 25 years respectively. The hybrid from the latter species and *P. rupicola*, known as *P.* 'Edithae', commonly survives for 6–8 years or more – indeed, one excellent specimen in a garden in Kent, England, was known to be 26 years old in 1997.

There are interesting and important parallels among the European Hybrids. Experience shows that one group, thought to be derived from *P. campanulatus*, and typified by *P.* 'Evelyn', *P.* 'Pink Endurance' and *P.* 'Papal Purple', usually survive for 4–6 years or more before replacement becomes necessary.

The broad-leaved hybrids are the most numerous and widely grown, but their persistence is never certain. They are most likely to overwinter well as one-year-old plants, but by their second growing season some gaps commonly appear in multiple plant groups of most varieties. A typical lifespan for satisfactory performance is 2–3 years, but there are so many varieties in this group it would be surprising if some did not have better persistence than others. The cultivars *P.* 'Burgundy', *P.* 'Knightwick' and *P.* 'Mother of Pearl' are varieties which are appreciably more persistent than, say, *P.* 'Osprey' or *P.* 'Countess of Dalkeith'. However, because of the generally low persistence of cultivars of the larger-flowered hybrids, from the late 19th century onwards many firms offered seed mixtures of this type of penstemon as half-hardy annuals for those who wished to bypass the issue of uncertain persistence.

Of special interest is yet another group of cultivars, typified by 'Andenken an Friedrich Hahn' (syn. 'Garnet'), bred with the deliberate aim of providing a hardier border penstemon, and a small number of

P. 'Papal Purple'.

similar cultivars have appeared since. They have set new standards for robustness and persistence. In the British Isles they commonly persist in good condition for six or more years; planted in particularly favourable positions, specimens have been known to attain an age of 17 years or more.

A final group, not European Hybrids, worthy of special mention comprises those varieties considered to be developed from *P. heterophyllus*. These typically persist for 3–4 years, 'Catherine de la Mare' and 'Margery Fish' being two examples. This persistence is still short-term and some gardeners may prefer to use seed strains within the group, such as *P. h.* 'Zuriblau' and *P. h.* 'True Blue', which are grown (and accepted) as biennials.

GARDEN HABITATS

Quite a number of dwarf shrubby species from the Pacific northwest of America are gardenworthy evergreens. Some, for example *P. davidsonii* and *P. fruticosus scouleri*, are very widely distributed in the wild and occur at all altitudes from high mountain peaks to sea level; as a consequence they are exceedingly variable. Others such as *P. cardwellii* and *P. barrettiae* are more localized, but these northwestern species characterize a wider group of alpine shrubs and herbs that have cool, mountainous, rocky terrains as a common environmental feature. Such conditions can be reproduced in both lowland and highland rock gardens. Sharp drainage and a rock crevice to fill or rock face to cover are the main environmental features necessary.

Full sun is not always essential, and indeed may be detrimental to some species.

Not everyone wants a rock garden, and fortunately there are alternative garden habitats that provide positions suitable for alpines. Any garden on sloping land offers the potential to create terraces, and terraces require retaining walls. Located to gain exposure to the sun and constructed preferably as 'dry' retaining walls, that is, made of brick, artificial blocks or local small stone without the use of mortar (even rot-proofed timber can be used) and backed by free draining soil, they can be highly satisfactory sites for low-growing alpine species, either planted along the top of the wall and allowed to spread, or planted in the wall itself.

For the garden that offers no opportunity for the construction of retaining walls and terraces the raised bed is an alternative. The only disadvantage is that such features in a garden are so obviously artificial that they are difficult to accommodate aesthetically, and the effect, even if the plants grow well there, is not necessarily satisfying to the sensitive eye. However, for some enthusiasts, this may be the only practical method for the garden culture of alpine species and their derivatives. Beds vary between 30 and 100cm (1–3¼ft) high, with walls preferably constructed in the same way as retaining walls.

If raised beds are not an appropriate choice, this approach can be scaled down – many gardeners find a plant trough more acceptable, or even a desirable attraction in its own right. There are two problems here. First, even small penstemon plants need a relatively deep root run, and many troughs are shallow. Secondly, there are few penstemon species diminutive enough at maturity to be in scale with a trough of typical dimensions of 90 × 60cm (3 × 2ft). Although low mat-forming species suggest themselves for this mode of culture, most of them, *P. caespitosus* being a good example, spread too vigorously. Some species have miniature forms which are more suitable, so, for instance, *P. procerus tolmiei* might be preferred to the normal type. *P. aridus* and *P. eriantherus* are ideal for size and *P. caryi*, although rather tall, has sparse foliage and therefore does not crowd its neighbours.

Scaling down the size of the container can be taken further; it is not such a big step from the trough to the pot. Many of today's larger penstemons, especially the European Hybrids, are sold in pots of 2-litre (6½in)

capacity. Such pots enable multi-stemmed plants to be grown which are often in flower at the time of sale. However, the 2-litre (6½in) pot does not provide the ideal home for large plants for a whole season.

In general the size and growth characteristics of the taller penstemon hybrids make them far from ideal subjects for pot culture, irrespective of the size of container. However, the characteristic growth pattern of *P. campanulatus* and its derivatives is much more suited to this form of cultivation. In these plants the principal shoots have readily extending side shoots from buds in the lower leaf axils, almost all of which will terminate in an inflorescence. Because they are formed successionally, they not only provide bushy growth, but also abundant floriferousness, combined with continuity of flowering. Recent breeding developments have now exploited this potential by providing a series of free-flowering cultivars of limited height with an erect but bushy habit, capable of taking their place alongside more traditional subjects for the sunny patio garden. One of the neatest and most compact of these new cultivars is *P.* 'Patio Wine', which reaches 45cm (18in); *P.* 'Patio Pink' exhibits similar qualities but is a little taller at 50–60cm (1⅔–2ft). Where a different plant profile is desired, the older *P.* 'Papal Purple' will form a low mound large enough to obscure the edges of the container.

Species of limited height with numerous branched inflorescences can also make excellent subjects for large containers. One example is *P. hirsutus*, good forms of which grow to 60cm (2ft). Such plants are very attractive while in bloom but they are not repeat flowering, and therefore have a different role in the patio garden, where they form part of a changing display.

For early flowering the production of container-grown specimen penstemons commences with early-autumn propagation. Young plants of the campanulatus group should be kept pinched, and grown cool throughout the dormant season. Pot on into the final container for flowering once the dormant season is past and new growth is developing. The number of plants to use in one container will obviously depend on its size – say three for a 20cm (8 in) diameter pot and five or more for larger pots up to 60cm (24in) in diameter. Correct

compost and feeding are very important, as is attention to further pinching up to the commencement of flowering and thereafter to dead-heading.

If the standard of culture has been good in the first year, and the plants are in good condition at the end of it, the pots can be retained for a second season without repotting, though they must be very adequately fed to perform well in the second year. The plants can be over-wintered out of doors if they receive protection from severe frost and cold winds. When new growth is well into its stride, cut the old shoots back hard, and top-dress with an appropriate slow-release fertilizer.

OPEN BORDERS

The most common garden habitat for European Hybrid penstemons, and the one that provides the best conditions for persistence, is the open sunny border. A soil that is naturally free-draining is more important than one that has high fertility. If the soil is not naturally free-draining, especially in winter time, a special area can be allocated to penstemons and the site improved by incorporating considerable quantities of grit and sharp sand. On a flat site it may also help to elevate the bed a little. Fortunately, growing penstemons on one site repeatedly is quite satisfactory provided healthy planting stock is used. The main danger with such a monoculture is the introduction of plants

P. 'Mother of Pearl', a cultivar with good persistence.

P. 'Edithae' in its third year growing on a dry stone wall.

that are infested with chrysanthemum eelworm.

Stony soils often grow good-quality, sturdy plants. Most penstemons are notably tolerant of soil alkalinity, and grow well on free-draining chalky soils. However, this habitat is not exclusive to the European Hybrids, typified by such older cultivars as P. 'Southgate Gem' or P. 'Rubicundus' and by modern ones like P. 'Blackbird' or P. 'Pershore Pink Necklace'; some kinds developed in America are suited to the same environmental conditions. Good examples of these are the cultivars P. 'Prairie Fire' and P. 'Prairie Dusk', plus the seed strains P. 'Scharf Hybrids' and P. 'Mexicali Hybrids'. Such borders are also the most obvious position for species which are too large for the more specialized and artificial garden habitats discussed above, so such species as P. angustifolius, P. heterophyllus and P. venustus are likely to find a home here too. A few kinds, for example P. barbatus and its derivatives such as P. 'Rose Elf', while suitable for the open border, need a dry situation.

The garden merit of a small group of species distributed across the eastern USA from the Midwest to Maine is being increasingly recognized. Many tolerate competition and grow in grassland on alluvial soils, while others tolerate some shade and actually enjoy moist soil conditions. These eastern species offer fresh opportunities for garden placement, based on their tolerance of these environmental conditions. Although they grow more lush with plenty of summer moisture, they can also resist drought. Good forms of P. digitalis can be sited in open positions in full sun or planted in damp shade, thus providing a very desirable degree of flexibility in siting. The related species P. hirsutus, P. tenuis and P. smallii flourish and persist under similar conditions. Such species make good candidates for borders containing mixed perennials which, like them, die back in winter to a basal crown. (See Appendix IV.)

SHELTERED BORDERS
Some of the larger species native to Mexico and all the European Hybrids are sub-shrubs, capable of retaining the previous year's top growth but also producing many new shoots from the base. It is a little surprising therefore that traditional techniques for the cultivation of such penstemons tend to ignore their sub-shrubby character. If the previous year's growth can be retained relatively undamaged through the winter and on into spring, flowering will start earlier in the season and a taller plant of different character will develop. Where these penstemons are planted as individual specimens it is worth treating certain kinds in the same manner as other semi-hardy low shrubs such as Salvia microphylla and Teucrium fruticans, which in many European gardens can only be grown with protection from neighbouring larger shrubs or the warmth and shelter of a south-facing wall. Such special provisions are unnecessary where penstemons are grown in warmer winter climates, for example in parts of Australia, South Africa and California.

PRAIRIE GARDENS
The early horticultural explorers in the USA came upon beautiful sights in the wild, for example Nuttall, who, travelling the Potaeau and Kiamichi valleys to Red River in May 1819, is quoted by Alice Coats in her book Quest for Plants as writing, 'The prairies were now enamelled with innumerable flowers . . . and charming

Pot culture – one plant each of the four 'patio' varieties fills a 60cm (24in) pot to overflowing. (See pages 122–3.)

as the blissful regions of fancy.' He was looking at a scene in which *Penstemon cobaea* intermingled with *Coreopsis*, *Oenothera* and *Rudbeckia*. The wheel has now gone full circle, for in the USA there is a current trend to create prairie plant communities in the domestic garden, though prairie gardening demands space and is seldom advisable on a plot of less than 0.4 hectare (1 acre). Under North American conditions the choice of penstemons centres round *P. cobaea* and *P. digitalis* on medium soils and *P. gracilis* plus *P. grandiflorus* for dry soils. Combine these with the grass *Schizachyrium scoparium* (little bluestem) with its blue-green hues, changing to a good orange-red in autumn, and *Sporobolus heterolepis* (prairie dropseed), the latter growing into an elegant emerald green foreground plant. These two are short grasses, which leave room for a variety of wildflowers such as *Solidago speciosa*, *Verbena hastata*, *Viola pedata*, *Ratibida pinnata*, *Rudbeckia hirta*, *Silphium perfoliatum*, *Lupinus perennis*, *Monarda punctata*, *Liatris aspera* and *Echinacea purpurea*. During the winter months the top growth will shelter wildlife and the silhouettes of spent flower stalks will give visual interest.

GROWING CONDITIONS

In the wild, penstemons have adapted to a wide range of soils. In the Pacific Northwest some species occupy neutral moist sites, others dryer, more alkaline ones; the many species that colonize open areas in the Great Plains succeed in rock-hard, dry clay soils; those distributed in the Great Basin succeed in soils derived from sands and limestone; species that stretch eastwards towards Maine encounter a wide range of soil types, while the species from the Mexican uplands can be happy in soils derived from volcanic ash; one or two species are initial sand dune colonizers and many are noted spontaneous colonizers of roadsides where road construction has left the edges lined with crushed and shattered rock. Thus, as a generalization, it is possible to conclude that soils of relatively low fertility can adequately support many penstemon species provided they possess sharp drainage, and hard clay soils can also do the same provided they are dry in winter. In addition many species have the ability to grow well over a wide pH range, from neutral to highly alkaline. To a large extent plants under cultivation show the same properties, whether they are species or garden hybrids.

P. smallii, a good front-of-border species from the eastern USA.

However, it is a longstanding tenet among American enthusiasts that penstemons are not happy if soil conditions are suddenly changed, and consequently they prefer to grow their own plants, or purchase only from local sources.

The tolerance of European Hybrids to at least moderate alkalinity has been proved by long experience – for example the National Collection at Kingston Maurward College in Dorset, UK, is grown on a gravel soil over chalk with a pH of 7.8. More extreme conditions occur at Highdown, the famous chalk garden near Worthing, UK, where alkalinity is at the upper limit for soils, pH 8.5. European Hybrid penstemons grow well at both sites.

It is a mistake to imagine penstemons will give the best garden display by slavish imitation of every aspect of natural habitats. Although porous soils of low fertility in low rainfall areas can provide adequate development in the wild, this should not be interpreted as the blueprint for achieving a maximum display under conditions of garden cultivation. Admittedly fertilizer is not essential and penstemons withstand drought, but it is only when both soil fertility and moisture availability are supplemented that the best performance, in terms of growth and flowering, can be seen. Generous treatment does not seem to reduce floriforousness – indeed the reverse is normally the case – but it can make the plants extra tall and leafy, making them more easily damaged by strong wind and rain. Over-generous treatment leading to excessive lushness is likely to reduce persistence.

SITE PREPARATION

It is a good practice to prepare sites for penstemons well before planting by forking the soil over and, especially where it is thin, gravelly or sandy, incorporating a bulky organic manure or, failing that, garden compost. Heavier, more fertile soils are less likely to need this addition but will benefit from forking through before planting, coupled with a light application of a general-purpose inorganic fertilizer. For summer-flowering penstemons the quicker the plants get away after planting, the sooner the floral display will begin and the more intense it will be.

Although drought resistance is one of the merits of penstemons as garden plants, irrigation can be distinctly beneficial during long dry periods. This is particularly true for the European Hybrids and seed strains, which is consistent with their derivation from Mexican species which experience summer rainfall in their native habitat. The benefits of irrigation can be seen in the new base and side shoot development necessary for long-term floral display. Where water for irrigation is scarce or expensive, priority should be given to new plantings until established.

Artificial growing media will be needed for plants to be grown in raised beds, troughs or patio pots. For sites in or at the top of dry retaining walls, the addition of generous quantities of grit and sharp sand will extend laterally the good drainage conditions close to the wall. Penstemons suitable for the rock garden are almost inevitably part of a plant mosaic, and accept the rooting conditions considered appropriate for alpines generally.

For troughs a mixture of three parts coarse grit with three parts sharp sand and two parts leafmould or moss peat, which suits many alpines, has proved satisfactory for penstemons. Initially no nutrients are added, but in the second and subsequent years growth can be sustained by applications of a general-purpose liquid fertilizer during active growth.

Fill large containers with a loamless compost mixed with 15 per cent of perlite granules. Add temperature-responsive slow-release fertilizer granules, following the manufacturer's advice for the quantity to use. Sharp sand or fine grit could replace the perlite granules and add weight to the compost if this were desired for stability.

Because raised beds are completely artificial, the gardener has control over the physical properties of the rooting zone in a way that is not possible in the open border. Heights vary between 30 and 100cm (1–3¼ft), the higher ones combining good root depth with the benefit of bringing the smaller types of plants closer to the eye. The emphasis here is on excellent drainage. Some advocates of raised beds use a medium of apparently extreme low fertility, a mix of 50 per cent small gravel with 50 per cent sharp sand to a depth of 15cm (6in) placed over soil. An alternative is to create an artificial rooting medium to a minimum of 20cm (8in) deep incorporating soil of a loamy texture up to 40 per cent of the total volume. The surface is coated with a 5cm (2in) deep layer of pure grit. Whatever the precise composition of the mixture, good drainage from the base of the bed is essential in order to avoid the roots being drowned.

PERIODIC REPLACEMENT

The point at which replacement becomes necessary depends upon which group the plants belong to. Persistence is best assessed in the spring when healthy survivors will show their good potential for the coming summer by having a generous number of new, dark green, healthy-looking shoots growing from the base of the plant. Very few new shoots or yellowish (chlorotic) basal shoots are sure signs that a plant has overwintered badly; dig it up and you are likely to find a blackened or almost non-existent root system. The top growth will normally have been left on over winter and it will often be damaged or dead to some degree by spring, except under ideal conditions. However, persistence is best

P. laetus, shown here growing in its natural habitat near Fresno, California.

judged by the vigour of basal growth, not by the greenness of the previous year's top growth.

If a batch of plants die at the same time the need for total replacement is obvious. The awkward problem is gappiness. Do not attempt to lift established healthy penstemons and plant them into the gaps; penstemons resent root disturbance and although transplanting carried out with care under good conditions may not lead to further losses that year, the transplants will be identifiable all season as weaker plants and inferior performers. Filling the gaps with new young plants is more successful, but they will be noticeably smaller than the older plants surrounding them and will come to peak flowering at a later date. Where the level of gappiness is not acceptable there is no doubt that the best policy is to scrap the whole group or border and make a fresh start.

As longevity cannot be reliably forecast, the most satisfactory approach is to plan a succession of plantings, ideally raising and planting a batch of plants annually – say 20–30 per cent of the total stock. This provides more than a practical strategy for combating losses; it can also enhance the display. Among the European Hybrids, plants two or more years old are the

first to come into flower. One-year-old plants, even large autumn-propagated ones, can take about three weeks longer to come into flower. Thus by maintaining a garden population which includes a mixture of one-year-old and older plants, the period of peak flowering display can be extended.

ANNUAL REPLACEMENT

One climatic factor fostering annual replanting is high summer rainfall combined with wet winters. Hybrid penstemons are resistant to the former but not the latter. In Scotland, where the National Trust has a garden at Threave, the annual rainfall is high at 1,279mm (50in). However a range of hybrid penstemon cultivars were deliberately introduced nearly 40 years ago because of their tolerance of high summer rainfall. They have continued to provide long-term colour in circumstances where alternatives, such as annuals, are often a failure. But the wet winter conditions mean that annual replanting is the norm.

In many continental European gardens winter conditions can be quite severe (low temperatures, soil frozen to a considerable depth, unreliable snow cover) compared to the British Isles. Here, following the large rise in popularity and standard of private domestic gardening in the last two decades, it is gradually being recognized that hybrid penstemons, grown necessarily on an annual replacement basis, are valuable as reliably replaceable elements in carefully designed and colour-coordinated borders. As elsewhere their appealing form and capacity to provide late colour make them valuable constituents of the design.

Sometimes there may be other reasons for cultivating hybrid border penstemons on an annual replacement basis. In the UK the European hybrids have enjoyed such a revival of interest that a surprising number of cultivar collections have been built up. Where this status leads to a 'centre of excellence' philosophy, it can become an aim to exhibit all cultivars in the collection in top condition every year. The gardens of Kingston Maurward College, Dorset, England, have been restored to their Edwardian appearance and thus considerable use of annual bedding is appropriate, forming a teaching base for students as well as a great visitor attraction. Any significant collection is bound to include cultivars of low, moderate and good persistence, so after managing their penstemons on the basis of periodic replacement for a number of years, the policy was changed in 1996 to annual replacement as the most consistent means of presenting the collection in prime condition every year.

Hybrid seed strains have been produced, some originating in the 19th century, which germinate and develop very rapidly, so that seed sown in warm protected conditions early in the year of planting can be in flower in about 14 weeks. In essence the use of seed strains is a convenience of scale, enabling large numbers of plants to be raised and used with less effort and lower cost. In large numbers they are often seen in preference to cultivars in municipal and other public gardens. However the use of seed strains is constrained by the restricted choice for there is a limited range of colours and plant types available, although new seed strains continue to appear in limited numbers. Most strains produce plants in mixed colours, which prevents their use in borders increasingly designed to provide colour harmony.

Normally penstemons raised as half-hardy annuals would be consigned to the compost heap at the end of the season. But there is an amazing reminder that seed strains for annual bedding produce plants that are essentially perennials. At one famous garden, Blickling Hall in Norfolk, England, several borders of seed-raised penstemons were a striking annual feature for two decades until 1995. Each year the same beds were replanted and each year the plants were dug out in autumn. The regularity of this feature attracted many visitors. A good number of them came annually to see the penstemons, and would return at the end of the season to buy the dug-up plants for their own gardens. This is not a recommended practice! But this account does not merely endorse the public appeal of penstemons, it has an unexpected practical point to make. Although established penstemons resent root disturbance, and transplanting is generally best avoided, if there is a compelling reason for doing so, undertake it in the early autumn and not in winter or spring.

PLANTING

A key point to remember is that the bigger the plant at planting time the better its first-year performance. To obtain a homogeneous effect right from the start, early and late-propagated plants are best planted in separate groups rather than mixed together because

they will reach peak flowering at different dates.

Spacing should be adjusted to suit the growth characteristics and size of the plant at maturity. This is particularly important where a large group or an entire bed of penstemons is being planned. Such groups may tend to look somewhat 'open' in the first year but this only emphasizes the need for large, well-grown plants at planting time. Vigorous hybrids, notably P. 'Andenken an Friedrich Hahn' and P. 'Schoenholzeri', which have stems which tend to arch over, require a spacing of 45–60cm (1½–2ft). Most of the medium and tall broad-leaved hybrids are satisfactory at 40–45cm (15–18in) apart, as are the smaller fine-leaved hybrids, for example P. 'Evelyn'. The sprawling P. heterophyllus types can be planted 45cm (18in) apart and allowed to merge, but more room is needed for such species as P. glaber and P. venustus, mature plants of which spread out at flowering time to cover an area 90cm (3ft) or more across. The flowering stems on mature plants of P. barbatus, and especially its vigorous hybrids, for

example *P.* 'Prairie Fire', usually bend outward under their own weight or the influence of wind and rain, suggesting wide spacing. However, it may be better to encourage mutual support by planting them 60cm (2ft) apart, or placing them among other upright plants which will provide some support. *P. digitalis* is becoming one of the most widely grown rosette-forming penstemons, each basal rosette having a diameter of nearly 40cm (16in) under good conditions. Since the rosettes themselves are of significant ornamental value, especially with the red-leaved form *P. d.* 'Husker Red', plant spacing should aim to achieve a ground cover of rosettes. Seed-raised penstemons treated as half-hardy annuals need to be planted at a closer spacing than their vegetatively propagated equivalents for the simple reason that they will not have sufficient lifespan to develop into such large plants; 30cm (12in) square is a reasonable spacing.

The weather at planting time will obviously have a considerable bearing on establishment. Properly hard-

A border of European Hybrids including *P.* 'Hidcote Pink', *P.* 'Blackbird', *P.* 'Stapleford Gem', *P.* 'Apple Blossom' (Type 2), *P.* 'Ron Sidwell' and *P.* 'Cherry Ripe'.

ened off plants can withstand some frost. Slow establishment will delay flowering and can reduce the number of flowering stems in the first year. This emphasizes the need for moist soil conditions, watering in and further waterings if the weather remains hot and dry after planting.

PRUNING

Where sub-shrubby penstemons have been planted in large groups in the open border, or where they are integrated with herbaceous plants that die down and rise again the next year, the old stems are not worth retaining for a second season. They should be cut off close to the ground, but the timing of this operation is very important; during winter they provide shelter and protection for the crown of the plant and so should be left uncut for as long as possible. The right moment to prune them is when new shoots are growing strongly and have reached 5–10cm (2–4in), and the danger of very severe frost is past.

Where a relatively small number of plants are grown in the presence of shrubs, or in a wall-backed warm sheltered border, another approach can be used to take advantage of their sub-shrubby habit. When growth restarts after the dormant season, the extent of any winter damage will be evident – it may be light or relatively severe according to climatic conditions in the preceding months. Prune back all obviously damaged shoots to new, strongly developing growth. This will temporarily leave a bare and perhaps unattractive stem structure, but if the plants are in good condition and pruning has been light, regrowth will be rapid and flowering will be earlier than where the stems had been cut to soil level. In years when winter damage has been rather severe, and pruning must therefore be likewise, the plants are likely to be slow to respond. It is the more characteristically persistent cultivars that are the best adapted to this treatment. With an old favourite in trouble it may pay to be very patient if it is not easy to replace, since it may well miss flowering altogether the next summer but be back to full vigour in the second.

Penstemons that form basal rosettes or basal mats and have no permanent 'superstructure' normally need to be handled differently. With these kinds the vertical growth takes the form of flowering stems only, varying in height from 30 to 150cm (1 to 5ft), depending on species. In most kinds, for example *P. barbatus* or *P. hirsutus*, these will die back naturally and will not provide useful protection for the basal rosette in the cold season. In addition the stems of the taller species are likely to blow over and present an unattractive appearance by the end of flowering. Unless you wish to collect seed these stems can be pruned to base as soon as their ornamental role is over, with the exception of the few species that have stiff stems and decorative seed pods, for example *P. digitalis*. Such structures make a significant contribution to the ornamental aspect of the garden in winter, and justify retention for as long as possible.

The lower-growing shrubby alpine species also benefit from pruning. However, the timing and treatment most appropriate for these plants needs to be considered within the broader context of other cultural treatments which are aimed at keeping the stock in vigorous and healthy growth. Without pruning, some of these plants – the majority of them in the Dasanthera section – tend to decline in cultivation.

Two good examples are *P. fruticosus scouleri* and *P. cardwellii*, which are low spreading plants that sometimes reach as much as 1m (3¼ft) in diameter if left alone. However, their performance, in terms of floriferousness and lifespan, is considerably enhanced if they are pruned hard immediately after flowering, and this is followed up by top-dressing with a gritty soil-based compost with some incorporated organic matter towards the end of the growing season. New growth is stimulated and the natural tendency to self-layer provides a young increased root system. Pruning is less appropriate for *P. rupicola* and *P. davidsonii*; with these, cutting is best restricted to the removal of cut-flowered inflorescences.

DEAD-HEADING

Dead-heading can be very beneficial to penstemons, but as this work comes at a busy time it is useful to know under what circumstances it will produce the best results. Although dead-heading is often taken to mean the removal of individual flowers past their prime, in penstemons it normally takes the form of removing whole out-flowered inflorescences.

It is the penstemons that have the capacity to blossom continuously from the onset of flowering until low temperatures halt growth that benefit most from dead-heading. The foremost reason for removing the old flower stems is the prevention of seed development, which acts as a brake on shoot formation and extension. Any growth factor that stimulates a successional supply of new shoots, many of which will terminate in an inflorescence, is likely to intensify and prolong the floral display. Dead-heading is one of these, the others being nutrition and water availability.

Thus the benefits of dead-heading are greater in drier growing seasons, on soils of lower fertility, and cultivars of moderate vigour and flowering performance, such as *P.* 'Raven'. It is more important for cultivars grown under semi-artificial conditions, for example raised beds, and essential if they are grown in patio pots. Dead-heading penstemons which form basal rosettes stimulates the development of the rosette in preparation for next season and increases the potential for a secondary flush of flower the same season in some kinds, for example *P. barbatus*.

Of course the other great consideration is the aesthetic appearance of the plant. The presence of out-flowered inflorescences turning brown markedly detracts from the appearance of light to mid-green-leaved varieties with white or white and pink flowers. The hybrid cultivar *P.* 'White Bedder' is a classic case where the display can quickly turn from attraction to repulsion if dead-heading, or even better, dead flower removal, is not attended to. At the other end of the scale are those varieties with dark green leaves and a brown-red coloration to their stems extending all the way to the tip of the inflorescence. When the flowers have fallen away the shape, form and colour of the flowering stem with its swelling coloured seedpods and attendant coloured calyces can be an additional attraction, as in *P.* 'Andenken an Friedrich Hahn'. These effects are enhanced in cultivars which also have red flowers, for example *P.* 'Schoenholzeri', for these will possess a subtle mixture of coloured new stems with flowers and older flower stems which have shed all their flowers, revealing the colouring and detail of the remaining floral structures. The impact of this effect is perhaps greatest in cultivars which have dark red flowers and highly coloured stems; *P.* 'Razzle Dazzle' combines these effects superbly. However, these benefits

P. barbatus has given rise to many garden forms. The swept-back 'sharkshead' shape of the flower is clearly visible.

can be enjoyed to the full only if growing conditions are excellent so that plant vigour is adequately maintained despite the formation of seed.

PENSTEMONS AS CUT FLOWERS

Soon after the showy hybrids were developed in the Victorian era there are references to their use as cut flowers. William Robinson, in his book *Hardy Flowers* (1871), included a chapter on 'Hardy Florists' Flowers'. Here he recommends the reader 'to use the choicer Penstemons, Phloxes, Pyrethrums and Anthirrhinums'. The high death rate in the large Victorian families made bereavement a familiar part of Victorian life, and thus all shades of violet, purple, dark crimson and maroon were popular flower colours.

Today, time and labour are in short supply and cut flowers are required to last as long as possible. For optimum longevity, water the soil round the plants the night before and then cut the stems early in the morning, standing them in water for a few hours in cool surroundings before use. A few flowers often drop, usually because they have been pollinated by bees prior to picking but sometimes because the plant has been growing in dry conditions. The rapid surge of water uptake when the stems are cut and put in water escalates the maturing process, hence this sudden drop.

Cut penstemons last longer if additives are used in the water, one of the most readily available being Universal Flower Food. With such additives *P. serrulatus* and *P. glaber* can last for at least six days in excellent condition, after which the colour can fade. *P. angustifolius* and *P. venustus* easily last as long, but in these species some flowers shrivel or suffer loss of colour. *P. tenuis*, however, does not easily drop or fade.

Commercial producers of penstemon seed often recommend certain penstemons as cut flowers. These include *P. barbatus* 'Coccineus', *P. b.* 'Rondo', *P. cobaea*, *P. digitalis*, *P. d.* 'Husker Red', *P. eatonii*, *P. glaber*, *P. gracilis*, *P. ovatus*, *P. parryi*, *P. scouleri*, *P. serrulatus* and *P. strictus*. Tests have been carried out at the University of Nebraska to evaluate penstemon species as cut flowers. These suggested that some had a markedly superior cut-flower life than others. Among those tested *P. digitalis* and *P. procerus* gave the best performance, lasting 13 days, *P. confertus*, *P. wilcoxii*, *P.* 'Scharf Hybrid' and *P. buckleyi* lasted 9 days, *P. barbatus* lasted 7 days, *P. oklahomensis* and *P. grandiflorus* lasted 6 days and *P. pinifolius* only 5 days. All were stood in water to which a proprietary preservative had been added.

It seems that the commercial production of penstemons as cut flowers is a fairly recent development. Since 1994 growers in the Netherlands have been marketing *P. barbatus* 'Jingle Bells' and *P. digitalis* and, since 1995, a selection of *P. digitalis* called 'Red Star'. Perhaps in years to come there will be more penstemons suitable as cut flowers for the mass market, with the qualities of lasting well in water and not dropping any flowers. Currently *P. digitalis* seems to be the principal kind that fulfils these criteria, and it is now grown commercially for cut flowers in the Netherlands and Switzerland. It is harvested twice, in early and late summer. A bonus is that the seed capsules are very attractive so that flower stems that have gone to seed can also be harvested.

5
PROPAGATION

The genus *Penstemon* is a plant propagator's delight. The great majority of species and hybrids cultivated in gardens can be readily propagated vegetatively, usually by cuttings. For this purpose a variety of cutting types may be used, for any part of the stem framework of penstemons has a natural propensity to form roots in warm, humid conditions. Furthermore, timing is seldom critical and both simple and sophisticated techniques and equipment can produce excellent results. Penstemons can also be propagated by seed – indeed for some it is the preferred or only suitable means – but in the case of named hybrids the progeny will not be true except for a few seed strains where the required consistency has been achieved by controlled development. In some cases propagation from seed is as quick as vegetative methods in terms of the time taken for plants to reach flowering size.

CUTTINGS

The cuttings of many penstemons, including the European Hybrids, root readily at any time of year given the right conditions. Nevertheless, gardeners who wish to grow stocks guaranteed to flower normally in the next season are restricted to late summer or early autumn of the previous year to start off their cuttings. Essentially the reason is plant size; cuttings struck at that time will be at a young bushy stage ideal for overwintering. Those taken earlier will tend to be too advanced and become straggly, while those taken later will not flower until late in the season.

TIP CUTTINGS

As the name implies, a tip cutting is the top portion of a vegetative shoot. It consists of the active growing point with three or four pairs of leaves, of which the lowest pair are removed. They are the commonest type of cutting made, partly because of their ready availability and partly because they consistently root faster than other types of cutting, two or three weeks being normal.

When possible, select tip cuttings from shoots with short internodes, erect tips and, if there is variation in leaf size, smaller rather than very large leaves. The ideal length for the larger species and hybrids is 7.5–10cm (3–4in), and about half that for alpine and other small types. If the leaves are large, they should be cut to half their length to help maintain turgidity. Most accounts of penstemon propagation by tip cuttings state that they should be 'nodal', which is to say the base of the cutting should be made by severing the stem immediately below a pair of leaves. This is a traditional propagation practice, of considerable importance for some kinds of plants. However, sub-shrubby penstemons at least root so readily that there is no need to slavishly adhere to this custom; cuttings severed in between two nodes (internodal cuttings) root equally well.

'SECOND' CUTTINGS

Tip cuttings are usually available in sufficient quantity for most gardeners' needs, but if for any reason this is not so further cuttings can be taken from the lower parts of vegetative shoots. The procedure is as for tip cuttings: sever a length of stem with 2–4 nodes and trim it as usual. Again, making the basal cut immediately below a node is optional, as equal rooting success can be expected from internodal cuttings. What is more important is that the upper cut is made close to the uppermost pair of leaves. A long length of stem above this point will eventually die, and pose a risk of disease through infection with grey mould (see page 52).

When second cuttings have rooted and started to grow, the twin buds at the top provide them with a characteristically different appearance from tip cuttings at the same stage of development. Second cuttings give rise to plantlets that are initially bushier. This has to be encouraged in tip cuttings by removing the growing point.

SINGLE NODE CUTTINGS

The size of the piece of stem removed to form a tip or second cutting is purely for convenience of handling; it is well above the critical minimum needed to succeed in establishing an independent plant, although there is always the advantage that larger cuttings tend to develop more quickly. The principle of using segments of vegetative stem to form cuttings can be miniaturized for the sub-shrubby species and hybrids. All that is required is sufficient tissue from which a root system can develop, and one or more growing points that will

Fig. 5. A single node cutting of a European Hybrid. Note root formation from the internodal area, and the development of twin shoots from axillary buds.

form shoots. The most obvious form of miniaturization is the single node cutting, that is, a single pair of leaves visible or latent buds in their axils at the top of a short piece of stem, which is needed for both anchorage in the rooting medium and for the formation of roots. Such cuttings need be no more than 2.5cm (1in) in length. This process can be taken one stage further, since to establish an independent plant from a section of stem, only one bud is vitally necessary; thus, once a single node cutting has been detached and trimmed, it is possible to slit the short piece of stem longitudinally to form two single bud cuttings. This is the smallest micro-cutting that can be readily handled by an amateur.

The practical disadvantage to miniaturization is that development is slower, and, compared to tip or second cuttings, it takes twice as long to establish a root system and adequate top growth before planting out. The most useful role of single node cuttings is as a multiplication technique for plants in very short supply – a rare species or new cultivar, for instance.

FLOWERING STEM CUTTINGS

Flowering stems are often regarded as inferior sources of cuttings, with little or no chance of success. However, in the case of penstemons, they can be used for propagation where other types of material are not readily available, that is, in the case of those penstemon species and their derivatives which form basal rosettes and basal mats from which only flowering stems arise. The fact that successful cuttings can be taken from just beneath an inflorescence in sub-shrubby species has encouraged us to investigate the propagation potential of flowering stems of rosette and mat-forming species. One of the most commonly cultivated is P. barbatus, where the leaves on the flowering stems have tiny dormant buds in their axils, just as on ordinary stems. Moreover, it is quite common for these stems to be beaten down by wind and rain, when portions in contact with soil often develop visible root initials. Experiment has shown that cuttings made from flowering stems of P. barbatus 'Prairie Fire' and P. digitalis 'Husker Red' will root with normal treatment and develop into flowering plants.

However, rooting and the development of such cuttings into plants is slow, and unlike the sub-shrubby species they seldom root unless their bases are cut below

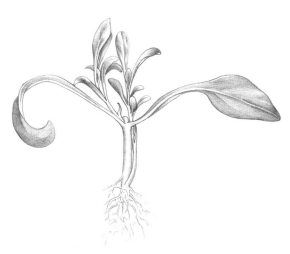

Fig 6. A two-node cutting from a flowering stem of a
P. barbatus hybrid. Note root formation at the lower node,
and the development of a lower axillary bud (buried in the
compost) into a strong shoot.

a node. The development into shoots of the uppermost
dormant buds, held above the rooting medium, is
erratic; of greater certainty is the development of the
buds at the base of the cutting, buried in the rooting
medium. One or both rise, break through the surface of
the medium, and develop into growing shoots (Fig. 6).

Because species of this type have long internodes, a
typical nodal cutting is a length of stem cut at the upper
end just above a pair of leaves and at the bottom just
below the next pair. Cuttings of *P. digitalis* appear to be
less ready to root than those of *P. barbatus* but produce
small shoots from the uppermost buds, even on
unrooted cuttings. In such cases it is better to regard
vegetative propagation as a two-stage process, initially
stimulating the new shoots to develop, and subsequently detaching these and inserting them as fresh
cuttings which have a greater rooting potential.

ROSETTE CUTTINGS
The overall appearance of a plant rosette conceals its
structure. In fact, a penstemon rosette is a compressed
stem on which the leaves are tightly bunched due to the
very short internodes. Short rosette shoots can be severed and inserted in a propagator as cuttings. They
normally root readily, but timing is restricted because
such propagation material is usually only to be found in
early spring and early autumn. The overall size of such
cuttings varies greatly from species to species because it

is the leaves themselves, not the minute shoot to which
they are attached, that determine overall size. For
convenience of handling, and to lessen any tendency
to wilt, large leaves should be reduced in length by half.
A similar approach is used for kinds which produce
basal mats.

PROPAGATION SYSTEMS
FOR CUTTINGS
Penstemons root readily in a range of media that
provide good aeration and free drainage yet retain
adequate moisture. These include mixtures of medium-
grade sphagnum peat and sharp sand in equal
proportions by volume, equal parts perlite and sharp
sand, and equal parts perlite and horticultural grade
vermiculite. Proprietary mixes using carefully graded
pulverized bark as a substitute for peat may also prove
satisfactory, although there are now reports that the
bark may inhibit growth once rooting has occurred.
Nutrients are not essential initially, but can later be
supplied to the cuttings by foliar spray. Commercial
propagators, who tend to use mist propagation systems,
mix equal proportions of perlite and a peat-based
potting compost containing nutrients.

Adequate warmth in the rooting medium encourages
rooting, and so a propagation system that provides bottom heat is beneficial, particularly if successive batches
of rooted cuttings are required. However, bottom heat is
not an essential requirement except for cuttings taken
in late autumn and winter. Otherwise, rooting may be
slower without it, but the results can be just as good.

a) A basal rosette, typical of some
species (e.g. *P. hirsutus*) at a stage of
growth when cuttings may be taken.

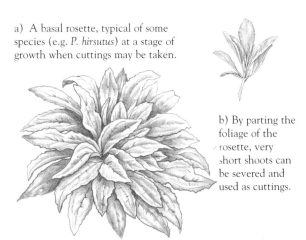

b) By parting the
foliage of the
rosette, very
short shoots can
be severed and
used as cuttings.

Fig 7. Taking a rosette cutting

It has become common practice to stimulate root formation in cuttings by treating their bases with a rooting hormone, usually as a powder. Our experience is that the use of rooting hormones is not essential, but it may be beneficial in circumstances where the material to be propagated or the propagation conditions are not ideal. As with all cuttings, the general rule holds that the woodier the material the more a rooting hormone is likely to be beneficial.

PROPAGATION FACILITIES

Large scale The system of mist propagation on shallow benches provided with bottom heat is well known and widely used. Cuttings are usually inserted in shallow trays or modules filled with propagating medium.

Medium scale Direct planting in a cold frame is a low-cost, low-input system very suitable for the gardener keen on maintaining a substantial display of penstemons, a part of which will be renewed annually. The principles are the same regardless of the scale, the key point being that the cold frame or frames must be dedicated to penstemon production. Choose a sunny site with good natural drainage, and excavate the soil under the frame to a depth of at least 15cm (6in). If possible line the hole with woven polypropylene sheeting, and back-fill with a rooting medium. A peat and sharp sand mix in equal proportions will give good results. Place the frame in position and add another 2.5cm (1in) of rooting medium to ensure a wind-proof seal where frame meets soil. Drench with water and the frame is ready.

Cuttings are traditionally taken in late summer or early autumn. In this system of propagation the spacing of the cuttings is much wider than normal, partly because the rooted cuttings will stay in the frame until planting time the following spring, and partly because there must be sufficient space round each rooted plant to allow you to use a sharp trowel at planting-out time and remove each plant separately with its root ball. A convenient spacing is 7 × 10cm (2½ × 4in). Choose a dull day for insertion if you can. Water the cuttings in progressively as you fill the frame, using a dilute foliar feed. When the frame is full or, less satisfactorily, after each batch if you spread the process over several days, lay a sheet of very lightweight clear polythene film directly on top of the cuttings and sprinkle it *lightly* with water from a fine-rose watering can. This will bed the plastic down into direct contact with the cuttings and minimize the air space round the tops, thus maximizing the conditions required to keep them turgid. Because the tops of cuttings have to support the weight of the polythene, the latter must be of the thinnest grade you can obtain – 15 microns is ideal. (The wrapping used by dry cleaning shops can be reused for this purpose.) Then close the frame and provide shading. Once you have gained confidence with the system you can safely leave the frame unattended for two weeks at this stage. The use of contact polythene greatly increases the efficiency and ease of cold frame propagation.

After about 14 days inspect the frame. The tops of the cuttings will have grown and bent over, but this is not cause for concern. Check the cuttings for rooting. If the weather is not too hot and sunny the shading can be removed if the polythene is left in place a little longer as the condensation which forms on its undersurface provides additional shading. The contact polythene film can be removed within a further ten days; all cuttings should by then have rooted. As the cuttings grow and develop, keep the tips pinched to produce multi-stemmed, bushy plants, look out for aphids and ventilate the frame during mild weather from midwinter onwards. Watch carefully for signs of grey mould infection, that is, cuttings dying back to soil level or below, and at the first sign spray with a suitable fungicide. In late spring the glass or plastic lights can be removed altogether. Keep the compost moist, periodically drenching it with further dilute foliar feed.

Of course there are alternative ways of using a cold frame. It has much in common with a small cold glasshouse, and both can be used in similar ways to accommodate cuttings inserted in modules, trays or pots. In the glasshouse these may be placed in a closed case, but in the cold frame some less bulky container is called for, such as a very large plastic bag used horizontally or a proprietary rigid cover designed to fit the size of tray being used. The cuttings will need to be kept shaded and high humidity maintained, and under ideal conditions they should be ready for potting up within four weeks. If the cuttings have been taken very late in the season, potting up will cause undesirable root disturbance at a time when growth is minimal; in such circumstances potting is best left until growth resumes in late winter/early spring.

Small scale When only a small number of plants is required, or where conventional propagation facilities are not available, you can use a domestic windowsill. Select 12.5cm (5in) diameter 'half' pots (shallower than the standard type), and after filling them with rooting medium, insert 4–5 cuttings round the edge and one to fill the middle. Enclose the pot in a polythene bag and place on a sunny windowsill, but be prepared to use a shade screen until rooting has taken place and the polythene can be removed. Keep in cool, well-lit conditions all winter and pot up in spring.

New possibilities – pots The very considerable advantages of the dedicated cold frame directly planted with cuttings that will develop in situ until it is time to plant out have already been emphasized. Can the same advantages (low inputs, low costs and really large plants ready for planting early in the season) be achieved in another way? Although it cannot be claimed that the following system has borne the test of time, experience with it so far has convincingly demonstrated its potential as an alternative approach.

This is a pot-based system designed for the sub-shrubby species suitable for the border and the numerous European Hybrids. Instead of starting with one small newly rooted cutting which must be potted up and later potted on, all this is bypassed by starting with the usual end point, a standard 2-litre (6½in) pot. This is only half-filled with a rooting medium containing nutrients, preferably as slow-release granules, leaving the pot rim standing 6cm (2⅓in) above the medium. Into this are inserted three or preferably five tip cuttings, with their tops just below the pot rim. Water the cuttings in and cover each pot over with tightly stretched kitchen clingfilm (plastic wrap). Stand the pots in a sunny position in the open, in a frame or on a glasshouse bench with bottom heat, and give them shade. The cuttings will root in about 2–3 weeks and start to produce extending shoots. Nothing further needs to be done until the new shoots make their presence obvious by pushing up the cover, indicating a successful 'take'. At this stage remove the shading and, to provide ventilation, make two cross-shaped slits in the cover. The pots can be left like this for about two more weeks, gradually increasing the ventilation by tearing the cross slits more fully open. After this the cover can be removed completely and the cuttings allowed to overwinter normally.

Plants with a small root system in a large volume of rooting medium have inferior overwintering prospects, so one of the objects of this system is to fill the relatively large volume of rooting medium with roots before growth stops. This is one reason for inserting several cuttings. When growth resumes at the end of the dormant season, you can take advantage of a notable feature of penstemon physiology – the ease with which many layer naturally. This is encouraged by a warm, moist environment and direct soil contact, so fill the pots to just below the rim with a suitable potting compost. This will cover the lower part of the stems, which will root into it. After roughly two further months of growth each pot will contain the equivalent of a single large multi-stemmed plant providing a high flowering potential. Experience so far shows that, in comparison with large plants raised in a dedicated cold frame, plants propagated by this technique establish themselves more rapidly and flower appreciably earlier.

New possibilities – open garden In the UK and Germany success has been reported with so-called 'winter cuttings' of European Hybrids inserted directly into garden soil. Sections of the lower, woody region of one-year shoots approximately 15cm (6in) long have been inserted for one-half to two-thirds their length in the open ground without protection. Timing has been late autumn in advance of the onset of frosts severe enough to freeze the soil. Under the cool damp conditions at this time of year the cuttings do not wilt and appear very resistant to low temperatures.

LAYERING

Among the species, layering is particularly effective with some members of the Dasanthera and Ericopsis sections. The plants layer themselves naturally and the rate of increase can be accelerated by mounding the multi-stemmed clumps. A similar procedure is also very effective with the commonly grown dwarf evergreen P. pinifolius. In western Europe the larger sub-shrubby species and the European Hybrids developed from some of them also root naturally from growing stems, but in a rather haphazard way. In parts of Australia and South Africa with good summer rainfall they self-layer very freely indeed. It is only the fallen stems that normally form roots, so you can take advantage of this natural tendency by carefully bending shoots over and, when they have matured and become firm in summer, mounding them with a rooting

Fig 8. Two-litre (6¹/₂ in) pot propagation.

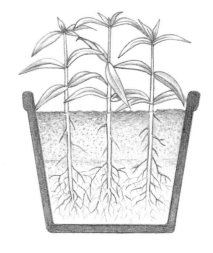

a) In 2-litre (6¹/₂ in) pot propagation, the pot is half-filled with compost into which cuttings are inserted. Their tips are below the cling-film (plastic wrap) stretched across the top.

b) Once the cuttings have rooted and extended well above the rim of the pot, more compost is added.

medium. Buds will break along the length of the horizontal shoot, the new growths forcing their way up through the compost. When good root systems have formed, the shoot can be detached, severed into its component units and each one potted or planted out. It is a useful technique for relatively small-scale propagation and valuable in circumstances where cuttings are not an easy option.

DIVISION

As a general rule most of the European Hybrids do not lend themselves easily to division, but this is no hardship because they root so readily from cuttings. However, for those species and their derivatives that form basal rosettes, for example *P. digitalis* or basal mats, for example *P. euglaucus*, division is a simple and important method. As growth commences in early spring, lift established plants and tease the crowns apart into sturdy units, each with at least one growing point. Some species form tough crowns that require equally tough methods to sever them; if necessary use a compact pruning saw. The individual sections can be directly transplanted into their new flowering positions, or potted, as desired.

The persistence of many of the dwarfer, early flowering penstemons suitable for rock gardens and raised beds, such as *P. cardwellii, P. linarioides, P. scariosus* and *P. barrettiae*, can be maintained by a process of rejuve-

nation which in essence is a form of division. Just after the plants have finished flowering and have formed new shoots, water them thoroughly. On the following day dig them up one at a time and split them apart so that every shoot has a section with roots attached. Each section can then be potted and kept in a plunge frame until planted out in autumn, or alternatively kept over winter in a cold frame and planted out in spring. If these potted divisions are planted closely in clumps, by flowering time they will appear as large thriving plants.

SEED

In recent years a much wider range of penstemon seed has become available. There are two broad categories of penstemon for which propagation from seed is the most convenient, or in some cases the only, method. By far the larger category is made up by the many species now being offered by specialist seedsmen and seed exchange schemes. The species offered range from dwarf subshrubs and others needing the specialized conditions of the rock garden, scree or raised bed to larger species. Among the latter are a number which comprise some of the principal decorative kinds that flourish in the modern penstemon border, for example *P. heterophyllus* and *P. hartwegii*, but for both of these vegetative propagation remains an easy alternative. A smaller category is the large-flowered hybrids offered by seedsmen. Although essentially perennials, these are normally offered as half-hardy annuals. They are largely derived from, and rival in display, many of the named hybrid cultivars (but these must be propagated vegetatively to preserve their individual identity, as their seed rarely comes true).

If seed comes from a commercial source, there is a natural tendency to take the advice given on the packet, or in the catalogue, regarding sowing conditions and timing. However, not all packets containing the same kind of seed carry the same kind of advice on how it should be handled, so some knowledge of the variation in germination patterns and requirements across various kinds of penstemons is useful to the gardener keen to try the wide range of penstemon seed available today.

GERMINATION REQUIREMENTS

Research has shown that among the many species and hybrids there are four main types of germination requirement:

1. Some kinds, including most mountain species from the Rockies, germinate best over a protracted period at 4°C (40°F); for these penstemons the normal glasshouse raising temperature of 21°C (70°F) can be fatal. To obtain adequate germination many kinds need to be subjected to an initial period of low temperature to stimulate subsequent germination at a higher temperature. This procedure is often referred to as chilling treatment, or stratification.

2. A few species, typified by P. whippleanus and P. pinifolius, and probably Mexican species such as P. hartwegii and P. gentianoides plus most of the large-flowered hybrid seed strains, germinate rapidly at 21°C (70°F). Chilling is ineffectual but not harmful if the seeds are subsequently germinated at the correct temperature. This is fortunate because some seed packets carry this instruction while others containing the same kind of seed do not. If sown early in the growing season under protected conditions, such as a glasshouse or frame where the necessary temperature can be maintained, flowering takes place the same year, in many kinds within 4–5 months from germination.

3. Some plains and lowland species, for example P. grandiflorus and P. hirsutus, have a decided requirement for a period of dry storage prior to germination. If the seeds of these kinds are sown

without prior dry storage they can wrongly be dismissed as non-viable. Dry storage is an ill-defined term, commonly taken to mean six months storage in a non-humid atmosphere at room temperature. It is worth noting that the seedpods of some species remain tightly closed while on the plant all winter, providing in situ dry storage.

4. It has recently been recognized that whereas the seed of most kinds germinates in the dark, there are some that need light to allow the process of germination to begin. An example of this group is P. digitalis.

Where the germination requirement of a batch of seed is unknown, it may be wise to adopt a two-part strategy. Pre-chill half the seed at 4°C (40°F) for at least four weeks, and then sow at 21°C (70°F). The other half can be stored dry for six months and then sown. It is also worth while returning pots of sown seed that have not germinated by the middle of the growing season to the refrigerator for a month, or just retaining pots of sown but ungerminated seed until the following season, or even the season after if weeds and liverwort can be kept at bay. You will often get a surprise!

In common with many other flower seeds, packets of penstemon seed bear no 'best before' or 'use by' date. The gardener is therefore usually unaware of the age of the seed he or she has acquired, as well as the duration of its viability. Fortunately penstemon seed usually seems to have long viability, and there is even some evidence to suggest germination may improve with storage for up to five years or more. There are well-authenticated records of the seed of some species remaining highly viable over long periods of dry storage – 22 years in the case of P. rubicundus and 10 years in the case of P. grahamii – so seed of unknown history is at least worthy of an attempt to germinate it.

PROCEDURES

Seed that is thought to benefit from chilling treatment prior to being germinated at 21°C (70°F) is most easily handled by placing it in a zip-lock plastic bag mixed with a small quantity of damp fine sand. Insert a plastic name label and reseal. A batch of such bags can then be rolled into a cylindrical shape and held together with an elastic band to make a convenient pack to place in the refrigerator. Inspect regularly as germination may often occur at this stage. After 4–8 weeks the seed is removed and sown in trays (flats) or pots, using an appropriate seed compost. As an alternative to a proprietary seed compost, use the same mix recommended for cuttings or a mixture of two parts by volume sharp sand, two parts horticultural perlite and one part moss peat. Press the seed into the surface of the compost and cover it with fine compost or fine grit to a depth of 2mm (1⁄16in) (except for light-requiring kinds, which should be left uncovered). Once germinated, keep both types watered with a general-purpose soluble fertilizer.

For rapid growth root disturbance should be avoided, so as soon as possible prick out the seedlings singly into small pots initially, and be prepared to pot on into larger ones. At this stage a general proprietary potting compost is normal, but if a peat-based compost is used, the addition of 15 per cent of fine horticultural grit is beneficial. Shade from bright sunlight until well-established. Seed sown in late winter can produce plants of the border hybrids ready for planting out by mid to late spring which will be in flower by early to midsummer. This is the traditional timing and method for seed-raised large-flowered border hybrids, though surprisingly good results can be obtained from later planted stock which will provide a later peak flowering in late summer and early autumn. This can be achieved by sowing later or holding plants back by keeping them pinched and potting on again.

Those kinds of penstemon which require a germination temperature of 4°C (40°F) need to be sown first and then placed in a refrigerator. They are slow to germinate and may do so gradually over a period of three months. Much still needs to be learnt about seed germination of many of the species.

All this said, there is still a body of enthusiasts who simply plant seed in pots in mid-winter and leave it in the open to be subject to all weathers, arguing that this is how it happens in nature. This takes some courage with scarce, tiny and sometimes expensive seed, but a layer of grit or a plastic bag over the pot will usually keep it safe. The results are often very rewarding. Once germination begins the pot should be given more sheltered conditions.

Plate III (overleaf). Hybrid seed gives good results, whether from commercial seed strains or from seed collected from the garden.

PLATE III

All flowers are shown at approximately ½ size

P. barbatus 'Nanus

Ex large-flowered hybrid

Ex P. 'Blackbird'

P. 'Scharf Hybrid'

P. 'Scarlet Q
form with gu

P. 'Scharf Hybrid'

Ex P. 'Cherry Ripe'

Ex large-flowered hybrid

P. 'Scarlet Queen' – form
with unmarked throat

6

PESTS, DISEASES AND DISORDERS

Under normal garden conditions penstemons are remarkably free from serious damage by pests and diseases, although from time to time problems do occur. This chapter is designed to help the penstemon grower recognize the symptoms of ill health and their causes and to take appropriate action. A knowledge of possible pests and diseases is also useful in avoiding the accidental introduction of problems on plants from suspect sources.

PESTS

APHIDS

Aphids (frequently called greenfly, although they occur in several colours according to species) are common garden pests but vary considerably in importance as pests of penstemons according to geography and culture.

In the more northern countries of Western Europe aphids can cause leaf discoloration but are not usually a serious pest of plants in the garden; control measures are seldom justified. However, they can be a dangerous pest during the propagation phase. Penstemons in frames, glasshouses or plastic tunnels are much more prone to attack. Here aphids can directly damage growth and pose the threat of virus infection by acting as vectors of such diseases. Keep a careful check and apply a suitable aphicide as soon as an infestation appears.

Aphids are a more serious pest of penstemons in North American gardens, where they may be found in large numbers feeding on leaves, stems and even flowers. Under such attack symptoms may include leaf curling and discoloration. The aphids may excrete honeydew, making the plants sticky and unsightly. In severe cases wilting and death may result.

EELWORMS (NEMATODES)

In Western Europe eelworm is commonly regarded as the most important pest of penstemons. It can be a serious pest in nurseries and some large public gardens, but in the small domestic garden it seems less of a problem. The principal species infesting penstemons in Europe is the chrysanthemum eelworm, also known as leaf and bud eelworm (*Aphelenchoides ritzemabosi*). This species can attack a wide range of garden plants including asters, chrysanthemums, dahlias, doronicums, phlox and verbenas as well as penstemons. Several common garden weeds, especially groundsel, sow thistle, chickweed and buttercup, are also hosts of this eelworm. Infestation can take place at any stage of growth from cutting to mature plant. Eelworms move over wet surfaces in films of water. These microscopic pests, about 1mm long, feed and breed externally in buds and leaf axils as well as internally within the plant's tissues, entering through small wounds and natural openings.

Because eelworms tend to move upwards, symptoms are first seen towards the base of the plant. Initial yellow-green blotching turns to leaf browning and gradually extends to leaves higher and higher up the stems. The older infested leaves dry out and turn brown, and some drop off. Severely infested and weakened plants consequently have a reduced number of shoots, which, together with leaf loss and many brown and dry leaves, can give the plant a very open appearance. At an advanced stage green leaves may only remain towards the shoot tips. Early infestation prevents flowering and can kill the plant in 2–3 months. Symptoms of chrysanthemum eelworm infestation in penstemons can be confused with die back (see page 52) and complicated by simultaneous infestation with spider mites (see below).

Although chemical control measures are available to the commercial producer they are not to the gardener, who must look primarily to avoidance and prevention. If you have not had chrysanthemum eelworm problems in other susceptible garden plants or weeds, the likelihood of infested plant debris blowing into your garden is normally remote. Therefore the best line of defence is to keep your garden eelworm-free by scrutinizing all newly acquired stock closely for symptoms that might indicate eelworm damage. Newly acquired plants are almost invariably potted ones and they will often have come from a nursery. Such plants are likely to have been standing in close proximity to other potted penstemons on a concrete or plastic surface and given overall watering. Because eelworms travel in films of water, the conditions on nursery sites favour their spread from pot to pot. If the plants are young and need to be grown on, stand them away from your own young stock and check that no symptoms appear before planting out. Destroy suspicious-looking plants by burning or deep-burying pot, compost and plant.

Long-term persistence in dry plant debris is possible, but eelworms normally only survive in dead leaves and other tissues for about three months, less in bare soil. If infested plants are found in borders or beds not only should the plant be destroyed but the site should be kept weed-free and not replanted with penstemons or other susceptible garden plants in the same growing season. Since most penstemons are planted early in the growing season this will effectively mean a time gap of six or more months during which all eelworms initially living in the soil should have died out. However, if you wish to replant penstemons on the same site, the soil should be deeply dug towards the end of the dormant season. Groups of one cultivar planted in a border showing symptoms of eelworm infestation where surrounding groups of other cultivars are healthy is a good indication of contamination or infestation at the propagation stage.

In North America different species of root knot eelworms (*Meliodogyne* spp.) attack penstemons, causing plants to wilt, turn yellow and die. The females enter the roots where they feed until mature, in the process causing small or large swellings to form on the roots. These galls (known as root knots) are the chief diagnostic symptom, but because root galls can be induced through other means, expert diagnosis may be needed. Destroy infested plants by burning. If contamination occurs in the propagation unit, steam-sterilize all materials and utensils used for propagation; in the garden, keep the infested site bare and fallow for at least one year. There are no chemicals suitable for garden use.

SPIDER MITES

The glasshouse red spider mite (*Tetranychus urticae*) is a severe pest of many glasshouse-grown crops and plants, and in long periods of hot, dry weather it can be an outdoor pest on many half-hardy plants, including penstemons. As they are only 0.6mm long these pale yellow to green mites are difficult to see with the naked eye, and a magnifying glass, or better still a hand lens, is a great help in identifying them. They may be easier to see if you stimulate movement by holding a suspect leaf close to your mouth and blowing on the under surface.

Spider mites breed and multiply very rapidly in hot, dry conditions after emerging from cracks and crevices in the glasshouse, where they overwinter. They feed on the undersides of the leaves, mainly along the veins, causing a mottling of fine white dots on the upper surface. If no action is taken the lower leaves of glasshouse plants will dry up and may fall off. In the border the leaves may curl downwards, with yellow or bronze patches appearing over the areas on the underside where feeding is most concentrated. In severe cases the worst affected leaves may turn brown, and some may fall off.

Infestation by spider mites is most problematic at the propagation stage. Small plants are more at risk of serious damage than large ones, and infested plants will carry the mites with them into beds and borders when they are planted out. On a domestic scale penstemons are most likely to become infested when propagated and grown on in glasshouses in the company of other plants. If necessary seek advice on the use of a suitable chemical control product. Because cool damp conditions suppress spider mites, it is a good policy to harden off glasshouse-grown plants as early as possible under outdoor conditions. The cool and damper conditions associated with cold frame propagation give this system of plant production the advantage that infestation by spider mites at the propagation stage is extremely unlikely.

DISEASES AND DISORDERS
DIE BACK
Some of the shrubby species, especially those forming evergreen mounds (notably those in the subgenus Dasanthera), may suddenly suffer the loss of a sector of their stem structure; the leaves turn brown and the affected part of the plant has a scorched appearance. The cause of this not infrequent phenomenon is not known, but it occurs in the wild as well as in cultivation. If you prune the affected part away, the remaining healthy sector may regrow. If die back is severe, repropagate from healthy shoots.

GREY MOULD
Grey mould (Botryotinia fuckeliana, or Botrytis cinerea) is primarily a disease of concern at the propagation stage. Cuttings wilting or dying back to compost level are often the first indications of infection. If left the stems and leaves become enveloped in a grey fur-like fungus. Inspect cuttings and young stock regularly, especially during periods when growth is very slow or at a standstill. Remove and destroy affected plants or cuttings and if necessary use a suitable fungicide, for example carbendazim.

LEAF SPOT
At least six fungi can cause leaf spot lesions on penstemons in North America, the most common and severe of which is Cercospora penstemonis. The spots, which are grey in colour, vary in diameter from 3 to 13mm (⅛ to ½in) and in cases of severe infection may coalesce to form large irregularly shaped dead areas or completely kill the leaf. Some of the leaf-spotting fungi cause brown rather than grey lesions, the centres of which may drop out, causing what is called a 'shot hole' effect.

All the leaf-spotting fungi overwinter on dead infected leaves and form wind-borne spores when the new season's growth begins, infecting fresh leaves. These new lesions produce more spores in their turn. Some species and cultivars are resistant to infection. Where these diseases are commonly severe, regular protective fungicide sprays may need to be considered. Seek advice on choice of chemical.

Leaf spot diseases are of a much lower incidence in Western Europe, probably because fewer of the fungi capable of producing spot-like lesions are present. European Hybrids appear free of these diseases, but leaf spot is noticed from time to time on some species, including P. heterophyllus and its derivatives.

POWDERY MILDEW
The disease Erysiphe cichoracearum appears as a whitish powdery coating over stems and leaves; in severe cases the latter may become distorted and discoloured and may even die. This disease infects a very wide range of ornamental garden plants, and penstemon species vary greatly in their susceptibility; a number of species, including P. cobaea, P. cyananthus, P. heterophyllus, P. grandiflorus, P. pallidus and P. tubaeflorus, are very prone to attack, while P. hartwegii and the European Hybrids seem very resistant when growing in the open air. However, even these kinds can become infected at the propagation stage if the cultural conditions are wrong. All young penstemon seedlings are highly susceptible, with the blue- or grey-leaved forms most at risk. The conditions that favour infection by powdery mildew in glasshouses and plastic tunnels are very high temperatures, little or no air movement and overwatering; ventilation and shading are therefore important. In severe cases pick off infected leaves and spray with a suitable fungicide.

VIRUS DISEASES
The only virus so far reported to infect penstemons is cucumber mosaic virus (CMV). This disease, manifested as stunting and leaf distortion, was found in plants of several species of the sections Anularius and Peltanthera being cultivated in Nebraska.

There are many ornamental plants that can become infected with CMV and that therefore act as reservoirs of the disease in the garden. These not only include such common perennials as campanulas, primulas and violas, but also a number of longer-lived favourites such as buddleias, daphnes and periwinkle (Vinca minor). Several common species of aphid readily transmit the virus as they feed, and become the agents of virus spread (vectors) as they move from an infected plant to a healthy one. The severity of CMV infection varies according to the species, and even between varieties; it is often disabling, but seldom lethal. The growth of some kinds may even be little or not at all affected, such cultivars or species being said to be virus tolerant, but all virus-infected plants remain infected for life. In climates where aphids are not an obvious pest of

P. glaber in early spring. Only light pruning has been necessary to achieve handsome ground cover.

cultivated penstemons the risk of infection to established plants may not be great. In any event, attempts to prevent the spread of virus infection in penstemons by aphid control would not be effective on a garden scale.

The absence of adequate investigation and accurate description of symptoms is an obstacle to the positive identification of infected plants, and to an assessment of the impact of virus diseases on penstemon cultivation. However, it is wise to regard any plant exhibiting stunting, leaf distortion, non-flowering or otherwise unexplained mottling or ring spotting of its leaves as possibly virus infected if no other cause is evident. It would be foolish to take cuttings or seed from such a plant, and the best policy is to destroy it.

The common occurrence of CMV in existing garden plants and the widespread presence of some of the aphid vectors suggest that the risk of virus infection in penstemons and its consequences should be better recognized. One commentator has put forward the theory that virus diseases have been the major cause of the loss of so many cultivars of the European Hybrids from the past,

but there are no reports of the demise of hundreds of cultivars through ill health and an alternative explanation might be changes in fashion and the effects of two world wars on the maintenance of garden plants that need constant repropagation.

WILT DISEASES

Some garden soils can become infected by soil-borne wilting fungi such as *Verticillium* spp., often introduced by planting infected crop plants. These fungi can infect a wide range of plants, including garden weeds and some garden shrubs and young trees, for example species of *Rhus* and *Acer*. Plants can become infected during vigorous growth and suffer dramatic symptoms of rapid collapse, the stems and leaves turning brown over the whole plant or large areas of it. Despite the name of the disease, affected plants do not necessarily wilt. Such symptoms can superficially resemble a severe infestation of chrysanthemum eelworm (see page 50).

If local sites of infection in the garden are known, avoid planting penstemons in them. Ideally such infested areas of soil should be left fallow for several years, or maintained as weed-free grass swards. There are no chemical treatments suitable for garden use.

7
PENSTEMONS ACROSS THE WORLD

USA

We have already discussed on pages 18–19 the development of gardening interest in penstemons in California in the 19th century, but what of the rest of the USA? The answer seems to be that not much occurred until perhaps the 1920s. A number of reasons suggest themselves for this. First and foremost, ornamental flower gardening is a leisure pursuit requiring settled conditions and at least a little spare cash. Life in the central states of the USA, where most penstemon species are found, was hard and uncertain in the 19th century. Although political and social stability was fairly well established by 1900, economic depression and drought between the two world wars hardly encouraged an interest in growing flowers.

Gardening in the eastern coastal states was rather less affected by these problems but this is where penstemons prove most difficult to grow – the western species because of high summer humidity and rainfall, and the European Hybrids because the winters are too cold. Climate is therefore another factor.

It is true that the east has its own indigenous penstemon species, but here we come up against gardening fashion as a third factor, and in particular the British style which was well established during the colonial era and continued to influence American taste thereafter. Gentlemen gardeners in the UK, faced by a local flora which is not in the top class for garden interest, craved for anything exotic they could find. Local species were allowed in if they had medicinal use but rarely otherwise. Translate that attitude across the Atlantic, and we can see that fashion did not favour penstemons.

This is not to say that no penstemons were in cultivation in the eastern USA during the 19th century – many US botanical gardens certainly grew them – and from early days the native American flora had its champions, but with limited success for our genus. The catalogues of the period show this: of about 100 species discovered by 1900, not many more than 10 were offered locally, compared to more than 50 in Europe from William Thompson alone (ironically enough obtained in many cases from New York seed exporters).

THE DEVELOPMENT OF INTEREST

Momentum seems to have picked up in the 1920s, principally in the alpines of the Coast and Cascade ranges of the north-west USA, and with the main focus on the Dasanthera group. Records of garden specimens of these species exceeding 25 years old are known from the early 1950s. The growth of interest was firmly underpinned by the publication in 1932 of Ira Gabrielson's seminal work *Western American Alpines*. The true garden worth of America's indigenous wild penstemons was finally beginning to be recognized, and in the case of the alpines this should not have been too difficult, since at every turn on a mountain road in the USA one is likely to be faced by a natural rock garden of breathtaking perfection – never attainable by human artifice, but temptingly inviting imitation. It was not long before many of these species were being successfully grown throughout the country once their special, and often individual, needs were better understood.

But what of *P. albidus*, tucked demurely among the grasses of the sparsely populated range country, or the more aggressive intrusions of *P. grandiflorus* in the better farmland on the Great Plains? All Americans know of the Great Plains, but relatively few have actually visited them, with the inevitable result that the garden value of such species has been slower to establish itself. That it should have happened at all is largely due to the energy and persistence of one man, Claude Barr. A South Dakotan of homesteader stock, Barr set out to do for the Great Plains flora what Gabrielson had done for alpines. It was a long haul. He set up a nursery business and published his first catalogue in 1932; he wrote many articles on penstemons – and other plains species – and gradually their popularity increased. Like Gabrielson, he wrote a definitive book, *Jewels of the Plains*, but it did not appear until 1983 – the year of his death at the age of 95.

It was a similar story with the desert penstemons of southern USA, but here it has been more of a collective effort, with no one name standing out. The eastern species, however, still lack a human champion notwithstanding the fact that the first American Penstemon Society president, Ralph Bennett, was based in Virginia. It is true that one of the first APS projects was the development of an improved strain of *P. hirsutus* in the early 1950s, but after that virtually nothing new happened until the arrival of *P. digitalis* 'Husker Red' 30 years later. Perhaps the enormous success of that introduction will persuade American gardeners to consider the merits of its near relatives more seriously.

As in most parts of the world, thankfully, the environmental value of indigenous wild flowers is now much better appreciated in the USA, with the happy side effect of encouraging people to be naturalists as well as gardeners and thereby understand better the relationship between botany and horticulture. The market is sufficient to support several seed firms devoted entirely to wild seed collection and sale, and the range and demand is increasing. State and county authorities have also responded by such measures as providing public amenity spaces devoted to wild flowers – including, most recently, the re-creation of prairie habitats in some Great Plains cities – and in using indigenous species for roadside replanting instead of over-vigorous, and on occasion disastrous, aliens. In both cases penstemon are to the fore, notably *P. grandiflorus*, *P. angustifolius* and *P. palmeri*. Apart from such planting, rock-strewn roadworks have been invitation enough for many species, including *P. eatonii*, *P. platyphyllus*, *P. virens*, *P. strictus*, *P. alpinus*, *P. cobaea* and *P. buckleyi*, to consolidate or even extend their natural distributions. In the eastern states the same process is thought to have extended dramatically the northward range of *P. digitalis* over several decades.

AMERICAN BREEDERS

The species are still the main interest of the average penstemon enthusiast in USA, but whenever a genus begins to be popular the plant breeders soon set to work. Can faults be bred out? Can improvements be bred in? In the case of penstemons, the ideal goal is a hybrid that combines the virility and persistence of a northerner like *P. serrulatus* with the superior flower power of the Mexican *P. hartwegii*. Attractive foliage would be a good bonus. Above all, if the result could be produced as a true seed strain rather than as a vegetative clonal form, then the breeder could die happy, not to say rich.

No American penstemon breeder has yet died rich, at any rate not as a result of breeding penstemons. The most successful results – not surprisingly given the extent to which they interbreed in the wild – have been with some of the Dasanthera species. Other examples of wild hybrids are fairly common, but always between species in the same section. This allowed breeders such as Bruce Meyers in Washington State to work towards improved sectional hybrids, for example an improved yellow Procerus like *P.* 'Goldie' (1971), the result of a cross between a deep yellow variant of *P. confertus* christened 'Kititas' and an unusual pink form of *P. euglaucus*. Breeding of such lines is fairly predictable because the cross usually shows intermediate features.

When it came to hybridization between sections, however, it was another story. From the 1950s onwards Professor Glen Viehmeyer of the University of Nebraska attempted to make many such crosses but with no success at all. There seemed to be a mismatch between the genes which tended to vindicate the taxonomists in the way they had divided the genus, but offered the hybridists no consolation whatsoever.

That might have been the end of the road, except for a chance breakthrough. This came in 1948 from an accidental cross of *P. barbatus* and an unknown species in the section Habroanthus, possibly *P. glaber*, which was christened *P.* 'Flathead Lake'.

In itself 'Flathead Lake' is not a top-rank variety, but Viehmeyer found that it accepted the pollen of almost any penstemon species, regardless of section. The result was that a cross of two species could be achieved by first crossing each with 'Flathead Lake', and then crossing the progeny together, when the next generation, or the one after that, might produce a small percentage of plants with blood only of the two desired species – a lengthy process but plant breeders are noted for their patience! This work has been continued until the present day by Professor Dale Lindgren and has resulted in a number of seed strains and cultivars which are recognized by the inclusion of 'Prairie' in their names.

Meyers himself has probably produced the most controlled penstemon hybrids of any breeder ever – in the hundreds at the last count. By the 1970s he was able, by sheer dint of trying, to produce a few inter-sectional crosses, from which the line he called the 'Mexicali Hybrids' has proved to be the most important. This name covers a series of hybrids, usually true from seed, in which the showy characteristics of various European Hybrids have been combined with the winter-hardiness of the earlier 'Mexicana Hybrids', themselves involving the cross of *P. campanulatus* and other Mexican species with, mainly, *P. palmeri* and *P. parryi*. If that sounds like a complicated programme it was – it took over 10 years to perfect the 'Mexicali Hybrids'.

The result of all this hard work and dedication by many people for 70 years or more has been to give American gardeners a complete range of penstemon types for their pleasure, whether they want the species, the selected strains thereof, the hybrids deliberately bred for US conditions, or the European Hybrids grown as annuals from seed. The Andersen Source List of Plants and Seeds for 1993–6 lists over 200 types of penstemons available from American nurseries, a far cry from the old days. Even so, it would be an exaggeration to say that penstemons are yet a common garden plant in their home country; what we can say is that conditions are right for the breakthrough.

FRANCE

No account of penstemons can avoid reference to the most remarkable role played by French nurserymen based in Nancy in developing, producing and popularizing hybrid cultivars from the earliest days. One man towers above all others in this sphere – Victor Lemoine, whose work we have already touched on in Chapter 3. In 1849, at the age of 26, Lemoine married and settled in Nancy to start a nursery business which was to bring him international fame. His first penstemons appeared around 1855. As is so often the case, no record of his

actual crosses survives, but we do know that even from this early date many of his introductions bore descriptions that could equally apply to some of the modern varieties available today. For instance, his cultivar *P.* 'Cardinal Richelieu' had very large scarlet flowers with white throats, while another of his equally large-flowered red cultivars, *P.* 'Vulcain', had typical carmine striations on the floor of the corolla tube.

Lemoine's productivity soon led to the offer of 10–15 new cultivars of his own breeding or selection per year, alongside older cultivars from the past as well as some produced by his fellow nurserymen in Nancy. Seldom did he turn to Germany or the UK for novelties, but then, as the penstemon giant of his time, he had no need to do so. No other Frenchman has taken up the baton since the nursery closed and sadly Lemoine's achievements are now but a memory, for none of his 520 cultivars seem to have survived to the present day.

One of the enigmas of this story is that Lemoine devoted so much time and energy to the breeding of plants that were unsuited to the climate of Nancy, where winter temperatures frequently reach –15°C (5°F). Clearly location was not a consideration. One explanation may be that local trade was unimportant since, in the 19th century at least, most of his plants were sold into the gardens of large châteaux in more temperate parts of France. Another may be that his customers were not only numerous but also international, for he published catalogues in both French and English. Many British and German growers certainly stocked his varieties in quantity.

Although Nancy was the penstemon capital of France for about 100 years, there was another site of production – in Angers. This was the base of another famous nursery firm, Vilmorin, who started to produce penstemon hybrids of the same type late in the 19th century.

A REVIVAL OF INTEREST

Even though the European Hybrids fell from grace for a long period from the late 1930s, a revival of interest is under way. A small number of new cultivars have appeared, namely *P.* 'Le Phare', *P.* 'Souvenir d'Adrien Regnier' (of Californian origin), *P.* 'Souvenir d'André Torres' and *P.* 'Gloire des Quatre Rues'. However, these modern French cultivars are only slowly establishing themselves in the national list: few, if any, nurserymen stock all of them. Much more widely available are a selection of British cultivars, and, not surprisingly, that robust pair from Switzerland, P. 'Andenken an Friedrich Hahn' (syn. 'Garnet' and, in France, 'Jupiter') and P. 'Schoenholzeri' (syn. 'Firebird'). The only 'historic' cultivar still available is the English P. 'Southgate Gem', bred before 1910.

An increasing number of nurseries now stock a range of both cultivars and species, and three of them are worthy of mention because they maintain large collections: the garden and nursery Le Clos du Coudray at Etaimpuis in Normandy; the perennials nursery Lumen near Bergerac, Dordogne; and the garden and nursery Lewisia in Lazer, Hautes-Alpes, which concentrates on species and their varieties only. Among botanic gardens, that at Nice maintains one of the better collections. Displays of hybrid cultivars are still a feature at a number of public gardens, notably Parc Floral de la Source in Orléans.

GERMANY

As in other major western European countries, German nurserymen took a very early interest in hybrids of Mexican species. One of the most prominent horticultural figures of the mid-19th century was Wilhelm Pfitzer, who founded a nursery firm in Stuttgart in 1844. From the outset he was attracted to the hybrid penstemons then starting to appear. The exact origin of Pfitzer's early introductions is unclear, but it was not long before he started to breed or select his own named hybrids. By 1861 eight cultivars with German names had appeared, which Pfitzer sold alongside the new cultivars from France. The number of new German offerings grew and grew with, for many years, 10–35 novelties per year being released, until towards the end of the 19th century Pfitzer was listing nearly 100 cultivars.

The range of European Hybrids offered by Pfitzer after 1900 remained predominantly of German origin, although P. 'Southgate Gem' was a permanent fixture and a few topical novelties from elsewhere appeared from time to time, such as P. 'Orville Wright' and P. 'Wilbur Wright' from Lemoine in France. The firm has remained in family hands for four generations, and by the time of its centenary in 1944, nearly 560 cultivars of penstemon had been introduced. So far we have not, with certainty, traced any that have survived to the present day.

The winter climate over most of Germany is very unfavourable to European Hybrid penstemons. But as elsewhere in Europe before the First World War, most customers for penstemons were wealthy landowners, not only in Germany itself, but also in Austria-Hungary, who could support the annual commitment of propagating and replanting. Certainly the interest in this kind of penstemon declined greatly before the middle of the present century; no doubt the social and economic consequences of two world wars were an important factor.

MODERN-DAY HYBRIDS

The present-day gardener in Germany is presented with a very restricted choice of hybrids. The white P. 'Eisberg' and the red P. 'Regina' seem to be the only two cultivars available of German origin, supported by a few English and Swiss ones, for example P. 'Evelyn', P. 'Hidcote Pink' and P. 'Andenken an Friedrich Hahn'.

Perhaps the main interest in penstemons today is focused on alpine types and robust species suitable for the border. Of these, over 50 species and their derivatives are available through large or specialist nurseries. The most popular borderworthy kinds are P. barbatus, P. campanulatus, P. digitalis, P. heterophyllus 'Zuriblau', P. hirsutus and P. serrulatus; currently P. cardwellii, P. davidsonii, P. rupicola and P. fruticosus scouleri are the alpinists' favourites.

Germany has long had the benefit of a good supply of penstemon seed through its own enterprising seed firms. In the first half of the 19th century plant breeding and seed production became traditional enterprises in the area of Erfurt, in what was then Prussia. One of the longest established firms primarily involved with flower seeds and still very active today was started in 1843 by Ernst Benary. His business expanded rapidly, enabling him to breed and produce a very wide range of flower seeds, including penstemons, which were traded in France and the UK as well as meeting home demand. Originally his list offered penstemon species, later expanding to include hybrids. The firm introduced the well-known P. 'Scharlachkoenigin' (syn. 'Scarlet Queen') in 1932, and it remains in production today.

SWITZERLAND

Swiss gardeners, like their neighbours in France and Germany, have been cultivating penstemons for probably well over a century, though we have found no evidence that the enthusiasm for breeding that led to the production of many hundreds of European Hybrids in the latter half of the 19th century carried over into Switzerland at that time. However, in the 20th century Swiss nurserymen and seedsmen have made particularly important contributions to the range of cultivars, some of which, although introduced 50 or more years ago, have qualities which still make them of special garden value, and universally popular.

In the interwar period in Europe, Arnold Vogt, a nurseryman of Erlenbach, took more interest in penstemons than most of his Swiss colleagues and seems to us to be the most likely raiser or introducer of a small number of hybrid cultivars, which elsewhere have been attributed to Carl Frikart. These included P. 'Brillant', in cinnabar red with a contrasting white throat, and the descriptively named P. 'Dogenpurpur' ('Doge's Purple'), now no longer offered. Countless gardeners in many countries owe a debt of gratitude to Hermann Wartmann of St Gallen for breeding P. 'Andenken an Friedrich Hahn' and it seems likely that he also introduced a second cultivar called P. 'Andenken an Anton Purpus'. Although Vogt's friend Paul Schoenholzer produced the fine P. 'Schoenholzeri', he never took his breeding further, and no one in Switzerland has succeeded him.

The well-known P. heterophyllus 'Zuriblau' must surely be a Swiss development, for this name is the local dialect word for the particular shade of blue that appears in Zurich's coat of arms. Seed of this strain has been consistently produced by the Swiss seed firm Samen Mauser for over 50 years, and it is still strongly in demand. Samen Mauser are also the sole producers of two large-flowered red strains, P. 'Rote Riesen' ('Red Giants') and P. 'Feuerzauber' ('Magic Fire').

In Switzerland several factors influence where, how and which kinds of penstemons are grown: low winter rainfall plus protection from wind and very low soil temperatures by means of snow cover are favourable climatic elements in upland areas. The softening effect on the climate of large water masses favours penstemon culture in the vicinity of lakes Constance and Geneva. Two other factors are soils and tradition: in contrast to southern Switzerland soils north of the Alps are better suited to penstemon culture, being neutral to alkaline, and it is here too that gardeners traditionally take the greatest interest in perennial plants in general.

The range of border penstemons available to Swiss gardeners today concentrates on the most robust cultivars. Naturally P. 'Andenken an Friedrich Hahn' and P. 'Schoenholzeri' still feature strongly and they are supported by derivatives of P. campanulatus such as P. 'Evelyn' and of P. heterophyllus, particularly 'Zuriblau', plus several P. barbatus types. The limited range of species that find favour includes such reliable representatives as P. hirsutus, P. pinifolius, P. strictus and P. ovatus but it is surprising that more are not grown, particularly alpines. Penstemons grown as half-hardy annuals are also popular, and every year a display of commercial seed strains is grown for public viewing in the Botanic Garden at Geneva.

AUSTRALIA

European Hybrid penstemons reached Australia well before the end of the 19th century, at which time John Forbes, the leading British source of penstemons, had customers in Victoria and Queensland who complimented him on the quality of the material they received after a voyage lasting several weeks.

In most parts of south-east Australia penstemons grow in a Mediterranean-style climate – long, hot, dry summers and autumns, with rainfall occurring predominantly in winter and early spring. Frosts are infrequent and the temperature seldom falls below –7°C (19°F). Many Australians regard their climate as much more suitable for growing these hybrids than that of Europe, even though that is where they originated. With species the situation is quite different – the mild wet winters are ill-suited to most, so few gardeners attempt to grow them apart from those mentioned below.

The European Hybrids flower for up to seven months in Australia, so it is no wonder they are highly regarded there. A representative range of about 25 hybrid cultivars is available to gardeners, and for those keen on plant conservation, the selection available is of some importance. At least one variety, P. 'Newbury Gem', raised in the UK shortly after penstemons first reached Australia, still thrives there, although apparently extinct in Europe for over a decade. Some of the other hybrids are also of particular interest. In the Australian climate hybrids with a very robust constitution flourish especially well. P. 'Andenken an Friedrich Hahn' (syn.

'Garnet') in particular can be found in many old gardens competing very successfully with allcomers (including weeds!), self-layering to make wide thickets many metres (yards) across. P. 'Willy's Purple' was found in an old garden in Scone, New South Wales. It has deep purple flowers borne on stiff upright stems 1.5m (5ft) high and is notably the tallest variety available in Australia, the only country where it is grown. The old scarlet cultivar P. 'Rubicundus' is available, and has a companion in P. 'Gladiator', which resembles it in habit and in flower size and shape but not colour, being a vinous purple with a white throat. Several modern British cultivars are available, for instance P. 'Blackbird', P. 'Midnight' and P. 'Papal Purple', plus some from New Zealand, most notably P. 'Susan' and P. 'Red Ensign'.

Although individual hybrid penstemons can be long-lived, gardeners find they obtain best results by treating them as short-term perennials, renewing them about every three years. Where frost is not a serious hazard there is less need to leave the top growth uncut in winter, and no harm is done by partially pruning back the plants after flowering has finished, provided about 45cm (18in) of growth is left. More ruthless treatment, however, does risk winter losses.

Of the species, derivatives of P. heterophyllus do not do well; although they are sold as perennials they are difficult to keep in good health even for one season, and rarely survive the mild wet winters. However, they are readily available as the seed strains P. h. 'Zuriblau' or P. h. 'True Blue'. P. barbatus and its hybrid forms are successful. Because there is such a long season to fill with colour the short flowering period of P. digitalis does not make it popular, although it persists well enough.

NEW ZEALAND

How and when penstemons first arrived in New Zealand is uncertain, but we do know that by 1912 Arthur Yates' nursery in Auckland was offering penstemons for sale, and not long afterwards, in 1916, penstemons featured prominently in a large ornamental display in Wellington Botanic Gardens. Although it is possible that these plants may have been raised from seed it is more likely that the original stock was imported from the UK.

It would seem that the initial interest when penstemons first reached New Zealand soon waned, and thereafter they were not very widely grown in gardens for some years. It was not until after the Second World War that new kinds were brought in. One of the first was P. 'Andenken an Friedrich Hahn' (syn. 'Garnet), which probably reached New Zealand about 1945 and is still the commonest variety seen, its robust constitution enabling it to outlive almost all other European Hybrids.

The availability of penstemons was broadened by nurserymen offering seed strains, such as P. 'Gloxinia Flowered', which has good persistence in the New Zealand climate. Gradually other European Hybrids arrived, including P. 'Schoenholzeri' (syn. 'Firebird'), and a few established cultivars of UK origin such as P. 'Pennington Gem' which regrettably has been renamed 'Pink Cloud'. Within the last two decades penstemons have risen in popularity, and more European Hybrids have been imported. Unfortunately, due to renaming and misnaming, confusion now reigns. However, a range of 20 cultivars is available, and new varieties of New Zealand origin are beginning to appear, two of which are P. 'Purple Passion' and P. 'Deep Velvet'.

New Zealand has a thriving Alpine Garden Society, with members (particularly those living in the cooler conditions of South Island) showing increased interest in alpine penstemons. Very few penstemon species were available in New Zealand until after the Second World War, and specialist society seed exchange schemes still form a primary source of material. In recognition of the growing enthusiasm, however, some nurserymen are now offering a good selection of species, some suitable for the rock garden and others of taller habit for use in the perennials border.

Several penstemon collections are open to the public. Dunedin Botanic Garden display 19 hybrids and 71 species. The Botanic Gardens in Auckland and Christchurch maintain smaller collections. Outside these public institutions one must turn to nurseries which have a special interest in the genus, notably Mara Nurseries of Hawera, Bay Bloom Nurseries of Tauranga and Eden Cottage Perennials of Wellington.

THE NEW ZEALAND CLIMATE

Although rainfall in parts of North Island is high enough to cause problems for penstemons – 1500mm (60in) in the New Plymouth area – 1175mm (46in) is more typical and of this two-thirds of the rain falls in summer, when penstemons are much more rain-tolerant. Average summer temperatures are typically 18°C (53°F) with winter temperatures averaging 10°C (50°F), higher in Auckland. Frosts are rare and, when they do occur, slight.

The climate in South Island is quite different. Rainfall in the population centres can be under half that in North Island; average temperatures in both summer and winter are lower by several degrees. There are more frequent and heavier frosts and, in many places, snow. Thus penstemons have a shorter flower-ing and growing period than in North Island and experience a winter dormant period.

Especially in North Island, the European Hybrids are thoroughly evergreen, and grow larger (by 20–30 per cent), live longer (by 2–3 years) and flower longer (by 3–6 months) than the same cultivars in the UK. Where penstemons are reliably persistent and frosts minimal, gardeners have the option of cutting their plants down to near soil level, pruning them moderately to lightly or leaving them alone. Most find they get the best results from either of the first two options, but because of long lifespans, they do become very woody at the base. Cutting hard back into the woody base is not damaging, but regrowth is slower, and the start of flowering is con-sequently delayed.

SOUTH AFRICA

How the first penstemons reached South Africa, and how long they have been cultivated in gardens, is a matter for speculation. The most commonly grown today are the European Hybrids, and it is proba-bly these types that first made their way to this part of the globe.

Despite sharp contrasts between soil and climatic conditions in different regions, penstemons are widely appreciated as long-term colour providers. Gardeners in summer rainfall areas such as the southern Transvaal and the Natal Midlands enjoy the best conditions for growing the European Hybrids. Growth is rapid, plant size is large and persistence good, 4–5 years if the plants are cut back annually. Certain cultivars grow luxuri-ously under these conditions – P. 'Stapleford Gem', for instance, may layer itself rapidly and reach 1.5 m (5 ft)

in diameter in one season. This cultivar starts to flower particularly early, and will continue for five months or more if dead-headed. In these regions penstemons are normally grown in full sun, with temperatures reaching 30°C (86°F). In places annual rainfall averages 1270mm (50in), falling mostly in summer.

Gardens in the Cape may have alkaline sands or acidic soils but gardeners manage to grow penstemons on both, perhaps the greater problem being drought induced by the hot, dry summers. Growth on the acidic soils is improved by treatment to increase the pH, and all penstemons here benefit from irrigation if it is avail-able. On very dry sites penstemon cultivation may only be possible if water stress is reduced by planting in light shade provided by trees. In the regions mentioned so far the frost risk is light to negligible, but the much colder winters which occur in the Eastern Free State do pose problems for penstemon culture. Here the European Hybrids are much less in evidence.

The range of cultivars available to gardeners in South Africa is rather restricted. Among the European Hybrids it extends to P. 'Alice Hindley', P. 'Blackbird', P. 'Evelyn', P. 'Andenken an Friedrich Hahn' (syn. 'Garnet'), P. 'George Home', P. 'Hidcote Pink', P. 'Burford Purple', P. 'Schoenholzeri' (syn. 'Firebird'), P. 'White Bedder' (syn. 'Snowstorm') and a selection introduced by the nursery firm of Malanseuns, located near Pietermaritzburg, called P. 'Strawberry Ice'.

Penstemon species are not commonly grown; the regions where the European Hybrids do well are not climatically suited to many of them. However, in the dryer area of the Cape, P. barbatus and P. digitalis, including the selection P. d. 'Husker Red', perform well as garden perennials.

Many outlets concentrate on mixed bedding plants raised from commercial seed, the most commonly offered being P. barbatus hybrids, P. 'Skyline', and large-flowered hybrids usually sold as P. 'Gloxinia Flowered' (sometimes startlingly mislabelled 'Gloriosa Flowered'). Although sold in small plant packs aimed at the market for annual bedding, they are a source of plants which in the South African climate are reliable short-term perennials, persisting for 3–4 years. Another seed strain, derived from P. heterophyllus called 'Blue Spring' seems shorter lived, however.

8

A SURVEY OF PENSTEMON SPECIES

In Chapter 1 we described the family position of the genus *Penstemon* and how its 272 constituent species, in spite of the considerable variation among them, could be told apart from those of related genera. We now go on to consider the genus itself, with two aims in mind – to give guidance on identification, and also to offer comments on gardenworthiness and special cultural requirements, if any.

Penstemons tend to group themselves into clusters of like species, with usually one species being the 'type' of the cluster if only because it tends to be commoner than the others. Many of these clusters have been recognized as having taxonomic significance, which is both helpful and unhelpful – helpful because having names for many of these clusters is a useful shorthand, unhelpful because it introduces to most gardeners the unfamiliar area of the ranks below the level of genus – in descending order, subgenus, section, and subsection. While this is admittedly a complication it does produce a logical structure for discussing the genus, and on balance is to be preferred to, say, a description of species in alphabetical order.

In *Penstemon* there are 6 subgenera, 12 sections and 23 subsections, arranged as shown in full in Fig. 11, Appendix VIII. Fortunately, for our purposes this structure is partly simplified because, first, a number of these groupings contain only one species, and, secondly, it is not necessary to consider every subsection. It will be seen that some names are repeated – for example, there is a subgenus Habroanthus and a section Habroanthus, while Penstemon itself occurs as a genus, subgenus, section and subsection. This is the result of a comparatively recent change to the international taxonomic rules, the advantages of which are less clear than the disadvantages are obvious.

THE RULES OF NOMENCLATURE
At this point it may help to note some rules of nomenclature relevant to this book. Most readers will be fully aware of the primary distinction in taxonomy between a naturally occurring species such as *P. digitalis* and a form of a species artificially raised or segregated for its garden value, such as *P. digitalis* 'Husker Red'. The italics indicate that this species has been 'validly published', which is to say that the name, with a technical description, has appeared in a recognized publication and that to date no one has published anything which invalidates that description. By contrast, 'Husker Red' in Roman script between single quotes tells us that this is a garden variety (a cultivar) and not 'botanically recognized'.

Italics are also used for validly published groups within a species, for example, *P. digitalis baueri*. Strictly speaking we should indicate whether *baueri* is a subspecies, variety or forma, but these fine distinctions are of no importance to most gardeners, and by omitting them it means that we can use the valuable words 'variety' and 'form' in their wider sense without fear of misunderstanding.

Between the levels of genus and species Roman script is used, so *Penstemon* indicates the genus, while Penstemon means the subgenus, section or subsection, according to context if not specifically indicated.

We have already mentioned the taxonomic confusion, and the consequent problems of synonymy in the genus. This introduces a further rule of nomenclature which is less well-known and applies when the same name has been used by taxonomists for different species of plant, a situation which can arise in one of two ways: either a taxonomist is not aware the name is already in use, or he makes a mistake in identification. When it is necessary to distinguish between publications of the same name the taxonomists' names are added. To give an example, *P. glaber* Pursh is the true *P. glaber*, whereas both *P. glaber* Gray and *P. glaber* Jeps (for Jepson) are today recognized as *P. speciosus*. Although we frequently touch on nomenclatural problems in this chapter, this particular complication will only directly affect readers who need to consult the list of common synonyms given in Appendix II, but the underlying problem is one which affects us all – for example, when we read of *P. glaber* 'Roseus' in an old catalogue was the author following Persh, or Gray/Jepson?

The distinction between botanical and horticultural forms, and the attendant rules, may at times seem pedantic but it has a definite value in regulating plant descriptions, and happily the use of the prescribed printing conventions is now almost universal. Some problems remain, however, of which two tend particularly to affect penstemons.

The first problem is when Latin names occur in a cultivar name. Before the rules were formulated the extravagant use of Latin names was rampant, and although this is now frowned on it is not practical to replace existing Latinized cultivar names. This leads to some confusion due to a common misconception that all Latin names have to be in italics. Thus *P. rupicola albus* is incorrect since that name has no botanical standing, and so should be rendered *P. rupicola* 'Albus'. It also works the other way: *P. heterophyllus purdyi* is valid, so the 'Purdyi' sometimes met with is incorrect.

The second problem is related to the first. To continue the example of *P. rupicola* 'Albus', this form occurs in the wild, and because of that some believe that 'Albus' should be italicized. However, the rule is clear – the form has no botanical standing and is therefore a cultivar. The same is true where a cross of two species in the wild is brought into cultivation and given a horticultural name. Such varieties, in contrast to the artificially bred lines of the European Hybrids, are normally readily identifiable with their parent species, and for this reason we describe them in this chapter.

Although Latin cultivar names are now discouraged, there is one exception. Very occasionally, a variety loses its botanical status, usually because further research reveals that it is not as distinct in form from its relatives as was first thought. In such cases it is acceptable to retain the Latin name for horticultural purposes. Two

examples in *Penstemon* are *P. hirsutus* 'Pygmaeus' and, very recently, *P. speciosus* 'Kennedyi'.

IDENTIFICATION

The variability of penstemon species was one of the reasons that so many mistakes were made in identification. Species have to be distinguished on the basis of constant botanical features and, as discussed in Chapter 1, these features have tended to get smaller and smaller. At least penstemon-lovers are spared the need to use an electron microscope to tell species apart, as is required of experts in certain members of the grass family, but all except those with the keenest eyesight will need a hand lens on occasion. The main problem concerns the distinction of the four main subgenera, since the mode of identification is based on the appearance of the anther sacs when they are ready to shed their pollen: dense woolly hair on the sacs indicates Dasanthera, small openings at the front of the sacs Saccanthera, partial opening from the rear Habroanthus, and full opening Penstemon.

Although this approach has the obvious disadvantage of leaving a very short season in which identification can take place, it is at least a reliably constant feature for each subgenus. However with penstemons there are always some exceptions, usually with species which are intermediate in form between groupings. At the level of subgenus this affects four species whose anther sacs do not behave as they should: these are explained in Fig. 10, Appendix VIII.

When it comes to sections and subsections within a subgenus, identification actually becomes somewhat easier because normal features become diagnostic – sizes, colours and shapes of flowers and leaves, serrated versus unserrated leaves, distribution of hairs, and even general habit. This will generally place a species in its 'cluster', but the identification of individual species in a cluster, particularly if rare, will involve a level of detail outside the scope of a book of this nature.

SUBGENUS DASANTHERA

This subgenus of nine species is probably the most important group of penstemons for American gardeners, and for alpinists generally. All but *P. lyallii* are small shrubs with small leaves, but their flowers are the largest encountered in the smaller penstemons – over 3.5cm (1⅜in) long and up to 2cm (¾in) in) wide. They flower in late spring, earlier than most penstemons, and the displays of flower can be spectacular. There is a hint of repeat-flowering, especially with *P. cardwellii*.

The focus for the distribution of the Dasanthera is the mountains of northwest USA, with some species crossing into Canada, and others reaching further south – *P. montanus* even into Utah. As an exception, *P. newberryi* inhabits only northern California.

This group is easily distinguished from other penstemons by their large woolly anther sacs (see Fig. 1, page 11), which give the appearance of pairs of arms plunged into white muffs. A few other species have hairs on the anthers, which can also be quite long, as in *P. strictus*, but they are much sparser.

There are many different named varieties, natural and artificial, so that it is quite difficult to tell the actual species apart. A very large number of the named forms are based on choicer colonies of the species, or on well-defined hybrid swarms, and the general rule seems to be that the former retain recognizable features of the species, while the latter show intermediate characteristics. We will describe the typical species forms first.

P. lyallii

We can begin by isolating *P. lyallii*, which is the only herbaceous, deciduous species, and the only one of the nine that is over 50cm (20in) tall. It has long, narrow, willow-like leaves, moderately serrated. The lavender flowers are borne in abundance in panicles. It does not have a wide distribution yet is very commonly offered as seed, and is one of the easiest of penstemons both to germinate and to grow on. It hybridizes readily in the wild with shrubby members of the Dasanthera, and the progeny as a result tend to be more shrubby than herbaceous.

P. barrettiae

This can also be isolated as the only species of the group which, except for its anther sacs, is hairless. In habit it is like a miniature evergreen azalea, mature plants usually being slightly domed mats up to 1m (3¼ft) across but less than 30cm (12in) high. The oval leaves are small but wide, leathery, and have a bluish tint. The short leafless flower spikes are held erect, and bear flowers in shades of white, lilac, purple and magenta. It is a choice subject growing at low elevations in the wild. It is not the easiest Dasanthera to grow, not liking hard winters, nor too much summer heat. Its wild numbers have declined in recent years.

P. montanus and P. ellipticus

These species are also small shrubs under 30cm (12in), but are distinguished from *P. barrettiae* by having flowering stems which are as leafy as their non-flowering branches – one of those features which sounds insignificant but, once seen, sticks in the mind's eye. They are differentiated from one another by two features: *P. montanus* has a bushy habit and greyish leaves, whereas *P. ellipticus* is a mat-former with bright green leaves. The leaves in both cases are serrated and elliptical, and the basal leaves often have distinct leaf stalks. *P. montanus* has perhaps the widest distribution of the Dasanthera, but is said to be temperamental in cultivation – semi-shade is recommended, and also a good root run to accommodate its large taproot. *P. ellipticus* is comparatively uncommon, and very much a scree plant with stems often buried under the stones. Both species have handsome deep lavender flowers, but not in such abundance as some other Dasanthera. *P. montanus* has a pretty subspecies, *idahoensis*, with clear blue flowers and smooth leaves – not to be confused with *P. idahoensis*, which is a quite different species.

The Big Five

The remaining five Dasantheras constitute one of the principal glories of the penstemonial world, and all are common both in the wild and in cultivation. Their persistence is not in question, but they are just short of being perfect alpines because they are prone to die-back (see page 52). They usually recover well enough but in the interim can look misshapen.

For identification purposes the typical forms of these five species can be split four ways: mat-formers versus upright shrubs and red or pink flowers versus purple. Thus:

Red/pink flowers, mat-forming: *P. rupicola*
Red/pink flowers, upright shrub: *P. newberryi*
Purple flowers, mat-forming: *P. davidsonii*
Purple flowers, upright shrub: *P. fruticosus*,
P. cardwellii

It remains therefore to distinguish between *P. cardwellii* and *P. fruticosus*, and this is not easy. *P. fruticosus* is bigger and bushier in habit with a flat-topped appearance, while *P. cardwellii* is more ground-hugging and irregular in shape; but *P. fruticosus* has two subspecies, *scouleri* and *serratus*, which are closer to *P. cardwellii* in habit, whereupon one has to resort to leaves – broad and with rounded serrations in *P. cardwellii*, narrow and

PLATE IV

P. cardwellii

P. hirsutus

P. attenuatus var.
militaris

P. richardsonii

All flowers are shown at approximately ½ size

toothed in *P. fruticosus scouleri* and broad and strongly toothed in *P. fruticosus serratus*.

With this basic classification in our minds we can begin to tackle the pink and red versions of the purple species, the purple forms of the red species, and the white forms of all of them! This leads inevitably to considering the named varieties, which number about 120. The complex relationships of the named forms to the species and to each other is illustrated in Fig. 12, Appendix VIII. Not all varieties may be totally distinct, nor have they all survived to the present time; but there can be no doubting the great degree of garden interest in the Dasanthera, to the extent of breeders making triple crosses in the case of *P.* 'Martha Ray' and quadruple crosses to obtain *P.* 'Pink Dust and *P.* 'Pink Holly'. To complete the picture, a number of unnamed hybrid swarms are known that comprise most of the available combinations not represented by cultivated varieties, such as *P. fruticosus* × *P. newberryi*, *P. barrettiae* × *P. fruticosus*, *P. ellipticus* × *P. newberryi*, and so on. Doubtless these will give rise to more named varieties in due course. Only *P. montanus* seems to stand aloof from this mating spree, possibly because its more easterly distribution gives it less opportunity.

With such a profusion of forms, space only allows us to describe a few of the better-known varieties still known to be in cultivation.

P. davidsonii has a rather uncommon white form, but the main garden interest lies in its subspecies *menziesii*, which is still often found as *P. menziesii* since it was for many years regarded as a separate species. Its leaves are smaller and glossier than the type, and more serrated. The forms *P. d.* 'Microphyllus' and *P. d.* 'Serpyllifolius' take the dwarfing process even further, being totally prostrate in habit with leaves which are minute. The subspecies *praeteritus* is similarly of small habit and leaf, but has flowers which are nearly 1cm (½in) longer than the type, and as a result is particularly striking.

P. rupicola has two very choice varieties in *P. r.* 'Diamond Lake', in a range of pinks, and *P. r.* 'Myrtle Hebert', a deep pink set against grey-green foliage which has the distinct advantage of being less prone to die-back than usual. 'Diamond Lake' is a wild selection and its seed progeny is not always pink.

P. cardwellii has two pleasing forms in *P. c.* 'John

Bacher' and *P. c.* 'Floyd McMullan'. The latter, registered in 1985, is a miniature up to 30cm (12in) in diameter which will appeal to gardeners who do not have the space to accommodate the strongly spreading habit of the type, which can quite quickly reach 90cm (3ft) in diameter. Its reddish-purple flowers are also distinctive. 'John Bacher', registered in 1961, is an outstanding snow-white variety superior in habit, form and constitution. It has the advantage of coming true from seed. The natural form *P. c.* 'Roseus' is just stunning, in a luminous but delicate mid-pink.

P. newberryi is rated by some as the best of all the alpine penstemons, and its common name of mountain pride is well-earned. The named varieties reflect individual choices from its normal range of pinks and reds, and the biggest colour break actually comes from the dark reddish-violet of the natural subspecies *sonomensis*.

P. fruticosus gives a number of possibilities in pink and lilac, but the stars for many enthusiasts are the creamy white *P. f. scouleri* 'Albus', and *P. f. serratus* 'Holly'. The latter has small deep green leaves very similar to miniature holly in appearance, and is grown mainly for its foliage effect since it is shy to flower. *P. f. scouleri* had separate species status for many years as *P. scouleri* and is preferred by many alpinists as a better form than the type, sometimes with flowers in a true blue. *P. f. serratus*, with purple flowers, is less commonly offered, and should not be confused in name with *P. serrulatus* or *P. subserratus*.

Of the hybrid forms *P.* 'Breitenbush Blue' appears like a dwarf form of *P. cardwellii*, doubtless because of the influence of the smaller parent, *P. davidsonii*. *P.* 'Edithae', a cross of *P. rupicola* × *P. barrettiae*, is one of the earlier hybrids (1948) and one of the best, being strong-growing with clear purple flowers. Even earlier is the not dissimilar *P.* 'Six Hills Hybrid', which emanated from the nursery of that name in Hertfordshire, England, around 1930. At the time Thompson & Morgan stated the cross to be *P. davidsonii* × *P. eriantherus*, but the raiser, Clarence Elliott, gave it a few years later as a cross of *P. rupicola* with an unknown species. A definite *P. rupicola* cross is *P.* 'Pink Dragon', raised at the nursery of Jack Drake in Aviemore, Scotland. It is very floriferous with large flowers in a solid shade of pink and is a vigorous plant, although given to some die-back in hard winters. Nevertheless, we would recommend it for every rock garden.

Plate IV. A selection of species with purple/blue flowers.

Finally, after this excursion into named varieties, let us emphasize that the five typical species are still among the best penstemons there are.

SUBGENUS HABROANTHUS

This subgenus falls into two sections: 43 species of section Habroanthus with dilated blue/violet flowers, and the contrasting seven species of section Elmigera whose flowers are narrow tubes in shades of red. The subgenus is distinguished by anther sacs which open partially, from back to front.

SECTION HABROANTHUS

The 43 species of the section Habroanthus form the largest undivided grouping within the genus Penstemon. They are classic dryland species of the western desert states with Utah as their epicentre, but with appreciable representation also further north in Idaho and Wyoming.

Several of these species are uncommon or localized, and some have only been described in recent years – six since 1980 – so taxonomic definition of the Habroanthus may not yet be complete. The older-established species still have their difficulties, with doubts still persisting in some minds over, for example, the separation of *P. deaveri* from *P. virgatus*, or *P. alpinus* from *P. glaber*. Taxonomic fall-out persists as a result, so that we have to cope with names like *P. glaber, P. subglaber* and *P. cyananthus* ssp. *subglaber* in close proximity, each describing a different plant.

This is a uniform section. The flowers are about 3.5cm (1⅜in) long, almost always in shades of blue with greater or lesser infusions of violet, although several species have rarer pink or white forms. The leaves are always smooth-edged. Ten or more species are fairly small alpine types, while the remainder are herbaceous, with flowering stems up to 1m (3¼ft) high, though generally less. Identification is not easy, and at times really demands a magnifying glass. The following simplified classification using gross features will offer some guidance, but beyond this there is really no alternative to the full botanical key. (A 'broad leaf' here means one that is five or less times as long as broad.)

Anther sacs have a small number of long white hairs, easily seen with naked eye
Leaves broad: *P. comarrhenus, P. cyanocaulis, P. moriahensis, P. navajoa, P. strictiformis*

P. fruticosus scouleri

Leaves narrow: *P. caryi, P. idahoensis, P. scariosus, P. strictus*
Anther sacs appear smooth to naked eye
Flowers hairy, leaves broad: *P. leiophyllus* ssp. *francisco-pennellii, P. leiophyllus* ssp. *keckii, P. mensarum, P. subglaber, P. uintahensis*
Flowers hairy, leaves narrow: *P. gibbensii, P. leiophyllus* ssp. *leiophyllus, P. parvus, P. wardii*
Flowers smooth, leaves broad: *P. absarokensis, P. alpinus, P. compactus, P. cyananthus, P. cyaneus, P. deaveri, P. debilis, P. glaber, P. laevis, P. lemhiensis, P. longiflorus, P. nudiflorus, P. payettensis, P. pennellianus, P. saxosorum, P. tidestromii*
Flowers smooth, leaves narrow: *P. ammophilus, P. fremontii, P. hallii, P. neomexicanus, P. pahutensis, P. paysoniorum, P. penlandii, P. perpulcher, P. pseudoputus, P. speciosus, P. virgatus*

The best of the section There are some splendid varieties in this group which have attracted gardening interest mainly because of their beautiful colouring, but, with a few notable exceptions, the difficulties of identification and cultivation tends to make the Habroanthi a province for the specialists.

Among the exceptions, *P. glaber* and *P. strictus* stand out for being unusually easy in cultivation. *P. glaber* appeared in the *Botanical Magazine* of 1813 under the name of *P. gordoni*, and has been in the catalogues since early times. It is a taxonomic nightmare, at least six other species having been mistaken for it or described as varieties of it, or both. In fact it is fairly easy to identify with its waxy, shiny and dense basal foliage, a feature that makes for excellent ground cover. Although it is classified as a broad-leaved type, the basal leaves can sometimes be quite narrow. As the flowers are generally in a purpler shade than is usual for the section it is not one of the best from the colour point of view, but it is free-flowering over a long period from early summer and this and its easy-going nature make it a favourite of gardeners. That it should be so easy in cultivation may be due to its being much more of a plains species than any other Habroanthus, its distribution extending as far east as Nebraska and the Dakotas.

Some garden varieties have been offered over the years, notably the pink form *P. glaber* 'Roseus' – more often than not found as *P. g. roseus*, although it never had botanical status. Thompson & Morgan offered it continuously from 1902 until 1966, a sure sign of its quality, and it is not difficult to visualize a strong pink flower against the glossy dark green foliage as having better garden value than the type.

The other varieties of *P. glaber* were mostly ephemeral in the catalogues, and the fact that they were usually described as bluer forms might indicate that they were some of the commoner Habroanthi, such as *P. alpinus* and *P. speciosus*, which were from time to time confused with it. Among these offerings it was curious that the old name *P. gordoni*, this time embellished with '*splendens*', reappeared in the 1890s and is still used in continental Europe. Also interesting from the 1890s is *P. glaber hybridus*, described as 'from white to blue' without any further information, so the exact origin of this strain will probably stay a tantalizing secret. In later years firms such as Suttons, Watkins & Simpson and Thompson & Morgan did offer seed of *P. glaber* in mixed colours – lavender, mauve and rose pink. If we appear to dwell on these lost seed strains of *P. glaber* it is in the hope that some reader may be persuaded that it

might not be too difficult to reintroduce colour varieties in a species with such good habit and constitution to build on.

P. strictus does not take quite so easily to European conditions. Its wild habitat is in sparse upland grassland and broken ground in Colorado and Wyoming, where the summer rainfall can be next to nothing. That said, it thrives in temperate climates, seems to accept moisture in soils with open drainage, and moreover is very easy from seed. This plant has narrow leaves, and in good conditions forms a loose basal mat from which the inflorescences rise to 70cm (2⅓ft). The loose clumps of blue-tinged-violet flowers make a good show, and can individually show a striking pure blue. This trait is even more pronounced in a variety of American origin known as 'Bandera' which is highly praised by all who grow it. The best distinguishing features of *P. strictus* are the hairs on the anther sacs which can reach nearly 2.5cm (1in) in length.

We should also mention *P. hallii*, the only alpine Habroanthus at all common in cultivation. It is a tiny 7.5cm (3in) high subject from elevated places in Colorado, but adapts well to lower altitudes where it flowers in early season. Its flowers are rather fat and show their white throats and hairy staminodes quite clearly. The rest of the flower is in the usual blue to violet shade for this group.

Of the Habroanthi less commonly in cultivation the trio of 'cyans' – *P. cyananthus*, *P. cyaneus* and *P. cyanocaulis* – come in particularly good shades of blue, with *P. cyananthus* possibly taking the prize because of its free-flowering nature and greater tolerance of moisture. *P. alpinus*, a more southerly version of *P. glaber*, also inclines to a true blue at times, but the pick of the bunch is *P. speciosus*. It is fairly common and widely admired, but almost always the admiration is accompanied by a rueful comment on its difficulty in cultivation. Readers of the *Gardener's Chronicle* of 1848 were admonished to the contrary, however: 'If properly treated, few plants are easier to cultivate'! The secret was the typical Victorian recipe which has already been described: treat as biennials and plant in very rich soil, with liberal watering – surprising treatment for denizens of decidedly arid terrain (and requiring considerable labour, but with a single penstemon plant costing the equivalent of half a day's wage for a labourer in those days, it was a natural assumption that the readership would have an adequate supply of gardening staff). Alpinists might be tempted to try the miniature form *P. speciosus* 'Kennedyi', which grows at 3300m (10,000ft) or more in the mountains of California and has pretty grey-green foliage to offset the deep blue flowers. This variety recently lost its status as a separate subspecies due to doubts about its being a genuinely distinct form, which does not detract from its beauty but does indicate the need for care in choosing a good source of material – the best forms are under 10cm (4in) in height.

SECTION ELMIGERA

Over the years the group Elmigera has been variously classed as a genus, subgenus, section and subsection, from which it can be concluded that it poses some tax-onomic problems. Its relatively recent inclusion as a section of subgenus Habroanthus is based on having similar back-to-front opening of the anthers, but all its seven species are easily told apart from the rest of the subgenus by their narrow tubular flowers in varying, mostly quite vivid, shades of red, indicating pollination by humming birds. Some of the species show this even more in having a 'shark's head' shape to the flower, that is, the lower lobes fold right back on to the underside of the tube, giving the bird's head maximum access to the style and anthers. These species grow tall, pushing up long inflorescences up to 1m (3¼ft) or more from crowded, large-leaved mats. The flowers are generally quite long, up to 5cm (2in).

The Elmigera are confined to the southwest USA and northern Mexico, where conditions vary from decidedly dry to areas with summer moisture not unlike Europe. If the soil is kept overmoist the growth tends to be lax and over-exuberant, leading to untidy collapsing stems as the season goes on. The flowering season is quite long, at least five weeks, peaking in Europe by high summer.

P. eatonii and *P. cardinalis* differ from the other five species by having flowers which are all but complete tubes, only the smallest lobes being present. In *P. cardinalis* the flowers are a subdued crimson, and the lower lobes are still retracted in spite of their small size to give the 'shark's head' appearance. In *P. eatonii* the colour is an uncompromising vivid scarlet and the lobes all point forward. The flowers are set almost vertically on gently arching flower stalks. The effect is like a shower of sparks, which has earned it the nickname of firecracker

penstemon. These are both superb garden subjects, and could be more strongly recommended if there were not doubts about their persistence, in spite of their ability to survive the severest winters at up to 2800m (8500ft) in their native habitats.

P. barbatus is far and away the most familiar species to European gardeners, being described first in 1794 – as *Chelone barbata*, a name under which it can still be found. It is widely distributed, from Utah well into Mexico. It has the 'shark's head' flower, produced on stately, almost leafless panicles up to 1.5m (5ft) tall. The flowers are set as in *P. eatonii*, giving an angular appearance at close quarters, and the leaves are quite broad, dark green and without serrations. In the wild the flower colour varies from deep pink to intense coral and bright scarlet, always with the lower lips picked out in yellow. Rare yellows, designated botanically as forma *flaviflorus*, and pure whites are also found. The whole

P. strictus. The hairs on the anther sacs, typical of a small group of the Habroanthi, can be clearly seen.

plant is virtually hairless except for prominent yellow tufting at the angle where the lower lips of the flower fold back, but there are variations on this theme in two common subspecies found in the more northerly part of its range; ssp. *trichander* also has long white hairs on the anthers, while in ssp. *torreyi* the mouth hairs are absent or very sparse. *P. barbatus* is particularly prone to sprawl and really only recommends itself to large gardens, but gardeners with less space have a number of dwarfer varieties to choose from.

P. henricksonii and *P. labrosus* are the two closest relatives of *P. barbatus*. The former is distinguished by having maroon or red-purple flowers, and the latter by somewhat less reflexing of the lower lip, as well as leaves which are much narrower. Continuing the trend to even narrower leaves are *P. imberbis* and *P. wislizeni*, but in addition neither has the reflexed lobes of *P. barbatus*, although, viewed from the side, the front of the flower still has a raked appearance as the lower lobes are much shorter than the upper. All four species are Mexican and quite local, only *P. imberbis* venturing into USA, and then only just into southernmost California.

P. barbatus varieties *P. barbatus* has been the subject of much attention from horticulturalists. In the UK, Flanagan & Nutting's catalogue of 1835 was already offering *Chelone barbata* 'in variety', suggesting at least some streaming of the wild variants, but unfortunately no details are given and the usual sources of information for those times are silent on the subject. William Thompson in 1865 listed 'P. barbatus splendens' as 'a brighter scarlet than the type', although whether as a wild selection or as a cultivated seed strain is not clear. Then for a few years in the 1880s and '90s came 'P. barbatus hybridus', said to vary from pink to dark red and violet, new'.

The mention of a violet barbatus, albeit a hybrid, is puzzling since it is unlikely in the wild. Moreover, from later reports, it seems that *P. barbatus* is not a ready hybridizer with other species, although a violet form, possibly *P. barbatus* × *P. virgatus*, was reported in 1939. However, in 1948 the situation changed with the arrival of the hybrid known as *P.* 'Flathead Lake', which we have already discussed in Chapter 7. Crosses using 'Flathead Lake' have led to a variety of new hybrids, some of them, such as *P.* 'Prairie Fire', continuing to show their barbatus parentage in unmistakable fashion, others such as the 'Mesa Hybrids' inclining more to their other parent(s) in both flower shape and colouring, including purples and violets. With the variety of seed available to hybridizers by 1880 it is quite possible that, by good fortune, a similar cross to 'Flathead Lake' was achieved and then bred on, in which case the violet forms are explained. Another possibility is that seed collectors mistook the purplish *P. henricksonii* for *P. barbatus*, since it has the same shape of flower and general habit, and was not recognized as a separate species until 1975.

Whatever the explanation, the fact is that seed strains became available, and still survive, under the name of *P. barbatus*, some having the 'shark's head' and some looking more like *P. glaber*. Among these can be included *P. b.* 'Hybrida', *P. b.* 'Praecox', *P. b.* 'Nana' or 'Nanus', and *P. b.* 'Rondo', alone or in various combinations such as *P. b.* 'Nana Praecox Rondo'. To what extent these different names any longer signify unique origins is uncertain, but they are usually excellent offerings, giving long-flowering displays on plants of good habit – even in the first year from very early sowings. However, to be sure of having shark's-head forms, it will be necessary to select seed with great care.

A second source of confusion over seed strains concerns *P. barbatus* 'Coccineus', or *P. barbatus coccineus* as it was originally named in 1839, before distinctions between horticultural and botanical names were made. This name seems to have been applied to the bright scarlet version of *P. barbatus* (which could well be William Thompson's *P. barbatus splendens* of 15 years later) but it seems also to have become applied to *P. wislizeni*, which comes in the same strong colour. The possible explanation goes back some way: the original (1848) name for *P. wislizeni* was *P. coccineus*, but it was renamed *P. barbatus* var. *wislizeni* in 1862, regaining specific status as *P. wislizeni* only in 1959. Given that 'wislizeni' is such a tongue twister, it may well be that 'barbatus coccineus' was preferred. Besides the different floral structure and narrower foliage already described, the most telling argument for separate species status for *P. barbatus* and *P. wislizeni* is that, although closely related and with overlapping distributions, they do not seem to hybridize in the wild.

As if this were not enough confusion for one variety, a strain distributed as *P. barbatus coccineus* has been

P. eatonii in the 'semi-wild', happily colonizing a heap of discarded road stone in Little Snowbird Canyon, Utah.

found which uniformly gives large scarlet and white flowers similar to the giant hybrid P. 'Rubicundus' but smaller. Again the explanation may lie far back in time, in what is now fashionably known as a 'double take': first, the name *P. coccineus* was also erroneously applied in 1839 to *P. hartwegii*, one of the parents of the large-flowered hybrids, and second, some famous nurseries in this century for some reason took to describing these large-flowered hybrids as forms of *P. barbatus*. This may not be the correct explanation, but any other is likely to be much more complicated. Readers may by now understand the feeling of many who study penstemons that, attractive as they are on the surface, these flowers have a malevolent streak deep-down, at least when they come into contact with taxonomists.

Several clonal forms with *P. barbatus* parentage have been described over the years, but the mistaken attribution of some unrelated hybrids, for example *P.* 'Alice

Hindley' and *P.* 'Firebird', means that where a variety has died out and no full description has survived, we cannot be sure whether it was related to *P. barbatus* or not. In the following list of named varieties the link to *P. barbatus* has been established.

'Albus' Pure white, striking. This form may derive equally from natural or cultivated sources.

'Arroyo' A registered (1969) American cross between 'Prairie Fire' and *P. cardinalis* with red flowers. An improvement on 'Flathead Lake' (see below).

'Bashful' Salmon-coloured flowers, first mentioned in 1978.

'Coccineus' See above. A seed strain with vivid scarlet flowers. Name not always correctly applied.

'Elfin Pink' An American hybrid only 30cm (12in) or so high, dating from before 1978, strongly recommended in the USA for dry situations. Flowers a strong but definite pink. 'Pink Elf' may be synonymous; if so it is an earlier name. Several earlier clones or hybrids also had 'pink' in the name but it is not certain they still survive. A seed strain.

'Flathead Lake' Its floppy habit is not good, but it has given rise to some outstanding progeny. Coral or scarlet flowers, up to 60cm (2ft) high. Later given the name of 'Johnsoniae'.

'Jingle Bells' Released around 1995 in the UK. A bright scarlet form, not easily told apart from the type.

'Johnsoniae' See 'Flathead Lake'.

'Nanus Praecox' See above. A multicoloured seed strain, not always having a clearly defined 'shark's head' flower. Earlier and dwarfer than the species, probably from hybridization.

'Praecox' A taller version of 'Nanus Praecox' in a variety of colours. A seed strain.

'Prairie Dawn' A light, clear pink hybrid. Raised at the Horticultural Research Center of the University of Nebraska at North Platte, registered 1969.

'Prairie Dusk' A product of 'Flathead Lake' × P. strictus with good characteristics of habit and hardiness. The flowers come in shades of deep purple or violet. Raised at North Platte, registered 1990.

'Prairie Fire' An outstanding hardy hybrid of four species, via 'Flathead Lake' × 'Seeba Hybrid', another North Platte product, registered 1958. Low but strong-growing and graceful, with scarlet flowers.

'Prinz Daniel' Reported to us as a new yellow variety of German origin, released in 1997. As with 'Schooley's Yellow' (qv), it seems to have a less robust constitution than the type.

'Rondo' A recent trade name for 'Nana Praecox'. Sometimes rendered as 'Rhondo'.

'Rose Elf' An early development from 'Flathead Lake' in a strong rose colour, dating from before 1951. A seed strain.

roseocampanulatus This name has been used to describe a coral-red version of P. barbatus which is reasonably distinct and attractive, but its description as an apparent separate species has no botanic justification.

'Scharf Hybrids' A complex cross of 'Prairie Fire' and two doses of P. cardinalis, giving a wide and striking range of colours from pink and red to purple shades. The shark's head shape is less pronounced and the flowers slightly more dilated than in P. barbatus. 'Saskatoon Hybrids' are a selected strain of 'Scharf Hybrids'. Originated in Canada c.1972 by Alan Scharf. A seed strain.

'Schooley's Yellow' Yet another North Platte creation, registered in 1983, and only recently introduced to Europe. A stunning plant, under 60cm (2ft), with compact spikes of pure lemon yellow flowers. It arose as a selection from crosses using only a single original wild yellow plant of P. barbatus, found by Gussie Schooley. It is clonal, therefore, and can only be vegetatively propagated. Its seed yields a wide range of colours, including other yellows which should not be confused with it. It is less robust than ordinary P. barbatus – some botanists suspect that the yellow colour is associated with a genetic defect – but it is well worth persevering with.

'Violet Beauty' Also known as 'Violet Flathead Lake'. A cross of 'Flathead Lake' with an unknown species. Erect habit with violet flowers very like 'Violet Queen'. Raiser Ralph Bennett, before 1952.

'Violet Queen' P. barbatus in all but the vivid violet flower colour. It predates 'Flathead Lake' as it is known from before 1945 (cf. earlier discussion concerning the origin of the 'violet barbatus').

SUBGENUS SACCANTHERA

The subgenus Saccanthera consists of 25 species in three unequal sections, comprising 1, 6 and 18 species respectively. They are united by the possession of anther sacs which split at the front and only open a little way from the centre backwards (see Fig. 1 page 11). This and the fact that the sacs stay parallel at maturity typify the subgenus. A keen pair of eyes can pick up these details without the use of a magnifying glass. Three species from subgenus Penstemon exhibit the same features, as shown in Fig. 1, but otherwise are readily distinguishable Most of the Saccanthera species tend towards a low, shrubby habit, not more than 75cm (2½ft) high and usually rather less.

By penstemonial standards this group is relatively untroubled taxonomically speaking. There are good distinguishing features within the group; most species were recorded quite early since many inhabit the more accessible parts of the western seaboard states; and only two new species and a few varietal forms have been described since 1945.

SECTION EMERSUS

The one species in the section Emersus, P. rostriflorus, is quickly told apart from the rest by being the only one with red flowers. The flowers have lower lobes which are sharply retracted, giving the 'shark's head' appearance typical of P. barbatus and its relatives. It grows to about 70cm (2⅓ft) and inhabits dry parts of California and the inland desert states. In spite of this it has proved quite accommodating in garden conditions, and is a popular subject with enthusiasts. It was known as *P. bridgesii* for many years, and this synonym is still very widely used. Orange, pink and yellow forms are occasionally found.

SECTION SERRULATI

As the name suggests, the six species of the section Serrulati have sharply serrated leaves. The three rarest in cultivation are oddities, each in a different way: *P. glandulosus* feels sticky all over due to the secretion from myriad small glands, even on the flowers; *P. triphyllus* breaks ranks with all other penstemons in having three leaves to each node, arranged at 120 degrees around the stem; and *P. diphyllus* goes further in risking even its family links by frequently having leaves which alternate around the stem instead of being in the customary opposite pairs for the Scrophulariaceae. Occasionally one finds similar features as sports in other penstemons, another suggestion that only small genetic changes are involved.

The leaf serration in *P. serrulatus* is particularly jagged and uneven. It is found as far north as Alaska in semi-shaded woodland conditions, and is one of the few penstemons that prefers moist soil. The habit is bushy and slightly coarse but it is a prolific bloomer and gives a second flush in most seasons, reliably so if spent flowering stems are removed. It is easy from seed and a self-sower when happy, even displaying a thuggish disposition in swamping less vigorous neighbours. The flowers are 2.5cm (1in) long, with a colour that tends to be a mottling of blue and deep purple – a little ordinary by the high standards of the genus. The first flush of flowers are packed tightly at the tops of the stems. With its profuse foliage and strong spreading growth giving excellent ground cover, it might best be used to fill in difficult areas in the less formal parts of a garden. It has a white form, 'Albus', which is reliable from seed, and pinkish varieties are sometimes encountered.

P. venustus is similar to *P. serrulatus* but the flowers are bigger and lighter in colour. The whole plant is more graceful in habit, and might be recommended as the better type were it not for the fact that its flowers are sparser, normally appearing only towards the top of the stems. It is less tolerant of moisture than *P. serrulatus*.

P. barbatus 'Schooley's Yellow', a selected clonal variety derived from the naturally occurring but very rare forma *flaviflorus*.

P. richardsonii is a penstemon that can be grown purely for its foliage. The plant is effectively a sub-shrub, regrowing a spreading, twiggy superstructure each year from tight basal rosettes. The slender leaves are neatly serrated, and often to be found shaded in attractive greyish tints. The flowers are 2.5–3cm (1–1¼in) long, flattened at the mouth and with strangely hump-backed tubes.

SECTION SACCANTHERA

The remaining 18 species of this subgenus fall into the section Saccanthera, all typified by unserrated leaves. In many species these are grey-green and somewhat succulent, indicating a preference for dryland habitats.

Four of these species are immediately distinguishable by having bearded staminodes – *P. gracilentus*, *P. papillatus*, *P. pudicus*, and *P. scapoides*. The last is mat-forming, while the others tend to be more herbaceous than shrubby. They are of a delicate habit with flowers in pretty shades of blue and purple, but not in great abundance. Only *P. gracilentus* is at all common, and seems to take to cultivation reasonably well.

In the other 14 species, which have hairless staminodes, we find variations of hairy versus hairless parts, broad versus narrow leaves, and the tendency for some species to be more herbaceous than shrubby.

Leaves and flowers hairy: *P. kingii* (herb.), *P. laetus*

Leaves hairy, flowers not: *P. cusickii* (herb.), *P. heterophyllus* ssp. *purdyi*

Flowers hairy, leaves not: *P. filiformis*, *P. neotericus*, *P. purpusii*

Flowers and leaves hairless: *P. azureus*, *P. caesius*, *P. floribundus*, *P. heterophyllus*, *P. leonardii*, *P. parvulus*, *P. platyphyllus* (herb.), *P. sepalulus*.

From this group, *P. azureus*, *P. heterophyllus* and *P. laetus* are the species most often found in gardens. However, some of the others have been grown by enthusiasts with some success and are worth mentioning. *P. cusickii*, for example, is a diminutive, and reportedly good-natured, species from driest Idaho with pretty blue to lavender flowers. *P. sepalulus*, similarly, does well in gardens, and is quite widely grown in the USA. It is the largest of the Saccanthera, making a medium-sized bush 1.2m (4ft) in diameter. *P. platyphyllus* is a smaller subject which gives superb displays of airy sprays of clear lavender flowers on rocky banks in the Wasatch Mountains of Utah, and ought to do well in gardens; seed is now available. The diminutive *P. purpusii* is a mat-former with handsome violet flowers that has done well on both sides of the Atlantic, but it must have its feet kept dry. It is unusual in liking acid soil. *P. neotericus* also likes dry conditions, and is striking in that its flowers are yellow-brown when young but suddenly become a clear light blue at maturity. Lastly, the uncommon *P. kingii* has only just entered cultivation, but is showing promise not least for having very attractive, wavy-edged foliage.

The common species Of the commoner species in cultivation, *P. azureus* is a plant that drives hardened men to poetry when they see its beautiful flowers, not for any great abundance or showiness, nor for their size, but simply for the shade of blue – truly a pure azure. It was at one time treated as a subspecies of *P. heterophyllus* – which can have almost a similar coloration – and is only distinguished by its lighter green and broader leaves. *P. azureus* comes from a relatively mild part of California and Oregon and likes some summer moisture.

P. heterophyllus must be one of the most widely grown of any of the US penstemons. It has roughly the same range as *P. azureus*. The name, meaning 'different leaves', refers to the fact that tufts of smaller leaves occur in the axils of larger leaves, but it is far from being the only penstemon to possess this feature. It is a very variable species, in habit hovering between herbaceous and sub-shrubby, in leaf from dark green to almost grey, in leafage from quite sparse to quite the opposite, and in flower can be found with practically any shade between pinky-lavender and a vivid electric blue – often on the same plant, and even between flowers on the same stalk.

Given all this variation, and the fact that it has been in cultivation since early Victorian times, it comes as no surprise to find that a large number of named varieties exist of *P. heterophyllus*, most of them still in cultivation – 25 at the last count. We are unable to offer any information about the origin of these varieties except in a few cases, and it may even be that in the course of time names have become attached to the wrong plants – how else might a type with 'blue' in the name now be widely described as purple? Conjecture leads us to wonder if some of these varieties might be due to the presence of related species in them, notably *P. azureus*, but our overriding feeling is that there are more names than there are reliably definable forms.

The following are names ascribed to *P. heterophyllus* to our knowledge, but there are almost certainly more: 'Amethyst', 'Blue Bedder', 'Blue Eye', 'Blue Fountain', 'Blue Gem', 'Blue Robin', 'Blue Spring(s)', 'Blue of Zurich', 'California Blue Bedder', 'Carmen's Choice', 'Catherine de la Mare', 'Eastgrove Wine', 'Erectus', 'Heavenly Blue', 'Hergest Croft', 'Le Phare', 'Margarita Bop', 'Margery Fish', 'Mrs Blakey', 'Purdyi', 'Regina', 'Roehrslev', 'True Blue', 'Walker Ridge', 'Zuriblau'.

Of these, 'Le Phare' can definitely be eliminated – it is a large-flowered hybrid of French origin (see page 118). 'Blue of Zurich' is a rechristening of the Swiss

'Zuriblau' for American consumption. It is sometimes described as a tufted alpine sort with brilliant gentian blue flowers, but it is also known in continental Europe as a small herbaceous variety. It is offered as a seed strain.

'Blue Bedder' (1948), and probably 'California Blue Bedder', are trade-inspired names for the natural sub-species *purdyi*, which also attracts the misnomer 'Purdyi'. *P. heterophyllus* ssp. *purdyi* differs from the type in two main features – it has hairy flowers, and leaves which are twice the normal length but only slightly wider. It is appropriate to mention at this point *P. heterophyllus* ssp. *australis*, an intermediate form with hairy flowers but normal sized leaves.

'Blue Gem' is usually described as having purplish flowers on quite a low flat-topped bush. The display of flower is spectacular but not over-long. 'Heavenly Blue' is similar but more herbaceous, although in the 1970s, when we first saw the name, it was a striking sky blue. Has there been a 'reselection'? Or a mixing of labels?

'Blue Spring' (not 'Springs' as often seen) received an award as a seed strain from the RHS in 1969, which subsequently included it in its seed list from time to time. It was raised by the French firm of Clause. It is rather twiggy and greyish in leaf, with flowers which in bud are a unique cobalt green, becoming a vivid blue in maturity. It comes true from seed.

'Amethyst' is a Bressingham selection, but is now considered unlikely to be from *P. heterophyllus* at all, and in any case has been dropped since it proved to be shy to flower. It can still be viewed in the Dell garden at Bressingham in Norfolk.

In spite of occasional claims to the contrary, 'Margery Fish' was not raised by Margery Fish of East Lambrook Manor, Somerset, although she sold it under this name for a few years in the 1970s, as a form of *P. heterophyllus*. It grows quite low but with great vigour and is extremely floriferous – an excellent front-of-border subject. The flowers are more purple than blue.

The same description might fit 'Catherine de la Mare' except that it grows rather taller, to about 70cm (2⅓ft). This may also be a hybrid. It originated with Richard de la Mare – son of the poet Walter – around the 1950s at Hadham House, Hertfordshire. The foliage is a darker green than normal for the species and very dense. It usually gives a good second flowering if

trimmed over after the first. Name variations are rife – Mere for Mare, all the known variations of Catherine, and even de la Rue for de la Mare!

Some present-day offerings of 'True Blue' seem indistinguishable from 'Catherine de la Mare', and yet the name is known applied to a variety listed by the Alpine Garden Society since the 1930s. A misappropriation of the name may well have occurred.

P. heterophyllus is a particularly good example of the price of horticultural fame when no proper 'stud book' is kept. Some serious work is required to clarify the provenance and naming of both wild and cultivated material, followed by a reintroduction of validated stock.

The last of the common garden species is *P. laetus*. Broadly speaking, this plant is a hairy version of *P. heterophyllus* with perhaps a woodier appearance about it. It is slightly larger in habit and slightly smaller in flower. It can be confused with the two hairy subspecies of *P. heterophyllus* described earlier. It is its subspecies *roezlii* which is the best known form because the flowers are in a stronger and more uniform shade of violet, albeit a little smaller still than the type. This and other differences led it originally to be described as a separate species, *P. roezlii*, and there are some authorities still inclined to this view. What is more worrying for European readers is that since the 1930s a good deal of material offered under the name of *P. laetus roezlii* seems knowingly to have been *P. rupicola*. More recently, *P. davidsonii* has also appeared under this name.

SUBGENUS DISSECTI

This subgenus has a single species, *P. dissectus*. It is the only penstemon to have dissected leaves, albeit these are confined to the upper stems, the lower leaves being whole and quite broad, similar to the big-leaved eastern penstemons. The dissected leaves are often described as fern-like, but are perhaps more like those of marguerites; at any rate, they look as if caterpillars have been at work, leaving only the main veins. It is a herbaceous plant of around 70cm (2⅓ft) in height with dilated flowers up to 4cm (1½in) long in lavender and white. Although in cultivation in both the USA and Europe it is a rarity in the wild, confined to one area in the Appalachian Mountains. It takes to poor, acid soils quite happily.

SUBGENUS CRYPTOSTEMON

This subgenus also has a single species, *P. personatus*, which is confined to only a small area of California and is of endangered status. It resembles *P. hirsutus* in habit and in its purple flowers with totally closed mouths, but differs in having very broad leaves and a very small, somewhat coiled staminode.

SUBGENUS PENSTEMON

This is the largest subgenus, with 185 species divided into 8 sections and 21 subsections, making it a very diverse group indeed. The unifying feature is that the anther sacs are hairless and, when ripe, they split fully end to end and line up at right angles to the filament. There are a few exceptions to this rule, but the chances are that if you see four tiny gaping mouths facing you when you look at a flower then you are in subgenus Penstemon.

The subsections for the most part need not concern us, but the eight sections are valuable guides both to identification and to garden characteristics.

SECTION FASCICULUS

To the European gardener the section Fasciculus is the most important part of the whole genus *Penstemon*, not because many of the species as such are widely grown, but because they were the foundation of the development of the European Hybrids. This subject is discussed in Chapter 3, so here we shall deal only with the species.

Fasciculus contains 28 species, including some of the largest penstemons known, in both habit and flower. This is what gave them immediate appeal when collectors started sending material to Europe in the early 1800s. In fact there is only one miniature in the group – the common and popular *P. pinifolius* – and some would even prefer to see that one placed elsewhere, for example in Ericopsis, with whose members it has much in common.

Fascicles unite this section, and give it its name. A fascicle is simply the botanical word for a secondary branch growing from a main stem which stays small to begin with but later grows out and produces flowers. In a good season this process can be repeated, with fascicles growing from fascicles, so from the gardener's point of view fascicles are very good things as they extend the flowering season and provide a rich source of cuttings in autumn. If only more penstemons had fascicles!

P. pinifolius is also the geographical odd man out, being the only member of the section found in the USA. The others are firmly of Mexican origin, although one is also found as far south as northern Guatemala. Several of these species are very similar, of limited range, and rarely encountered, leaving only half a dozen which are of importance in cultivation.

The terrain in which the Mexican species grow varies from the usual dry semi-desert conditions to verdant woodland, often at high altitude. The species most familiar to British gardeners are certainly those which come from areas which experience some summer rainfall, and where the climate is more clement than in the USA, except California. Thus, persistence under British conditions is reasonably assured, but not totally guaranteed. It also means that, although they are far from being water-guzzlers, the occasional drink in dry spells will be appreciated, by young plants at least.

Taxonomically the section is divided into four subsections – Fasciculati, Campanulati, Perfoliati and Racemosi – but for identification purposes, it is better to think of a simpler, and by now familiar, classification: serrated versus unserrated leaves combined with broad versus narrow leaves. Thus:

Serrated/ broad: *P. bolanius, P. hidalgensis, P. moro-nensis, P. perfoliatus, P. schaffneri, P. tepicensis*
Serrated/ narrow: *P. campanulatus, P. gentryi, P. hintonii, P. kunthii, P. potosinus*
Unserrated/ broad: *P. coriaceus, P. gentianoides, P. hartwegii, P. isophyllus, P. leonensis, P. miniatus* ssp. *miniatus, P. mohinoranus, P. plagapineus, P. vulcanellus*
Unserrated/ narrow: *P. amphorellae, P. fasciculatus, P. filisepalulus, P. occiduus, P. pinifolius, P. miniatus* other than ssp. *miniatus, P. saltarius, P. skutchii, P tenuifolius*.

Occasional narrow leaves occur in the broad-leaved species, and serrated leaves in the unserrated, often in young leaves. The serration can be minute, and confined to the ends of the leaves.

The six main species

Only the six regularly offered species merit specific comment, several of the others being known only from one or two sightings.

P. campanulatus* and *P. kunthii These species are often regarded as synonymous, but this is not so. Their

P. richardsonii. Even before flowering, the striking foliage of this species offers good garden interest.

habits are similar: bushy, slightly floppy, up to 70cm (2⅓ft) high, and narrow, very finely notched leaves in bright green. However, in bloom they are totally distinct. The flowers of *P. campanulatus* are about 3.5cm (1⅜in) long, and widely dilated, in shades of purple with white throat and fine guidelines. *P. kunthii*, in contrast, has narrow tubular flowers with a high arch to the mouth, in deep red, purple-red or deep pink. In other words we have the classic difference between a bee-pollinated and a hummingbird-pollinated species.

P. campanulatus was first described in 1791 (as *Chelone campanulata*), and *P. kunthii* in 1817 (as *Chelone angustifolia*), so how could this confusion have come about? The reason seems to be that they hybridize together so freely in the wild that most later 19th-century authorities felt they had to be one species. Often no differentiation was made, but sometimes *P. kunthii* was split off as *P. campanulatus angustifolium* or *angustiflora* – murdering Latin grammar in the process, but let that pass. Nowadays the evolutionary

significance of the different flowers is better appreciated, and their status as separate species is not seriously challenged.

As if this were not enough, both species separately have laboured at some time under the name of *P. atropurpureus*, and *P. campanulatus* also as *P. pulchellus* and *P. elegans* – all names which are still sometimes seen, as is the invalid name *P. campanulatus roseus*. This latter was a pink variety offered for many years, sometimes as 'Roseus', but some material circulating in the UK under this name appears to be *P. kunthii*, or very near it. But, as if in compensation, some introductions of 'kunthii hybrids' in recent years are quite clearly forms of *P. campanulatus*!

Such confusion is unnecessary. The rule is simple enough for 99 per cent of cases:

Slender flowers in strong pink or red = *P. kunthii*
Bulbous flowers in violet, purple, or lightish pink = *P. campanulatus*

Plate V. Five named forms of *P. heterophyllus*, with the species for comparison (see page 73).

PLATE V

P. heterophyllus 'Zuriblau'

P. heterophyllus 'Blue Gem'

P. heterophyllus 'Blue Spring'

P. heterophyllus 'Catherine de la Mare'

P. heterophyllus 'Blue Fountain'

P. heterophyllus

All flowers are shown at approximately ½ size

Bulbous flowers in strong pink or red tones = a hybrid.

These two plants are a good way of starting a collection of penstemon species since they are graceful, floriferous, robust and easy-going. In USA they give a good account of themselves, survival down to –18°F (0°C) having been reported.

P. hartwegii and **P. gentianoides** This pair of species suffers equal confusion. The latter was first described in 1817 (as *Chelone gentianoides*), and the former in 1840, based on a collection in 1839 by Hartweg for the Royal Horticultural Society. Although related, the two species differ in a number of features. Moreover, they come from different parts of Mexico – *P. hartwegii* from a quite small area north of Mexico City, and the much commoner *P. gentianoides* from a large area south of the capital, and into Guatemala.

The chances of mixing up the two species might not therefore appear to be very great, but it was nevertheless very comprehensively achieved. For in 1838/9 three illustrations appeared in botanical periodicals under the name and description of *P. gentianoides*, but which were all clearly *P. hartwegii*. The correct naming of *P. hartwegii* followed within the year, whereupon it was widely assumed that *P. gentianoides* was a synonym, no doubt aided by the fact that no safely attributable illustration of the true *P. gentianoides* seems to have existed before 1851. By 1855, however, William Thompson was confidently writing about the differences between the species, and he is well worth quoting:

'[Gentianoides] is of very tall habit, frequently reaching the height of six feet, or even more, and its blossoms are of a dull purple, the tube being shorter and less drooping than in hartwegii. They are numerously produced, but the plant does not remain very long in flower. It is singular that hartwegii, and its varieties, now so common in our gardens, should ever have been mistaken for the preceding; for although its foliage is somewhat similar, the habit of the plant is very different, and also the colour and form of the flowers, which are pendant, and of various shades of scarlet and purple-crimson . . . flowering from the beginning of July to October, or even later.'

The modern botanist would also note the difference of flower shape: the fat and wide 4.5cm (1¾in) long

The illustration that still causes confusion, from the *Botanical Magazine* of 1838 – part of a painting of *P. hartwegii* wrongly identified as *P. gentianoides*. (Photograph by kind permission of the Linnean Society of London.)

flowers of *P. gentianoides* compared to the longer but narrower tubes of *P. hartwegii* – in other words, flowers adapted to different pollinators.

In spite of William Thompson's vehemence, by 1863 at the latest he seems to have bowed to fashion since thereafter he always listed *P. gentianoides* as a synonym of *P. hartwegii*. In gardening terms, *P. gentianoides* effectively lost its true identity, or rather almost lost it, since some nurseries got confused and used *P. gentianoides* (syn. *P. hartwegii*) instead!

It can be inferred from all this that *P. gentianoides* as a pure species fell out of commercial cultivation quite quickly as more compact and floriferous garden variants became available during the 1850s, possibly earlier. That the same fate befell *P. hartwegii* not much later is perhaps more surprising, given that it is a plant of great intrinsic beauty with distinct features that set it apart from its hybrid progeny. Nevertheless, all the evidence suggests that offers of *P. hartwegii* by the big seed-houses from the 1860s onwards was actually hybrid seed. Subsequent wild collections in this century may have reintroduced that species commercially to Europe, but not, as far as we can tell, *P. gentianoides*. (The situation may be different in California.) So when we read, say, that *P. hartwegii* was a parent of some particular hybrid in 1900, was it in fact the true species, or *P. gentianoides* under the wrong name, or some hybrid form of one or both? Such are the problems of researching penstemons.

There may be even more to this story, but enough of it has been told to show how a nomenclatural error in 1838 can still have repercussions over 150 years later. Perhaps it may also serve as a warning to those who believe that conservation of rare wild species is best done under cultivation. This may be true in establishments with adequate budgets, continuity of policy and dedicated staff, such that accredited stock is obtained, cared for, and bred pure. Otherwise the pressures of manpower and/or profit and/or ignorance and/or lost interest will soon bring about total loss, or the oblivion of hybridization.

A pure white form of *P. hartwegii*, given the name 'Albus', is particularly fine, producing long pure white tubes at maturity from buds which are cream or pale yellow. It is possibly the oldest surviving cultivar – see page 17. It is true from seed, but in common with many white varieties suffers the drawback of being susceptible to frosts. A *P. gentianoides albus* introduced by Ernst Benary of Germany c.1910 was in fact a large-flowered hybrid.

P. isophyllus and P. pinifolius

The remaining two species for detailed consideration are mercifully less controversial. *P. isophyllus* is a charmer growing quite close to Mexico City, which makes it all the more surprising that it was not discovered until 1901. At the risk of over-simplification, it might be regarded as a smaller-flowered version of *P. hartwegii*, around 3.5cm (1⅜in) long, and even narrower in the tube. The leaf is also noticeably shorter with a blunt end, and with a hint of blue in the colour. The foliage is more uniform in size, but possibly not so much so as to justify the name 'isophyllus', implying leaves all being equal. In English gardens *P. isophyllus* is really more herbaceous than shrubby unless very well sheltered, since, having flowered itself silly from early summer onwards, it usually gets cut back by the early frosts, only to regenerate from the base the following spring without any apparent loss of vigour.

In *P. pinifolius* we probably have the easiest-going and hardiest alpine in the whole genus. From seed or cuttings it rapidly forms a shrubby mat 10cm (4in) or so high, out of which the flower stalks reach 30cm (12in) or less. It has bright green needles for leaves – more like those of heather than of pine as its Latin name might suggest. In the flower it is unique, having very narrow tubes up to 5cm (2in) long, the anthers crowded into a mouth which, if not true 'shark's head', is definitely undercut: only hummingbirds need approach! The normal species is a bright but refined pillar-box red, but in the cultivar *P. p.* 'Wisley Flame' it is more a scarlet vermilion. A second cultivar, *P. p.* 'Mersea Yellow' is of English origin, from Mersea Island in Essex. It can lay claim to being the best yellow of any penstemon – a medium shade of daffodil with good substance and texture.

Quite recently a wild strain of *P. pinifolius* with orange flowers has come into cultivation. It has been christened 'Magdalena Sunshine' after the location in New Mexico where it was found. The orange shade is subdued, distinct and interesting. The plant yields a lot of variation from seed, with flowers of pink, orange, yellow, and red as well as bicolours. There is also a considerable incidence of sporting. Selected variants from this range, if they can be stabilized, will be of considerable gardening interest.

The one criticism levelled at *P. pinifolius*, mainly from American sources, is that it can be shy to flower, so stock should be carefully inspected for flowering shoots when purchasing. But even if it never flowered, those neat mounds of bright green would still be well worth having in gardens for foliage effect. And there is always the botanical talking point of how a native of the USA's semi-deserts can be quite so at home in temperate, humid Europe – a 'hardy' gene left over unwanted since the last Ice Age, or one that arose later and lay dormant with no purpose until man started dabbling?

Of the other 22 Fasciculus species little need be said: they tend to be very similar to one or other of the species already described, but on the whole less showy. Descriptions of *P. miniatus*, *P. leonensis* and *P. hintonii* suggest possible garden interest, and an opportunity to show off the giant *P. hidalgensis* might be appreciated by those who like to have something different. Add to that – if we are right – the loss to cultivation of the pure *P. hartwegii* and *P. gentianoides*, and a clear need emerges for a serious endeavour to establish a more representative range of these species in cultivation on a fully accredited basis. However, with the current clamp-down by the Mexican government on plant exports, due mainly to the indiscriminate predations of cactus hunters, it may be some time before that need can be met.

SECTION PELTANTHERA

The section Peltanthera is the first of two in the subgenus Penstemon which are distinguished by possessing leaves in shades of grey- or blue-green, usually with a decidedly succulent look – thick and fleshy or leathery. It is not surprising, therefore, that all 29 species in the section inhabit the desert states of south-western USA and parts of northern Mexico. More surprisingly, a number of these do well in cultivation in Europe, showing a gardenworthiness never less than interesting. Their main problem is a tendency to a floppy habit when growing in garden conditions if over-watered.

Nomenclature of the Peltanthera has never been a big issue, but the accepted split into four subsections has been placed in some doubt by recent genetic studies. Classically, serrated leaves versus unserrated leaves is a valuable diagnostic, as is flower colour, but there are complications not helped by interbreeding in the wild, producing natural hybrid swarms which blur identification. The following breakdown of species is as simple as possible:

Leaves serrated

Flowers white or light pink: *P. eximeus, P. grinnellii, P. palmeri*
Flowers deep pink, red or purple: *P. angelicus, P. bicolor, P. clutei, P. clevelandii, P. floridus, P. petiolatus, P. pseudospectabilis, P. rubicundus, P. spectabilis, P. stephensii, P. vizcainensis.*

Leaves unserrated

Narrow-leaved shrubs: *P. fructiformis, P. incertus*
Narrow-leaved herb: *P. subulatus*
Medium to broad leaves, purple or red flowers: *P. alamosensis, P. centranthifolius, P. cerrosensis, P. confusus, P. havardii, P. murrayanus, P. parryi, P. patens, P. rotundifolius,P. superbus, P. utahensis, P. wrightii.*
Apart from the rare or inaccessible species confined

to Baja California or the remoter desert areas of USA, each of these species has its own band of ardent supporters. Each may have its detractors too – reported experience varies, so that it may be necessary to experiment to find the best species for a given situation.

Serrated-leaf species Of the serrated-leaf species, *P. palmeri* is a favourite with most gardeners. It reaches 1.5m (5ft) high in the wild, but less in European gardens. It colonizes bare ground with gusto, and as a result is being chosen for amenity planting of new highway verges, which means its distribution is artificially expanding. The flower colour is white or pink. The flowers are arranged in neat pairs, and have a decidedly clownish appearance – fat and lined in the bud which makes them look like smiling whales, to be followed at maturity by flowers with gaping mouths out of which loll great hairy staminodes looking for all the world like worn-out toothbrushes. *P. palmeri* is one of the very few scented penstemons. Although it tolerates extreme winter conditions in its natural habitat it shows a distinct tenderness in the European climate, probably through the roots not being kept dry enough. In this respect the closely related *P. grinnellii* may be an improvement.

P. rubicundus from Nevada is similar to *P. palmeri*, but exhibits rather more of the classic penstemonial elegance. The flowers are less bulbous, and in much deeper shades of rose and purple – and with a much tidier toothbrush! It was named in 1937 by David Keck, who was probably unaware of the pre-existing and popular European hybrid *P.* 'Rubicundus' with which it has no connection whatsoever.

The remainder of the serrated leaf species in Peltanthera have much narrower tubular flowers, sometimes with much-reduced lobes, in choice and unusual shades of red and pink. *P. pseudospectabilis* is one of the best of these, its main drawback being its awful name. Its flowers are a glowing, almost luminous, shade of ruby red, such that a single flower can easily be seen from 50m (164ft). Nevertheless, the colour is in no sense garish. It is easy from seed and soon forms an exotic mound of blue foliage, with airy flowering stems to 70cm (2⅓ft) in gardens, more in the wild. Its name comes from its resemblance to *P. spectabilis*, another beautiful subject, but perhaps not quite as hardy and with more purple in the flower.

P. clevelandii is a similar species with a good constitution. As a contrast in habit but not in flower, the shrubby *P. petiolatus* grows no more than 20cm (8in) high and likes to perch in crevasses in limestone rock. It is noticeable for having pretty, rounded leaves on long petioles, hence the Latin name.

P. clutei deserves particular mention for the unique colouring of its flowers – a deep pink with hints of purple and brown – and the regular saw-tooth serration of its leaves. It comes from a small area of Arizona, where it is coming under threat from the popularity of ORD (off-road driving) in the USA, an activity which entails causing much damage to the countryside without an apparent destination in mind: '*Cui usi?*' as John Mitchell might have put it. Conservation measures are in hand, but gardeners can also play their part by preserving and increasing cultivated stock, of which, fortunately, there seems to be a good quantity. *P. clutei* has a good reputation for hardiness in the UK. A white cultivar named 'Albiflorus' is known.

Unserrated-leaf species A number of the Peltanthera species with unserrated leaves have the red tubular flowers of their serrated-leaf cousins. *P. centranthifolius* is perhaps the showiest of them, and gains from being quite compact in habit. *P. alamosensis*, *P. utahensis* and *P. parryi* are all well recommended, the last-named in particular giving spectacular displays on hillsides in its native Arizona. This group has in general quite small flowers – under 2.5cm (1in) – and attractively crinkled or waved foliage. Records of a blue (or white) *P. utahensis* are dubious, the error possibly stemming from confusion with *P. glaber* ssp. *utahensis*, now known to be *P. subglaber* or *P. speciosus*.

Although the flowers of *P. superbus* are only some 1.8cm (¾in) long, its name is justified by its majestic habit; it produces radiating flowering stems up to 2m (6½ft) high with flowers in whorls for most of their length. This stature is not easily obtained in moister climates, for if the growth is at all sappy the stems are soon blown over. The closely related but more compact *P. wrightii* from Texas and Arizona might be a better choice for such conditions, and it has the advantage of particularly fine foliage, with basal mounds of broad undulating leaves in an attractive shade of grey-green. This was a Victorian favourite which held its own against the fashionable hybrids until the First World War. It is commonly known as the Texas rose, and the stock sometimes offered under this name is probably not the result of any special selection.

P. murrayanus, also from Texas, was enthusiastically received when it first reached Europe in 1835, but it was soon attracting bad notices for being short-lived – in England at least: apparently it fared better in Scotland. Possibly the problem was more one of it having a very short life unless specially treated, for example by ruthlessly cutting out old flowering stems before seed formation can occur in order to encourage early basal growth. Any plant that sends its stems up to 2m (6½ft) in a season then flowers and seeds profusely must take a lot out of itself, and may not have much left come the autumn. It is stately in habit, and a kaleidoscope of colouring: a basal mat of blue-green leaves, often with purple edges; dilated flowers up to 3.5cm (1⅜in) long in orange-scarlet with green anther sacs on red filaments and a red staminode; and flower buds in greenish yellow. It nevertheless appeals to many gardeners, as do the closely related but less common *P. havardii* (not harvardii, as it is often spelt) and *P. rotundifolius*. The pinewood habitat of *P. murrayanus* indicates some tolerance of shade.

Growing conditions To sum up the Peltanthera, there is much to recommend these species to any gardener who likes the exotic look, together with reasonable to good persistence – which is not, after all, a very common combination. For those who are equipped for growing plants in dry conditions, with sand beds and the like, the problem will mainly be to stop them overwhelming any less vigorous companions. In temperate gardens, however, their unusual colouring and dry-ground requirements militate against normal herbaceous border treatment, and most gardeners will probably prefer to grow them separately as specimen plants, or in large pots.

SECTION ANULARIUS

Anularius forms the second section in subgenus Penstemon having grey- or blue-green foliage. In contrast to the Peltanthera the flower colour is in the blue to lavender range, with several species also having common pink or white forms. The two sections have some overlap of distribution in the desert states, but the focus for Anularius is noticeably further north and east, in the Great Plains and the Canadian prairies.

The section contains 18 species, all herbaceous and leafy in appearance, with large thick leaves in the basal rosette and on the flowering stems. The flowers are packed into whorls close to the stem, often encircled by the stem leaves in natural posies. Apart from two or three desert species, the growth is sturdy, usually to 70cm (2⅓ft), in some species considerably more. The whole effect is of plants that can look after themselves, which indeed they have to when in competition with the grasses of the plains and prairies. Some (notably *P. grandiflorus*) are vigorous enough to cause problems to farmers.

Some distinctive species Identification within the section is quite difficult since some species are so variable. Thus, no simple groupings offer themselves, but a few species do have distinguishing features. *P. secundiflorus*, for example, has flowers that all point in one direction, 'secund' being the botanical term for this phenomenon. Whether this is done as a convenience to visiting bees or to gain maximum light for rapid seed-ripening is not clear. Secundity frequently occurs in other penstemons, including several European Hybrids. It is also found in other genera, but whereas in, say, freesias it is due to the flower buds all being on one side of the stem, in a penstemon it is the flower stalks doing U-turns and growing at right angles that produce the phenomenon. It is an intriguing mechanism, although one not welcomed by hybridists, who generally see this one-sided look as a disadvantage. Nevertheless, *P. secundiflorus* is nothing less than handsome, with blue or lavender flowers up to 2.5cm (1in) long massed on stems 70cm (2⅓ft) high. It is common in the eastern Rockies from Wyoming to New Mexico.

P. grandiflorus, which grows widely from North Dakota to Texas, stands out for having the largest flowers of any US penstemon bar, possibly, *P. cobaea*. These are 5cm (2in) long and widely dilated, held on stems up to 1.2m (4ft) tall radiating from a strong basal rosette. This gives a striking vase-like geometry to the habit. The flower colour varies from blue through lavender and light purple to pink and white, perhaps the widest variation of any penstemon. Trials at North Platte have demonstrated 31 different and distinct colour shades. Attempts to develop reliable seed strains by colour are in progress, the main success to date being with a pure white found in the wild, which has been isolated and

registered as *P.* 'Prairie Snow' in 1990. This comes true from seed if the pollen of other forms is excluded. *P.* 'War Axe' is a new seed strain for which colours of improved substance are claimed. *P. grandiflorus* is a very considerable presence in a garden, and needs a lot of space; for the smaller garden *P. angustifolius* (see below) gives the same colour effect, but is more compact.

By contrast, *P. cyathophorus* is the smallest-flowered species of this group and its relative, *P. harringtonii*, is only slightly larger. They are only found in one part of Colorado, and are not all that common. Their distinguishing feature is in the stamens, which project well beyond the mouth of the flowers. Closely enveloping leaves clasp each whorl of flowers in a tight embrace. The flowers themselves come in a range of pastels from purple to rose, and the combination with the grey-blue leaves is striking.

Pretty as they are, three Utah species of limited distribution – *P. bracteatus*, *P carnosus* and *P. flowersii* – cannot detain us long since their specialized near-desert habitats have proved difficult to reproduce in gardens, and in any case material is unlikely to become commercially available. However, *P. pachyphyllus*, another desert species, is more widespread and relatively easy in cultivation. Its name suggests broad leaves, but this is a little misleading except in the variety *mucronatus*. It is quite small of stature, no more than 30cm (12in) high. The related *P. osterhoutii* is quite similar, but grows to twice the size.

Returning to the plains, *P. nitidus* grows along both sides of the 49th Parallel from Manitoba westwards, and down to South Dakota. It is small for a plains species, under 30cm (12in) high, and seems to survive by being an early bird, flowering and seeding quickly in the expectation of a short life. In Europe, flowering in mid-spring is not unknown, the 1.8cm (¾in) flowers being held in a good shade of mid-blue over quite a long period, until purple creeps in after maturity. It needs a combination of minor features to identify it, particularly as it has broad- and narrow-leaved forms, but it is another of those 'once seen, never forgotten' penstemons. It is widely grown in gardens all over USA, even as a front-of-border bedder. It flowers well in Europe, but seems more difficult to keep alive in wet winter conditions. Fortunately it is quite easy from seed and cuttings.

If we overlook a number of minor differences, we can describe *P. acuminatus* as a double-size version of

P. nitidus. It grows in some fearsomely dry and barren places in inland Washington and Oregon, yet is reported to do well in cultivation, even in areas of quite high rainfall. William Thompson had it in his catalogue for 50 years from the 1860s, a sure sign of its popularity in those days.

The Angustifolius cluster All but one of the remaining Anularii – *P. angustifolius, P. arenicola, P. buckleyi, P. fendleri, P. immanifestus* and *P. lentus* – form a loosely similar group with *P. angustifolius* as the defining type, if only because that species is so variable that it can resemble any of the others in one or other of its forms. It has probably the widest distribution of any penstemon species, from Montana to Arizona via the Great Plains, with excursions into the eastern Rockies. Inevitably, with such a range a lot of subspecies exist, with cross-bred variants to boot. As a generalization, the northern communities have the distinctive narrower leaves from which the Latin name derives (*angustus* meaning narrow) and the purest blue shades, including a turquoise which some rate as the best blue of any penstemon. The flowers are not the largest, yet it is a showy species, very robust once established, and justly popular with enthusiasts on both sides of the Atlantic. Some taxonomic confusion needs to be borne in mind when buying: *P. angustifolius* was for many years also known as *P. caeruleus*, a name which was also applied horticulturally, not to say grotesquely, to *P. hartwegii*; while *P. kunthii* was termed *P. angustifolia* by some authorities until quite recently.

Of the remaining members of this informal subgroup, *P. arenicola, P. immanifestus* and *P. lentus* occupy barren terrain in various areas to the west of *P. angustifolius*. They are good subjects, but very much for the specialist in xeric alpines. Not so *P. fendleri*, which is found either side of the Mexican border, and comes strongly recommended by several growers. It has larger flowers than *P. angustifolius*, usually exceeding 2.5cm (1in), which are prettily pencilled on the upper as well as the lower lip – a feature confined to relatively few other species. *P. buckleyi* has also found favour as an easy-going garden subject, best thought of as a very broad-leaved version of *P. angustifolius*. Its natural habitat is the southern Great Plains, but it seems to be spreading northwards along roadworks, and has now reached Nebraska.

P. haydenii We have left *P. haydenii* until last because it celebrates a movement and a man. It cannot be recommended at present as a garden plant since it is on the Federal list of endangered species, which means prohibition of all distribution of material including seed, even from garden sources. While some might regard this as draconian to the point even of negating the conservation intent of the law, at least the rules are clear; but, more to the point, the law is backed up by action and public money. Thus, as a result of grants, the University of Nebraska has been able to raise several thousand seedlings for wild repopulation.

That is the movement: the man is Claude Barr (1887–1983), whom we have already met as the man who, virtually single-handedly, raised a nation's awareness of a neglected flora in its own Great Plains heartland. *P. haydenii* was a particular favourite of Barr's, and it was through his efforts that Federal intervention came about. This plant looks sturdy, and is intermediate between *P. grandiflorus* and *P. angustifolius* in appearance, with quite large and fat flowers mainly in pink or white and slightly scented. Some authorities believe it arose as a natural hybrid of these species, but, if so, it developed in the process its own very special quirk: a need to grow in pure sand. It lives only in the sandhill district of north-west Nebraska, where it is first on the scene when a new 'blow-out', or sandhole, appears, disappearing as soon as the dune grasses set up too much competition with their matted root systems.

It seems that *P. haydenii* is able to colonize bare sand because its root system develops rapidly and deeply until it reaches better subsoil. In old times most blowouts came from wind erosion where the activities of bison, and later domestic cattle, laid bare small areas of the sandy soil. But the number of blowouts decreased dramatically with the enclosure of land for arable crops by homesteaders, and also because of different cattle management practices. Claude Barr observed these trends over his long life, and with it the decline of the *P. haydenii* population. Fortunately he sounded the alarm in time, and *P. haydenii* looks to have been saved. It is both a classic and a unique story revealing the fragility of the natural environment and man's unwitting impact on it. Happily but strangely, since it is not in an area noted for blow-outs, *P. haydenii* may be seen at Kew Gardens near London.

The comments made about the Peltanthera apply pretty well to the Anularii. Their exotic appearance is at the heart of their appeal; and many gardeners may prefer the subtler, mainly pastel, blends of flower and leaf colour.

SECTION ERICOPSIS

The section Ericopsis contains 14 species, all of them rather small in habit, leaf and flower, and all of them shrubby or sub-shrubby in character. Several species are real miniatures, and comprise some of the best alpine subjects outside the Dasanthera. They hail principally from the desert states from Utah southwards, but, by the standards of severity that can apply in that area, these species do not occur in the most extreme habitats. They are, nevertheless, definitely drylanders and should be treated accordingly.

The endangered *P. haydenii* thriving in pure sand. In this location, numbers increased by 20 per cent in a year. The much narrower leaves on non-flowering stems can be clearly seen in the foreground.

Two of the species, *P. ambiguus* and *P. thurberi*, stand out as the tallest growers, even reaching 1m (3¼ft) in good conditions. *P. ambiguus* is fairly common from Utah down to northern Mexico and puts up spectacular displays in the wild, at times turning whole hillsides pink. With its many thin stems, very narrow leaves and delicate panicles of pink flowers, its whole habit imparts a truly graceful appearance. The flowers are about 2.5cm (1in) long, and unique in shape for a penstemon: very narrow pink tubes, each ending in a flat, upward-facing, white disc formed by a retracted upper lip and a projecting lower one – very similar to *Achimenes*. *P. thurberi* is similar, but both smaller, and a shade deeper, in the flower. For gardeners who can offer hot sandy conditions *P. ambiguus* presents little difficulty, but for the rest of us it is a tricky subject. It germinates easily enough, but the problem comes when it has to be weaned out of the seedling stage into permanent quarters.

Another pale-coloured species, *P. laricifolius*, is a little easier in this respect, and probably is hardier as well. A

Wyoming native, it puts up its flowering stems to no more than 20cm (8in), from small tufts of narrow leaves. The flowers are in white, sometimes very light purple, about 1.8cm (¾in) long, with the projecting lower lip of *P. ambiguus* but not the retracted upper lip. *P. laricifolius* is a delightful miniature, not showy but very graceful.

P. linarioides is quite a robust member of the section. It comes in a number of varieties, some being mat-formers and floppy with it, others being more upright with stems to 50cm (20in). The leaves are so thin and spiky as to be heather-like, in shades of grey-green. This makes it like a greyer version of *P. pinifolius* – until it comes to the flowers, which are quite different. These are grouped no more than three to a stem in shades from blue to violet, usually paler than deeper. They are about 1.8cm (¾in) long, quite bulbous and open-mouthed, with the lips at right angles to the tube. The lower lips have guidelines. Given stony soil it seems very hardy under British conditions. *P. californicus*, once counted as a subspecies of *P. linarioides*, is similar but the flowers have no guidelines and the leaves are less needle-like. *P. discolor* is also similar, but its flowers are only 1cm (½in) long, and in a cream, or occasionally pale lilac, shade. All three species are noticeably hairy.

A group with slightly broader leaves is centred on *P. crandallii*. The flowers are blue or dark blue, with relatively few guidelines, the main difference from *P. linarioides* being the forward-projecting upper lip. It also seems to take well to garden conditions. *P. ramaleyi* and *P. retrorsus* are similar to *P. crandallii*, but restricted in range to parts of Colorado, and not known to be in cultivation. *P. abietinus* is another comparative rarity, this time from Utah, but is reported in cultivation and does well. It prefers a little shade since its natural habitat is open woodland. It is told apart from *P. crandallii* by having flower lobes all the same size, and much narrower leaves.

The alpine Ericopsis The four remaining species of Ericopsis are all choice alpine subjects less than 15cm (6in) high, and blessed with fairly good temperaments, with the exception of the tiny *P. acaulis*. This is a leafy mat-former not over 2.5cm high (1in) even at flowering time, because the flowers have only tiny stalks. The leaves are narrow, and the flowers small, bright blue, tubular and dotted singly in the herbage. It grows

around the area where Utah, Colorado and Wyoming meet. In cultivation it is greatly prone to rot, and the pleas in the literature from experienced alpinists for tips on how to stop this might bring a wry smile from those less expert were it not for the growing concern that its natural habitat is coming under threat from land development.

P. caespitosus, *P. thompsoniae* and *P. teucrioides* are much more amenable and widely grown. They represent variations on a very similar theme of low mats and small but well-coloured flowers in various blues and violets. *P. thompsoniae* is distinguished by its small oval leaves covered in white hair, while in *P. teucrioides* the leaves are much narrower and with greyer hair. With *P. caespitosus* the hair is also greyish but much less in evidence, even absent in some forms. Their habitats vary, with *P. caespitosus* finding perhaps the easiest living in the Rockies when compared to the much drier conditions experienced by the other two. In cultivation the alpine house might be the best place for them in Europe, but they have been successfully grown outside, particularly *P. teucrioides*, which is quite vigorous.

Two cultivars of *P. caespitosus* have been released in recent times – *P. c.* 'Claude Barr' by Siskiyou Nursery in the USA in about 1987, and *P. c.* 'Bruce Alexander' by Denver Botanic Gardens in 1991. 'Claude Barr', also known as 'Denver Botanical Gardens', is a miniature form of a miniature with round leaves under 6mm (¼in) long. ('Cloud Barr' is a misnomer.) 'Bruce Alexander' is a pure white-flowered variety forming small mats of yellowish-green leaves. A native of central Colorado, it has probably been known since about 1945, although it was not named until 1991.

SECTION AURATOR

The 31 species of section Aurator are not broken down for taxonomic purposes, but for gardeners they fall into two distinct and unequal sections. Six of them are lowland species, all discovered before 1902 and all but one in cultivation, while the other 25 are drylanders from the Great Basin and the desert states, all but three discovered after 1903 (nine since 1960), and only one at all widely grown as a garden plant.

All Aurators are herbaceous with basal rosettes, and have notably hairy flowers and herbage, the flowers borne in loose spikes. The common theme that unites them in a separate section is the eye-catching golden or

P. grandiflorus. An example from the middle of the colour range, which extends from white to deep purple.

orange hairs on the staminode, which are often long and bristly. The staminode is usually prominent in the mouth, in several species actually protruding beyond it.

The lowland species Of the lowland species, *P. cobaea* stands out in importance as the parent of many of the European Hybrids bred in the 19th century. Found in Texas around 1835, its range stretches northward throughout the Great Plains, with signs that it is also spreading westward into New Mexico. It is sturdy, no more than 70cm (2⅓ft) high, with large, broad leaves both in the basal rosette and up the stems. The flowers are very large, often over 5cm (2in) long and widely dilated, with staminodes which are less hairy than most Aurators. The colour is white, sometimes flushed

pink or violet, with prominent guidelines on both upper and lower lips. A subspecies, *purpureus*, with deeper purple flowers, is confined to the southeast part of the species' range.

P. cobaea caused great interest when it was first received in Europe, and Thompson & Morgan had it in their catalogue until 1923. After that it seems to have waned in popularity, and it is now more talked about than grown, probably because it is, frustratingly, not quite hardy even in southern Britain, but not really an alpine house subject either. In the USA, however, it is still widely grown, and has a reputation for being good-natured, long-flowering and long-lived. Seed germination can be erratic, and commonly does not occur until the second spring after sowing.

P. albidus is similar in colouring and habit to *P. cobaea*, but with narrow grey-green leaves, and flowers which are only half the length and width. It is widespread in the Great Plains and the Canadian prairies. Under garden conditions in the USA it has proved tough and long-lived, giving good displays of flower in early summer. It was one of the species listed by John Fraser in 1813, but it has not been much offered since in Europe.

Two species, both Texan, complete the group of light-coloured Aurators – *P. guadalupensis*, which is not in cultivation, and *P triflorus*, which is rarely so, strangely, since it is very fine. *P. triflorus* comes in white, pink or red-flowered forms, with tubes about 3.8cm (1½in) long. The throat and both lips are strongly marked with three clear lines per lobe. Seed is occasionally available for those who wish to experiment.

P. eriantherus, another of John Fraser's introductions, is perhaps the most gardenworthy of the lowland group, found in drier areas of the northwestern Great Plains, and into Canada. It is rather variable, with a number of botanical varieties, but is typically up to 50cm (20in) high, with grey-green foliage and medium-sized flowers which are as wide at the mouth as they are long. The mouth is filled with golden hair from the prominent staminode, and makes a pleasing contrast to the overall lavender or blue-violet colouring of the tube. Fine guidelines in deep violet complete a colourful but refined display that would grace any border. Varieties of *P. eriantherus* also exist in shades of pink and reddish-purple. *P. gormanii* is a related hardy sort which hails from Alaska and the Yukon. It has smaller flowers in a slightly lighter colour range. A useful, but not unique, aid to identification of both species is that the flowers are sticky to the touch.

The dryland species Turning to the 25 dryland Aurators, only *P. jamesii*, from New Mexico and Colorado, is at all widely grown as a garden plant. It can reach 50cm (20in) but it is usually much smaller, so that its 3.5cm (1⅜in) lavender flowers appear very large in comparison, the more so since they are strongly dilated both vertically and horizontally. The staminode protrudes out of the mouth, and the overall effect is not unlike *P. eriantherus*. *P. jamesii* is sometimes described as synonymous with *Chionophila jamesii*, but this is not so: both were first described as totally separate species in the same 1846 publication, but unfortunately given the same species name.

P. breviculus, *P. cleburnei*, *P. grahamii*, *P. janishiae*, *P. miser* and *P. ophiantus* are all related to *P. jamesii*. A second group, not much further removed, comprises *P. auriberbis*, *P. dolius*, *P. duchesnensis* and *P. pumilus*. All these sorts tend to be quite miniature and desirable dryland alpines which from time to time become available. Under European conditions they are probably best treated as alpine-house subjects.

The remaining 14 species contain some little gems, but because of rarity and difficulty in cultivation it is unlikely they will ever become common garden subjects, although occasionally seed may be offered by the native seed collectors. As a rough guide, we list them by wild locality:

California: *P. calcareus*, *P. monoensis*
Nevada: *P. barnebyi*
Northern Mexico: *P. pringlei*, *P. punctatus*
Utah: *P. atwoodii*, *P. concinnus*, *P. franklinii*, *P. goodrichii*, *P. marcusii*, *P. nanus*, *P. pinorum*
Utah/Colorado: *P. moffattii*.

The usual lavender/purple shades dominate this group, except for the two Californian species, which have red flowers.

SECTION DENTANTHERA

This section comprises four dryland species which are united by an unfortunately small feature for which a hand lens is needed to discern – the split edges of the open anther sacs are strongly toothed, as in some Saccanthera. They also resemble the Saccanthera in that the anthers stay parallel at maturity, but differ from

P. albidus in good heart despite the competition from prairie grasses.

them in having fully instead of partially opening sacs. Fortunately for gardeners the Dentanthera are not commonly encountered, although all have been cultivated at some time or other.

P. lanceolatus is the commonest of the four species, being widely distributed in dryish situations in northern Mexico and just into Texas. It is herbaceous, not above 60cm (2ft), with quite narrow leaves. Its flowers are deep red, slightly dilated and 3.5cm (1⅜in) or more in length – not unlike *P. hartwegii*, but it suffers in comparison with that species by being much sparser in flower. It has been frequently mistaken by botanists for *P. imberbis*, mainly due to the differences of anther detail being overlooked. *P. ramosus* is a slightly larger version all round of *P. lanceolatus*, differing mainly in having even narrower, grass-like, leaves. It is confined to a small area on the New Mexico/Arizona border.

P. stenophyllus and *P. dasyphyllus* also have grass-like leaves, but differ in having flowers in shades of violet and lavender. The latter is notably hairy all over, while *P. stenophyllus* is hairless and is also distinguished by having strongly dilated flowers. Their distribution straddles the Mexico/USA border.

SECTION BACCHARIFOLII

P. baccharifolius is the only member of this section, and is one of those awkward exceptions which complicate the genus – it is shrubby, and the anther sacs only open part-way from the front, as in the subgenus Saccanthera. However, as a red-flowered species it only has one counterpart in that group – *P. rostriflorus* – and there are several distinct differences to guide us. *P. baccharifolius* has hairy dilated flowers, and the leaves are small, broad and neatly serrated, whereas *P. rostriflorus* has small 'shark's head' flowers and long, narrow leaves.

P. baccharifolius is a little beauty from the Texas/Mexico border. Its natural habitat is limestone cliffs, and it consequently needs great care with drainage. In Europe it is probably best in the alpine house.

SECTION PENSTEMON

The remaining 63 species of subgenus Penstemon fall into this section, and include many useful gardening subjects. Here it is necessary to consider subsections for the first time. This is less daunting than it

P. triflorus. The triplet of guidelines on each lobe is particularly clear in this example.

may sound, because four of the nine – Arenarii, Deusti, Gairdneriani and Harbouriani – are small specialized groups, and two – Multiflori and Tubaeflori – contain one species each which are both very close to the subsection Penstemon, indeed at one time were part of it.

This leaves the three main subsections, which are Proceri, Humiles, and Penstemon. In general terms these are respectively small, medium and large in terms of stature, leaf and flower, but a more precise distinction is obtained from the characteristic of the inflorescence as a whole, and in particular the flower stalks – the peduncles and pedicels – branching from the main stem.

In Proceri the flower stalks are much shorter than the flowers, with the result that the latter are crowded in whorls around the stems to give a tiered effect to the inflorescence. In the Humiles they are about the same length as the usually bigger flowers, giving a more open appearance. In Penstemon the flower stalks are much longer and are usually branched once or twice, to give an airy panicle often of considerable size. Roughly equivalent arrangements in well-known genera might be *Erica* for Proceri, *Alyssum* for Humiles and *Thalictrum* for Penstemon.

Subsection Proceri

The 17 species of the subsection Proceri are largely confined to the northwestern states of the USA, with two showing up in western Canada. They are mainly tufted or mat-forming, and generally inhabit dry uplands, although they will not refuse moist situations if offered – one or two species actually prefer damp soil. The result of this is two-fold. First, there can be a wide disparity in the size of individual plants depending on how fortunate they are in their micro-habitat, and secondly they adapt pretty well to European conditions given, as usual, good drainage. Their frost-hardiness is not in question.

The flowers are under 1.2cm (½in) long, making them rather difficult to examine, but fortunately the species are separable by other features. The leaves are smooth-edged and are borne on distinct stalks. This is quite a uniform group, so inevitably there have been frequent changes of classification with at least six of the currently recognized species having been treated as variants of others in the past, and naturally these, being the commonest and most desirable, are the ones most

P. *eriantherus*. Delicate and diminutive, it nevertheless thrives in some of the grimmest badlands imaginable.

often found in cultivation to confuse the gardener.

P. *procerus* is the type species of this group, although for some time it was treated as a variety of P. *confertus*. It is an alpine mat-former, seldom more than 30cm (12in) high. It tolerates shade but may not flower as well as in full sun. It comes in six subspecies, making it a study in itself, but the constant features are narrow tubes which are totally hairless, and tiny black anthers which tend to protrude through the mouth. It is very

variable in colour, from deep violets and true blues which are very pretty through purples and pinks to rather washed-out whites and creams which do little to commend themselves as garden plants. The sub-species *tolmiei* can be a real miniature, often no more than 3cm (1¼in) high: it has a good pale yellow flower, but also comes in pink, white and lavender blue, not to mention bicolours. The pink form has been segregated as the variety P. *p.* 'Roy Davidson'. With such variety on hand P. *procerus* is a gamble from seed, but if that does not appeal it pays to buy from a specialist who has done the selecting for you.

P. *rydbergii* can reach 70cm (2⅓ft) in height but is otherwise close to P. *procerus* in form. Its flowers are also bigger, and the tubes more expanded. The colour range is similar, but excludes the paler shades, making it a safer buy, although rather too large to be considered a genuine alpine. A good feature for recognition are the sepals, which are very large, and wide, toothed and papery. It is definitely a moisture-lover, although one of its three varieties, *oreocharis*, tolerates dryish conditions. It has spread further south than other Proceri, being found in Arizona and New Mexico.

P. *confertus* has the rare distinction among penstemons of being a true yellow but is otherwise similar to P. *procerus*, though perhaps 10cm (4in) taller on average. The variety P. *c.* 'Kittitas' was registered in 1959 as a dwarf deep yellow variety, and this or a similar form can sometimes still be encountered in the wild.

P. *flavescens* is another yellow species, but not found outside the borders of Idaho and Montana. The yellow is often in a brownish shade. The tubes expand to give a wide mouth, unlike most Proceri. Similar, but with white flowers, is P. *pratensis*, which is also quite localized.

Three purple pairs Three pairs of species with flowers in the purple spectrum again show close affinities with P. *procerus*. P. *peckii* differs in having much narrower leaves but shows the same wide range of flower colour. P. *cinicola* is a smaller relative of P. *peckii* with sparser flowers, but in stronger colours. Neither is particularly common in the wild, but P. *peckii* is frequently found in gardens and is said to be even a touch invasive.

The second pair comprises P. *watsonii* and P. *laxus*. Unlike P. *procerus*, these are herbaceous plants which can reach 70cm (2⅓ft). They do not retain any basal leaves, and thus look rather sparse in habit. The flowers of *P. laxus* are small, with narrow tubes in a shade of magenta. It was originally described as a subspecies of the much commoner *P. watsonii*, which mainly differs in having flowers of a bluer shade and with a slightly more dilated flower tube.

The third pairing is of *P. attenuatus* and *P. globosus*. The former is an easy-going garden subject, a mat-maker like *P. procerus* but distinguished by its hairy flowers. It has the same variability of flower colour and habit, although some forms tend to be rather taller, up to 75cm (2½ft). There are four subspecies, of which ssp. *palustris* is interesting in preferring moist conditions, while ssp. *militaris* comes in erect spikes of a striking deep blue colour. Unfortunately its military title belies a certain taxonomic indiscipline because, in company with *P. globosus*, it has broken ranks with the rest of the Proceri by having anthers which do not fully open – as in the Subgenus Saccanthera. However, the form of the inflorescence would never allow them to be taken for anything but Proceri. *P. globosus* was originally described as a subspecies of *P. attenuatus*, but now has separate status. Its blue-violet flowers are 2–2.5cm (¾–1in) long and have moderately expanded tubes, making it the largest-flowered of the group. As its name implies, the flowers are bunched into a single tight ball on each stem. It likes moist conditions.

The Euglaucus cluster Two species have bluish leaves – *P. euglaucus* and the Oregon rarity *P. glaucinus*, now officially an endangered species. There is little to choose between them in appearance. *P. euglaucus* is much commoner, and is a vigorous, frost-resistant mat-former under 10cm high (4in), with flowering 50cm (20in) stems sporting whorls of purple or blue flowers. The foliage is attractive in its own right for its colour, compact regularity, and neatly elliptical leaf shape.

The final four Proceri make a group of essentially mat-formers of similar character to *P. euglaucus*, except that the leaves are smaller and in a true green. Only *P. heterodoxus*, a high alpine found in dry situations at 3660m (12,000ft) or more in the Sierra Nevada, is well-established in cultivation. It is highly rated by those who can grow it. It forms low mats of foliage covered in the flowering season by dense whorls of deep blue flowers, the whole never higher than 15cm (6in). The subspecies *cephalophorus* is a slightly larger form growing at lower altitudes. *P. heterodoxus* has been placed

under *P. procerus* in the past, but can be distinguished by the hairiness of the flower tubes.

P. shastensis, *P. washingtonensis* and *P. spatulatus* differ in minor details from *P. heterodoxus* and each other. They are all somewhat localized in the wild, *P. spatulatus* in particular being rare.

Subsection Humiles

This group of 17 species is modest in stature and in name, derived from *humilis*, meaning humble. The flowers tend to be more violet or blue than purple. Humiles are never found east of the Rocky Mountains. Five of the 17 species are definite alpines, but even the herbaceous species are never much over 50cm (20in) unless they are lucky enough to find good soil and shelter. The group divides into eight species with serrated leaves and nine where they are smooth-edged, although individual plants of some species are known to break this rule.

Serrated-leaf species Of those with toothed leaves *P. ovatus* has had a permanent place in seed catalogues since Victorian times and is the most frequently encountered. Its leaves are oval, with or without points, hairy, and born on long, slightly winged stalks. The flowers are a good bright blue and are profuse but small-ish, up to 2.5cm (1in) long. It has a reputation for not being long-lived, but it comes from an area of comparatively high summer rainfall, from Oregon to British Columbia, so some additional watering may help its longevity in dry gardens.

P. wilcoxii perhaps even outshines *P. ovatus* in colour, but is most easily told apart by having leaves which are not hairy. Both these species can grow to 1m (3¼ft), although half that is more typical. *P. pruinosus*, *P. albertinus* and *P. subserratus* are also quite closely related but their flowers are held nearer to the main stem, giving a narrow and clustered effect. In the last two species the leaves have very little serration. *P. elegantulus* is a miniature in much the same mould, but not known in cultivation. Unusual colour breaks in *P. subserratus* have been named in the past: 'Neve' (pink), 'Snow-flake' (white), 'Super Sub' (yellow and peach) and 'Dog Mountain', a dwarfer form of 'Super Sub'.

The last two Humiles with serrated leaves, *P. rattanii* and *P. anguineus*, are closely related, the latter once being regarded as a miniature variety of the former. The red-purple flowers of *P. rattanii* are the largest in the group, over 2.5cm (1in) long and widely flared, but it is not considered a showy species because of the crowding of the flowers by its leaves.

Unserrated-leaf species In the group of Humiles with serrated leaves there are four beauties generally rated in the first rank of penstemons – and three of them are not difficult to grow. All four fall into a subgroup in which the basal rosette persists throughout the season.

P. whippleanus is one of the most variable of all penstemons in both flower colour and leaf shape, yet it has a character about it that ensures instant recognition. One giveaway is the profuse hairiness of the flowers; another is that they are noticeably crowded and droopy; and if that is not enough all the lobes point dead straight ahead, the lower ones making a prominent 'landing stage', albeit nearly vertical. The flowers are 2.5–3cm (1–1¼in) long and half as wide. They come in a wide range of colours – white, cream, yellow, blue, violet, wine, purple, chocolate, even almost black. If anything the darker shades prevail, and this makes them too gloomy a subject for some tastes, but for others it adds to their fascination.

This species is tall for a high alpine, up to 70cm (2⅓ft) being common, but alpine it most certainly is. It is a plant of the high places, not apparently happy to grow below 3280m (10,000ft) if it can get higher – if left to itself, that is, for it also seems equally at home at sea level in our European climate, in cold soils at that. Perhaps this is to do with a preference for the cooler conditions at altitude, with also the presence of subsurface moisture from melting snow almost the whole summer. It seems to tolerate, even enjoy, a certain amount of shade. This is worth noting when growing it from seed: it germinates easily enough, but has a tendency to collapse at the seedling stage if at all stressed. Once established it spreads and self-seeds happily.

P. whippleanus is found throughout the Rocky Mountains from Montana to New Mexico. As it inhabits widely spaced mountain tops – the Rockies being far from one continuous range – there cannot be much interbreeding between colonies, and this, according to theory, is the classic situation for evolution of new species to occur. However, *P. whippleanus* has not read the rules, and remains one species, although each separate colony does tend to consist of only one flower colour. Rarely, a colony of mixed white and darker colour flowers will be found, but strangely very few intermediate shades occur in such cases, contrary to the usual rule with penstemons. One intriguing theory, not as yet proven, is that bees pollinate only the dark flowers and night-flying moths only the white ones, thus keeping the lines pure. Whether to botanist, naturalist or gardener, *P. whippleanus* has much of interest to commend it.

Coming down the mountains a little, but still not much below 2440m (7000ft), we encounter two more superb alpines from this group – *P. virens* and *P. humilis*. Both form tufts of basal leaves and send up a number of flowering shoots to about 30cm (12in), and both like it stony – although, as with *P. whippleanus*, one suspects that they are canny prospectors for subsurface moisture. The flowers are quite small, 1.8cm (¾in) long if that, but borne in profusion. The flower lobes are flared. *P. virens* has the more limited range, being found only in the eastern Rockies of Wyoming and Colorado. Its flowers are a rich blue violet verging on almost a true blue. It has a penchant for road cuttings where it can make truly spectacular displays in high summer, also benefiting from a little shade given by the steep banks for part of the day.

P. humilis takes over from *P. virens* in the western Rockies and also the coastal ranges of California and Oregon, venturing down to 1520m (5000ft) in cooler areas. It has a wide range of flower colour, from deep violet to a bluish lavender, quite pale. The throat is white and lined with fine deep guidelines. From a distance the effect in the mass approaches a powder blue. The variety 'McKay's Form' is a compact dwarf version.

P. aridus is the fourth of the good Humiles. As the name implies it likes dry conditions, and is found in the more inhospitable mountainous parts of Idaho, Wyoming and Montana. It is seldom over 20cm (8in) high and comparatively sparse in flower. The flowers are close to those of *P. humilis*, with perhaps a touch more purple in the shading, although individual flowers may show up as bright blue until they reach maturity. The easiest distinguishing feature is that the leaves of *P. aridus* are thin and rolled to become almost grass-like. It is a common rock-garden subject in those parts of the USA where its native dry conditions are not too difficult to simulate, but in Europe it seems to be quite tricky. The problem may be that the seedlings are easily

PLATE VI

P. rydbergii

P. wilcoxii

P. laetus ssp. *sagittatus*

P. newberryi ssp. *sonomensis*

All flowers are shown at approximately ¾ size

drowned by 'normal' watering since they quickly form enormous root systems. Nevertheless, they come quite easily from seed, and are well worth persevering with. P. radicosus has similarities to P. aridus but lacks a basal rosette. The stem leaves are grey-green and the whole plant is hairy.

The flowers of P. oliganthus reach 2.5cm (1in), and are tubular with lower lobes pointing forward. They are effectively bicolors, blue or purple upper parts contrasting with white throats and tube undersides. It is a graceful but not spectacular subject, reaching perhaps 70cm (2⅓ft). It inhabits high clearings in New Mexico's upland forests, and is unusual in tolerating even deep shade. P. inflatus, P. degeneri and P. pseudoparvus are uncommon and of very localized distribution, differing only in minor features from P. oliganthus.

SUBSECTION PENSTEMON

This subsection of 18 species represents a geographical break in the genus since, with one exception, they are found only in eastern USA and eastern Canada. They are mostly big subjects with chunky basal rosettes of leaves which persist through the year. These impart a distinct air of bulk and permanence. The flowers are 2.5–3.5cm (1–1⅜in) long, borne in profusion on long stalks in airy panicles. These species are more demanding of moisture than their cousins from west of the Mississippi, and consequently tend to find more favour in European gardens than in North American. They are all herbaceous and reliably hardy. There is a tendency towards coarseness in late season without, usually, the bonus of a second flush of flower to make up for it. Nevertheless, they are good candidates for the herbaceous border, having no special needs.

The subsection breaks down neatly into four groups by flower colour and mouth shape:

  White, open: P. alluviorum, P. arkansanus, P. deamii, P. digitalis
  White, closed: P. laxiflorus, P. oklahomensis, P. pallidus, P. tenuiflorus
  Purple, open: P. brevisepalus, P. calycosus, P. canescens, P. gracilis, P. laevigatus, P. smallii, P. tenuis, P. wisconsinensis
  Purple, closed: P. australis, P. hirsutus.

Plate VI. Species flowering in early summer in blue and purple shades.

White-flowered species These often show a distinct tinge of purple in the white, and guidelines when present, although fine, are quite deep in colour. Given the chance, the group interbreeds with abandon, and plants of garden origin may not easily be attributable to a single species.

P. digitalis is the best known of the whites. It grows to a stately 2m (6½ft) in the wild, but half that is more usual in gardens. The stout rosettes are up to 50cm (20in) in diameter on a tough woody base. The flowers can be 3.5cm (1⅜in) long (the biggest in this subsection) and are massed in large, but quite narrow, panicles. The flower tubes are short and dilate abruptly close to their inner ends. The lips are longer than the tube. There are supposed to be no guidelines, but in the cultivated version these are frequently found, possibly due to hybridization. The flower colour, too, is more likely to be very pale lavender rather than pure white, giving an overall misty, greyish appearance at a distance which is surprisingly attractive.

A garden variety, P. digitalis 'Husker Red', is a distinct improvement on the species in having pure white flowers and striking deep wine red leaves and flower stalks, this colour being retained for most of the growing season. The variety was developed at North Platte, Nebraska, in the 1980s from a partly red-leaved plant found in that state. It is strictly speaking a clonal form, but such was the demand for it – it was selected as American Perennial Plant of the year in 1996 – that selected seed-raised stock was resorted to by some nurseries. It has also been widely offered in seed form. Unfortunately, at present only a relatively small percentage of seed comes true to type, sometimes leading to inferior material being offered. The name refers to 'Corn Husker', the nickname given to Nebraskans for what is supposedly their main pursuit in life, hence 'Husker', not the often-found 'Husker's'. Another red-leaved form of P. digitalis, called 'Red Star', has recently emerged in the Netherlands, where it is grown for the cut-flower trade. We are unsure of its origin.

Of the remaining whites, P. alluviorum, P. deamii and P. arkansanus are similar to P. digitalis, showing minor variations in detail, but mainly distinguishable by being smaller in both flower and overall size. Of the four whites which have the more closed mouth, only P. pallidus has found much favour with gardeners. It might be described as a white-flowered P. hirsutus, but is

P. virens turning a road cut at 3,300m (10,000ft) in the Rockies into a perfect alpine scene. By late afternoon, as here, the bank enjoys some shade.

even hairier than that species, with the mouth slightly open and both anthers and staminode extending beyond the mouth. It is very profuse in flower.

The purple-flowered species *P. hirsutus* is perhaps the best-known of the purples in subsection Penstemon and is among the most widely grown of all the species, being as tolerant of soil conditions and as hardy as one can hope for in a genus with a reputation for temperament. It can reach 70cm (2⅓ft) or more in good soil, and flowers for several weeks in early summer. The whole habit is quite delicate, with olive green foliage which is attractive while young. The flowers are hairy, around 2.5cm (1in) long, narrow, and totally closed, resembling small snapdragons. They grow in profusion in dense panicles. The predominantly lavender and white colouring in the wild tends to be wishy-washy.

However, cultivated plants usually show much darker and more handsome shades of blue to violet, these being largely derived from a seed strain developed around 1950 by some early APS members, using selected stock.

Various named cultivars of the normal *P. hirsutus* have been offered based on good colour selections, mainly from the early 1960s and earlier, but they do not appear to have survived. Some pink forms exist, one, *P. h.* 'Olinda Pink', originating from Australia. There is a recognized botanical form, *P. h. albiflorus*, in which the flowers are pure white, but it is in the two miniature forms *P. h.* 'Pygmaeus' and *P. h.* 'Minimus' that most gardening interest lies. These were originally proposed as botanical forms by Ralph Bennett, but were rejected because they were not distinct enough, a continuous gradation in size being met with in the wild. Seed of 'Pygmaeus' comes about 65 per cent true to type. There is some confusion as to which is which: originally 'Minimus' seems to have been applied to the dwarfer form, but now is taken to mean plants 15–38cm

(6–15in) tall in which the flowers form tighter clusters than in the type, while 'Pygmaeus' is reserved for the tiny rock plant – a state of affairs perhaps not to be disturbed even if it was not Bennett's intention, particularly since a reference to a 'Pygmaeus' of very similar appearance has recently come to light, dating from before 1920. Both have white forms. What makes them so valuable is that the flowers are as big as in the normal type, thus giving a really striking display. There is a tendency for 'Pygmaeus' in particular to shed its leaves after flowering in a convincing display of death, but in 2–3 weeks new leaves generally appear.

P. australis is in cultivation but less frequently encountered than *P. hirsutus*, which it resembles. It differs in having the mouth slightly open, and anthers which protrude – rather like a purple *P. pallidus*.

The subsection Penstemon is completed by eight purples with dilated tubes and fully open mouths. Three of these have a prominent 'bee's landing stage' formed by the lower lobes sticking out stiffly ahead, the flowers being held in a horizontal position. Of these, *P. canescens* has relatively short flowering stems – to 50cm (20in) – compared to the large basal rosette of leaves. The deep red-purple flowers usually begin only just above the deep gray-green leaves, which makes a good colour contrast for the front of the border. *P. smallii* is similar in flower but has distinctive leaves in quite a light green with pink edging and veining. For sheer weight of flower it must come high up the league table of penstemon species; moreover, it self-sows readily so that, if the hoe is not used too enthusiastically, the young seedlings from the previous autumn will give a second flowering in the late season. *P. brevisepalus* is similar to *P. smallii* but is not in cultivation, being relatively rare.

The last five purples lack the 'landing stage', all lobes being flared at more or less right angles to the tube. *P. calycosus* is the largest of the four in habit, up to 1 m (3¼ft) tall, and the largest in flower – over 2.5cm (1in) long, with good strong colours varying between deep purple and violet. *P. laevigatus*, as we have seen, was the first recognized penstemon, but this rather than its gardenworthiness is its chief point of interest. In habit and flower it is a smaller version of *P. calycosus*.

P. tenuis is limited to parts of the south-eastern states not noted for their penstemons. It has a graceful habit up to about 70cm (2¼ft), with the flowers borne in airy panicles. The leaves are quite papery – *tenuis* means thin – with a hint of pink veining and a narrow, twisty triangular shape to the stem leaves which is quite distinct. The flowers are small, no more than 1.8cm (¾in), but borne in profusion. The colour is an almost luminous deep rosy purple, reminiscent of some verbenas. It lives in dampish conditions in the wild, and also tolerates shade. It is easy from seed, and blooms in late season from an early spring sowing.

Lastly, *P. gracilis* is unique in the subsection for not having a persistent basal rosette, and for living in drier plains conditions than the others, from the Dakotas to New Mexico. It grows to no more than 50cm (20in), producing small panicles of 2.5cm (1in) flowers in a very pale lilac, almost white at times, with prominent guidelines in the throat. The mouth is quite narrow but open, giving it more affinity with *P. australis* than *P. hirsutus*. It is easy in cultivation, but said not to be long-lived. *P. wisconsinensis* is a hairy-leaved version of *P. gracilis*, otherwise so close that it has been rated by some as a subspecies. As the name suggests, it is a Wisconsin native, and of very local distribution.

Subsection Tubaeflori

P. tubaeflorus, the sole member of this subsection, is similar in habit to *P. digitalis*, under which it used to be classified as a subspecies. It grows tall, to 90cm (3ft), and upright from a large basal rosette. The inflorescence is more open, and the white flowers smaller, without hair or guidelines, but the real distinguishing feature is the shape of the flower – a narrow trumpet with a gradually flared tube, without sudden dilation. It is widely distributed from Louisiana to Ontario, and given not too dry a soil makes a striking garden display.

Subsection Multiflori

This subsection also contains just one species, *P. multiflorus*. It is even closer to *P. digitalis* than *P. tubaeflorus*, its flowers being dilated and open-mouthed. It is slightly smaller, however, both in habit (up to 75cm/ 2½ft) and flower size (under 2.5cm/1in). The spiky deep brown hairs on the staminode help to tell it apart from its near neighbours, and the leaves tend to be bluish. It is confined in the wild to Florida and Georgia. The flowers are borne profusely over a long period.

Subsection Deusti

The three species of this group are small-flowered denizens of arid places in western parts of the USA. *P. deustus* is the commonest of the three, and its local name, the hot-rock penstemon, says it all. This species and *P. sudans* are subshrubs up to 70cm (2⅓ft) tall with branching stems, a feature unique in the section Penstemon. The flowers are whitish to pale yellow with darker guidelines. *P. sudans* is decidedly the hairier of the two, otherwise they are quite similar. *P. deustus* does quite well in American gardens offering the dry conditions which it likes, but in the British climate it is a challenge. The rare *P. tracyi* reaches only 12cm (4¾in) in height, and has pink flowers on stems carrying small oval leaves which are a light blue-green in colour.

Subsection Arenarii

Although this subsection is placed in section Penstemon it shares many of the features of section Anularius, being distinguished mainly by the sheer paucity of flower and leaf in its two species – *P. arenarius* and *P. albomarginatus*. They are found mainly in Nevada, where they show a strong preference for growing in, and almost covered by, pure sand. Small and sparse herbaceous plants 7–15cm (2¾–6in) high with small flowers in pinkish/purplish hues, these difficult species hardly commend themselves as garden subjects, though some enthusiasts have made the effort with *P. albomarginatus*. This is possibly because it is the only variegated wild penstemon, the margins of its leaves, as the name implies, being white.

Subsection Gairdneriani

This group comprises two alpines which, although classed under section Penstemon, are difficult to tell apart from some members of the separate section Ericopsis. *P. seorsus* we can perhaps overlook as it is rarely encountered, but *P. gairdneri* is rated highly by alpinists as a trough subject. It has a non-standard feature in that it often has some leaves spaced alternately instead of in the usual opposite pairs. It is a low mat-former with narrow, hairy, grey-green leaves, those on the flowering stems tending to hug them closely. The inflorescences reach 35cm (13¾in) long, with clusters of flowers held clear of the foliage. These are in shades of blue, lavender and purple, with tubes about 1.8cm (¾in) long, and quite large lobes held at right angles to the tubes, giving a noticeably flat appearance to the front of the flowers. *P. gairdneri* inhabits dry, rocky terrain in parts of the northwest USA, and seems to do best in poor soils in cultivation.

Subsection Harbouriani

This subsection contains a single species, *P. harbourii*, which again has affinities with another section, this time Aurator. This is due mainly to the staminode, which is typically Aurator-like – prominent and golden-haired – compared to the more subdued form found in the rest of the section Penstemon

P. harbourii is well-regarded by alpinists: it is a low, neat, spreading mat-former from 3660m (12,000ft) or more in a remote area of the Colorado Rockies, where it is found cascading spectacularly over steep rocky faces. The fresh grey-green foliage forms a perfect background to the 1.8cm (¾in) flowers, which are in effect purple/yellow bicolours because of the showy staminode. Its natural terrain might be slightly acidic, and those who have grown it recommend some addition of crushed granite to the growing medium.

Plate VII. Examples of taller-growing species in the subsection Penstemon.

PLATE VII

P. alluviorum

P. digitalis – probably
hybridized

P. smallii

P. calycosus

All flowers are shown at approximately ⅓ size

P. digitalis – normal
appearance

9

A–Z OF GARDEN FORMS
OF PENSTEMON

In this chapter we have recorded in alphabetical order all names known to us of garden forms of penstemon still in cultivation, including seed strains of controlled composition. For those varieties which have already been described under the relevant species in Chapter 8 we give a cross reference only, but for the European Hybrids details of habit, flower, and, as far as possible, provenance, are recorded. Unless indicated otherwise, our descriptions are based on our observation of plants from reliable sources, although in some cases we have been unable to view material personally. In other cases we are aware of certain names having been applied, but we have been unable to gather enough information to justify an entry in the A–Z. Those names are listed in Appendix VI.

There are still some varieties where considerable doubt remains as to which of several forms is the correct one for a particular name, and others where more than one name applies to what is apparently the same form. We have taken the view in these cases that it is more valuable for readers to know of these uncertainties rather than to record *ex cathedra* judgments in favour of a particular form or a particular name to the exclusion of the other possibilities. At times this means having to suppress a strong feeling that in some cases there are too many names chasing too few genuine variants. This is not to condone the careless misnaming of plants, but where there is genuine doubt it is a different matter. To give an example, of the four uses of the name 'Ruby', we know one to be misapplied; one to apply to a dwarf form of the alpine *P. newberryi*; and two to European Hybrids, without clear evidence as to which of them is the 'correct Ruby' according to the rules of nomenclature.

The problem of colour identification is notorious, but has to be faced when dealing with penstemons since cultivars are often distinguished by small shade differences. To do this we have to go beyond the ubiquitous 'purple' to stand for any colour from pale magenta to deep violet, nor can we regard red, scarlet, cherry, carmine and vermilion as freely interchangeable. Some imposition of order is necessary. The excellent Royal Horticultural Society (RHS) Colour Chart is available, but unfortunately not at a price to suit most pockets, besides which many find the use of code numbers in place of names a drawback. Our solution is to turn to philately, where consistent colour descriptions have been in use for many years, and for which reference guides are not difficult to come by. Where strict accuracy is necessary we quote the name from the Stanley Gibbons Stamp Colour Key (see Appendix III) in italics, followed by the closest equivalent RHS Colour Chart number in brackets. We always record the colour as seen close up in diffused light. The result is sometimes surprising, as when an obviously 'pink' variety under normal viewing is found as 'rose' in an old description and 'red' in the colour chart. (Partly this is due to how the eye averages the colours available, and partly it is due to fashion: the RHS in the 1930s trials saw only rose-coloured penstemons, not a single pink one!)

In offering such detailed descriptions, it has to be said that variations, especially of colouring and throat markings, do occur. The eye is easily attracted by the unusual, but we have done our best to resist this temptation in order to ensure that our descriptions relate to typical mature material. Type of soil, weather conditions, and plant health and vigour all appear to play a part in producing such variations. We have seen differences of flower colour and size in the same plant from year to year, and even between early and late flowerings in the same season. The same stem of flowers at maturity may have individual blooms with and without throat markings. Most importantly, differences between varieties are more evident in some seasons than others (the summer of 1997 in England was particularly noticeable for the way in which some varieties that are normally quite distinct appeared to be identical, mainly because varieties in light colour shades bloomed somewhat darker than is normal).

CLASSIFICATION

Although there is an International Registration Authority for penstemons, no official classification of the various types has been proposed for the European Hybrids. The RHS trials of 1991–3 used a classification based on flower shapes, and this, combined with other features, has led us to the tentative conclusions on parentage discussed in Chapter 3. Based on this analysis, we use the following groupings to make for easier reference and avoid tedious repetition, allowing that many varieties show intermediate characteristics.

1 Small-flowered

Flowers under 3cm (1¼in) in length, varying in shape from narrow trumpets to quite bulbous forms with abruptly expanded tubes close to the base. Flowers borne in compact panicles, colours from pink to mauve and violet. Leaves narrow, fine, pointed and serrated, those on flowering stems being up to 7.5 × 0.5cm (3 × ¼in). Leaves without stalks, and widest at the base. The early outgrowth of axillary shoots leads to a neat, compact habit, normally under 60cm (24in), but in favourable conditions can be much more. Examples: 'Evelyn', 'Papal Purple', 'Pink Endurance'.

2 Medium-flowered

A. *Narrow-leaved* Flowers 3–4cm (1¼–1½in) in length, tubes abruptly expanded from near the base, mouths wide, in narrow panicles. Leaves narrow and pointed, those on flowering stems being up to 8.5 × 0.5cm (3⅜ × ¼in). Leaves without stems, widest near, but not at, the base, and usually showing minute and sparse serration in the distal (outer) half only. Habit a branched structure, tall and spreading, up to 1m (3¼ft) tall and often more in diameter. Example: 'Schoenholzeri' (syn. 'Firebird').

B. *Broad-leaved* Flowers 3–4cm (1¼–1½in) in length, tubes abruptly expanded from near the base, mouths wide, borne in narrow panicles, sometimes in separated whorls leaving much of the flowering stem visible. Stem leaves pointed, up to 8 × 1.2cm (3¼ × ½in), appearing broad because the widest point is halfway along the length of the leaf. Leaves often quite dark green, shiny, and sparsely serrated on the distal (outer) half only as in 2A. Habit varies, but most commonly a spreading mound, rarely over 75cm (2½ft). Examples: 'Mother of Pearl', 'Pennington Gem', 'Burgundy'.

3. Large-Flowered

A. *Narrow trumpet* Flowers long and narrow, over 4cm (1½in), tubes not over 1.2cm (½in) wide at the mouth, lobes pointed. Flowers held in quite loose panicles, colours red or pink. Varieties differ in length of leaf, 4.8–7cm (1⅞–2¾in), and one-fifth as wide, appearing quite broad. Leaves without stalks, pointed, sometimes sparsely serrated on the distal (outer) halves, and often showing a bluish hue. Habit tall and erect, over 1m (3¼ft) being common, and may grow shrubby if left undisturbed. Examples: 'Connie's Pink', 'Taoensis', 'Cherry Ripe'.

B. *Wide trumpet* Flowers over 4cm (1⅝in) in length, tube gradually expanding to exceed 1.2cm (⅝in) at the mouth, lobes usually rounded and pointing forward to a marked extent. Bright reds, purples and violets predominate, throats often heavily marked. Flowers in narrow panicles, but well separated due to having long pedicels. Varieties vary in length of leaf, 7.5–11.5cm (3–4⅝in), and one-fifth as wide, pointed and smooth-edged. Habit upright, reaching 90cm (3ft). Examples: 'Blackbird', 'Flame', 'Rich Ruby'.

C. *Bell-flowered* Flowers over 4cm (1⅝in) in length, short tube expanding abruptly to a wide mouth, lobes large, rounded, more or less equal in size, flared at right angles to the tube or very slightly forward-pointing, the whole giving a quite symmetrical bell-like appearance

Plate VIII (overleaf). A range of the small-flowered Group 1 hybrids with examples of *P. kunthii* and *P. campanulatus* for comparison (see also Plate II.)

PLATE VIII

P. 'Threave Pink'

P. kunthii

P. 'Lynette'

P. 'Pink Endurance'

P. 'Mint Pink'

P. 'Patio Pink'

All flowers are shown at approximately ½ size

P. 'Papal Purple' × P. 'Evelyn'

P. campanulatus 'Roseus'

P. 'Evelyn'

P. 'Papal Purple'

received as P. campanulatus
'Roseus'

P. 'Pershore P/2/93' –
unreleased

P. campanulatus

P. 'Abbotsmerry'.

to the flower. Flowers usually tightly packed on the stem, hiding it from view. Wide colour range. Throats usually silvery white, unmarked or lightly pencilled. Leaves broad, up to 12.5 × 3cm (5 × 1¼in), bluntly pointed and smooth-edged. Habit an open clump, not spreading, heights varying by type 75–90cm (2½–3ft), but can be higher in favourable conditions. Examples: 'Osprey', 'Rubicundus', 'Flamingo'.

EARLIEST KNOWN RECORD (EKR)

Finally, we should explain the initials 'EKR', which occur quite often in the descriptions, e.g. 'EKR Forbes 1935'. 'EKR' stands for 'earliest known record', and is a shorthand designed to avoid having to explain each time that we do not have any reliable information on provenance but, to date, the earliest mention we have found is as indicated. This is in contrast to 'introduced by Forbes 1935', or 'raised by Forbes 1935' where our information is much more certain.

AWARD OF GARDEN MERIT

The symbol ♀ indicates the Award of Garden Merit (AGM) by the Royal Horticultural Society.

'Abberley'

A striking new variety, in a strong but not garish deep red shade which is quite easy to blend into a mixed border.

Group 3B of normal habit for its group, the foliage neater and in a deeper green than sometimes encountered. Flowers 4.5 × 3.5cm (1¾ × 1⅜in), the lower lobes larger and slightly forward-pointing. The lobes are broadly pointed. Tube and lobes *deep magenta* (72A), with a lightening of the colour towards the base and underside of the tube. The throat is pure white, strongly marked with smudged guidelines along its whole length in *lake* (59A), tending to join at the throat into a blotch on each lobe.

Propagated by Perhill Nurseries, Great Witley, Worcestershire, from a selected seedling, and introduced by them in 1994.

'Abbotsmerry'

An excellent cultivar of recent origin bearing large flowers of an uncommon shade of dark red.

A fairly typical member of Group 3B, forming an open and sometimes lax clump to 75cm (2½ft). Flowers 4 × 4.5cm (1⅝–1 ¾in), *deep carmine* (60A) on upper surface of tube and reverse of upper lobes, paling slightly on remainder of corolla. Interior of tube heavily pencilled on lower surface and lightly on upper. Upper lobes strongly overlap. Pencilling coalesces in mouth into a broad transverse band of *brown lake* (184A), extending partway onto the upper lobes. Lower lobes carry a pigmented central line almost to their outer edges. White staminode prominent and ornamental.

A seedling discovered in the garden of Mrs Margaret Wallis, near Tunbridge Wells, Kent. The heavy throat markings strongly suggest 'Rich Ruby', growing nearby, in its parentage. Informally distributed since 1994 and commercially introduced in 1998.

'Agnes Laing'

An old variety with attractive carmine flowers, held downwards in loose panicles.

A typical member of Group 3B, the flowers held well above the foliage. The flower measures 5 × 3.5cm (2 × 1⅜in) overall, with the lower lobes slightly angled forward. Tube and lobes are a uniform *carmine* (185B) of perfect substance, throat silvery white. The lobes are rounded.

Raised by Downie, Laird & Laing before 1870, and believed to be the oldest European Hybrid still in cultivation. The interest of this variety is that the large size of flower, and good colour, were achieved so early in the development of what was apparently a new breeding line – possibly incorporating *P. cobaea*. See also page 23.

Not yet in general circulation, pending improvements in the quantity and well-being of the stock.

'Alice Hindley' ♀

A firm favourite for the delicate mauve to violet colouring of its large white-throated flowers, often chosen for blue borders where the planting scheme is carefully colour co-ordinated. It needs good nutrition to reach its full height and produce multiple flowering stems, and benefits from close planting.

Group 2B, habit often a sparse open clump, unusually tall and erect to 1.2m (4ft). Flowers 4 × 3.2cm (1⅝ × 1¼in) Unopened buds *reddish violet* (83B), top of tube and rear of upper lobes *bright lilac* (86D), front of upper lobes and both sides of lower lobes *lilac* (85A). Underside of tube white, throat white without markings.

Introduced by Forbes in 1931. Synonyms: 'Lady Alice Hindley' (Handley, Lindley and Hindlip occur as mis-spellings). 'John Nash' (*qv*) has identical flowers.

'Amethyst'

See *P. heterophyllus*, page 73.

'Andenken an Friedrich Hahn' ♀

One of the most successful cultivars ever introduced and grown in virtually every country where European Hybrids are cultivated. More persistent than most, and notably floriferous, even when not deadheaded. Indeed the dark-coloured stems and seed pods which are revealed when the flowers fall are an added attraction to some. It also produces an attractive mass of fine green leaves and grows in the shape of a loose mound, points which qualify it as a plant of garden interest even when out of flower.

The classic 2A cultivar. Habit typical for group, height to 90cm (3ft) Flowers 3.8 × 3.2cm (1½ × 1¼in), *bright crimson* (63A). Tube pencilled *deep carmine red* (53A), terminating in three crescents in the lower mouth. Edges of lower lobes slightly irregular.

Raised by Hermann Wartmann, St Gallen (Switzerland) c.1918 – see page 25 for discussion of provenance. Synonyms: 'Garnet' (several countries), 'Jupiter'

(France). The name 'Garnet' was not applied until about 1950, and no record exists of its having been sold in the UK before 1939 under its original name.

'Apple Blossom'

Two different cultivars claim this name, not surprisingly in view of the frequency with which the classic apple blossom colouring occurs in seedling penstemons. *Type 1* ♀ A small-flowered pink and white cultivar of distinctive appearance when well grown, but needs good attention to cultural details to maximize its performance.

Group 1, forming a dense, upright multi-stemmed clump to 75cm (2½ft), its noticeably dark green leaves helping to distinguish it from most others in its group. Flowers 2.8 × 2.2cm (1⅛ × ⅞in), tube abruptly expanded, essentially creamy white, its upper surface *carmine-rose* (51C). Throat lightly pencilled *bright crimson* (63A). The position of the staminode is unusual; it

P. 'Apple Blossom' Type 2 (large-flowered).

may hold a central position, or lie close to the roof of the tube.

EKR Graham Stuart Thomas 1972, who likened it to a paler form of 'Evelyn', but the flowers of 'Evelyn' are noticeably less bulbous.

Type 2 A large-flowered cultivar of modest height, slower growing in spring than many others. Flowers so densely packed that dead flowers which have turned brown may fail to fall. Needs very prompt deadheading.

Group 3B, forming strong, dense, slow-growing clumps to a height of 60cm (2ft) with dull green leaves densely packed on stiff green stems. Buds and immature flowers strongly coloured, greatly enhancing appearance, particularly in the early stages of flowering. Flowers 4.2 × 3.2cm (1¾ × 1¼in), tube moderately expanded, the lobes rounded and crinkled, the lower ones larger and more forward pointing than the upper. Lobes *cerise* (63A) to *brown lilac* (185C), the colour most intense on the lobe margins, paling towards the tube and suffusing on to it. Tube otherwise white. Lower lobes overlap.

EKR Macpennys Nursery, Hampshire, 1951, but its origin may be much earlier. There are similarities with 'Barbara Barker', 'Peace' and 'Thorn', the main differences being that in 'Barbara Barker' the whole upper side of the tube is uniformly coloured and the flower is wider in the mouth; in 'Peace' the colouring is confined to a band on the lobes; while in 'Thorn' the lobes are in a cream shade, and the habit is taller.

'Arroyo'

An American variety of the 'Flathead Lake' type – see page 69.

'Astley'

This is a paler version of 'Mother of Pearl' (*qv*), having the same bold pencilling of the throat, but with the overall flower colour in off-white instead of pale lavender. 'Mother of Pearl' itself will occasionally have panicles in the same off-white colour, but in 'Astley' the colour is constant.

Propagated by Perhill Nurseries, Great Witley, Worcestershire, from a selected seedling, and introduced by them in 1994.

'Barbara Barker'

A classic large-flowered hybrid in cerise and white, found to be quite persistent by the standards of the group if grown hard, i.e. in well-drained soil with no feeding. It has proved to be internationally popular.

Group 3C, bushy habit to a height of 60cm (2ft). The flowers measure 5.2 × 3.8cm (2⅛ × 1½in), very open-throated, the lobes flared and equal in size. Lobes *cerise* (63A) on both sides, the colour suffusing down the length of the upper tube, but paling to white on the sides and underside. Throat pure white, totally unmarked. The panicles are crowded due to the short pedicels and large flowers.

Propagated by Hopleys Nursery, Hertfordshire, from a selected seedling in 1985 and introduced in 1987. The cultivar 'Beech Park' is very similar and can easily be mistaken for 'Barbara Barker'. In view of the provenance of 'Beech Park' (*qv*) we are of the opinion that 'Barbara Barker' is a valid name.

'Bashful'

A hybridized form of *P. barbatus* – see page 69.

'Beech Park' ♔

A large-flowered cultivar in Group 3C, very similar to 'Barbara Barker', but said to differ in having smaller flowers, and smaller leaves in a deeper green. The flower dimensions for 'Beech Park' quoted in the 1991 RHS trials report tend to confirm the smaller flower.

It would seem that this cultivar was grown at Beech Park in Dublin as long as 50–60 years ago, but was never sold, and was only named just prior to being entered into the 1991 RHS trials. EKR *Plant Finder* 1992. Much of the material sold as 'Beech Park' appears to be from 'Barbara Barker' stock renamed.

'Bisham Seedling'

A synonym for 'White Bedder' (*qv*) but also found as a smaller-flowered version of 'Barbara Barker' (*qv*), distinct enough to be offered as a separate cultivar. EKR in the latter version Hopleys Nursery, Much Hadham, Hertfordshire, c.1993 but not raised by them.

'Blackbird'

A tall dark-flowered cultivar popular in several countries, with extra-dark tips to its buds increasing its appeal. The long flower stems, thin for their length, lean and sway in the wind, giving the plant an open, willowy appearance. Deceptively floriferous – a well-grown specimen may have 75 flowers per panicle.

On fertile sites a large-growing member of Group 3A, developing into an open multi-stemmed plant to 1.2m (4ft) high, noticeable for its long leaves, up to 14cm (5¾in), widely spaced. Flowers moderately pendant,

P. 'Alice Hindley' – outstanding in its colour range.

P. 'Burgundy'.

3.2 × 1cm (1¼ × ⅜in), *deep reddish purple* (71A), a little paler on the undersurface of the tube and lower lobes. Upper interior of tube coloured a third of distance back from mouth. Lower interior heavily lined, same shade as lower lobes. A central coloured line extends almost to outer edge of lower lobes.

Raised c. 1960 by Ron Sidwell, Evesham, Worcestershire.

'Blue Bedder'
'Blue Eye'
'Blue Fountain'
'Blue Gem'
'Blue Robin'
'Blue Spring'
'Blue of Zurich'
All forms of *P. heterophyllus* – see page 73.

'Bodnant'
One of several purples in its group with features suggesting *P. gentianoides* in its genealogy. 'Bodnant' has good habit and persistence, and particularly fine markings on its flowers.

Typical Group 2B habit. Flowers 3.8 × 2.3cm (1½ × ⅞in), lobes forward-pointing, mouth broad. Tubes and throat *reddish-violet* (83B) when young, but later a suffusion of *bright purple* (72B) develops and the base of the tube becomes *bluish violet* (93B). Throat white with a few strongly marked lines in *purple* (79C), not coalescing at the mouth and not joining up with the purple part of the lobes.

EKR Perhill Nursery, Worcestershire 1992. Comparable with 'Hidcote Purple', 'Burford Purple', 'Priory Purple', and one form of 'Sour Grapes'. 'Russian River' is darker.

'Breitenbush Blue'
A natural cross of *P. cardwellii* x *P. davidsonii* – see page 63. Also found as 'Breiten Bush Blue' or 'Breitenbrush Blue'.

'Broken Top Mountain Form'
A natural form of *P. davidsonii* var. *menziesii* – see page 65.

'Bruce Alexander'
A form of *P. caespitosus* – see page 85.

'Burford Purple'
A variety very similar to 'Burgundy' (*qv*), but our information suggests that it had an independent origin in a garden in Burford, Gloucestershire. Compared to 'Burgundy' the only discernible difference is that it has more white in the throat, since the guidelines are more clearly marked and less smudged.

'Burford Seedling'
The original name for 'Burgundy' (*qv*).

'Burford White'
A synonym for 'White Bedder' (*qv*).

'Burgundy'
One of the most distinctive medium-flowered penstemons with deep magenta flowers, almost a self colour, also one of the most persistent. A totally reliable variety, but not the easiest to place in the border due to its uncompromising colour.

Group 2B, with a strong bushy habit, but we have seen taller-growing plants with inflorescences reaching 1.5m (5ft). Flowers 4 × 2.8cm (1⅝ × 1⅛in), rather fat in appearance, the exterior coloured *deep magenta* (72A) overall. Throat strongly marked in *brown purple* (183A), heavily suffused so that very little white shows. The staminode, however, is a vivid white which makes a strongly contrasting feature that is both decorative and an aid to identification.

Raised by Treasurer's of Tenbury Wells, Worcestershire, in 1971 under the name of 'Burford Seedling', introduced by them in 1973 as 'Burgundy'. The original name is still used by some nurseries.

'California Blue Bedder'
A form of *P. heterophyllus* – see page 73.

'Candy Pink'
A misnomer for 'Old Candy Pink' (*qv*).

'Carmen's Choice'
A form of *P. heterophyllus* – see page 73.

'Castle Forbes'
A striking old cultivar with strongly coloured scarlet and white flowers. The wide mouths and horizontal set of the flowers combine to reveal very clearly their splendid white interiors.

Group 3C but flowers a little small at 3.7 × 3.7cm (1½ × 1½in), *bright rose red* (45D); the colour of all lobes can sometimes be modified by a bluish tint on the reverse, which becomes more pronounced as each flower ages. Interior of tube opaquely white, extending onto lobes. The centre vein of each lower lobe runs in a faint white groove. All lobes overlap.

Raised by Forbes, introduced 1925. 'Castle Forbes' should not be confused with 'Rubicundus', the latter being larger, in a slightly deeper colour, and often with slight markings in the throat. One version of 'Scharlachkoenigin' (*qv*) is also similar.

'Catherine de la Mare'
A form of *P. heterophyllus* – see page 73.

'Centra'
An uncommon cultivar with moderately pendant tubular red flowers. These are arranged in loose panicles in an uncrowded, open manner, which gives the plant a graceful appearance.

Group 3A, leaves mid- rather than blue-green. Side shoots produced very freely, providing a bushy habit. Height 80cm (2¾ft). Flowers 4 × 2.7cm (1⅝ × 1⅛in), *rosine* (46C) on all external surfaces. Lower lobes widely flared with finely irregular edges, and bluntly pointed. The whitish interior extends on to the lower but not the upper lobes. Small coloured smudges appear near the mouth.

EKR Kermack, Saltash, Cornwall 1994.

'Charles Rudd'
A purple and white cultivar of great presence, not quite achieving the recognition it merits due to confusion with other varieties.

Typical group 3C habit. Flowers 4.3 × 3.7cm (1¾ × 1½in), lobes flared and equal, wide mouth. Tube *deep magenta* (72A), lobes *purple* (80B) shading to deep magenta. Throat pure white.

Raised by Charles Rudd before 1962, when it was entered in the RHS trials. It is often confused with 'Countess of Dalkeith' (*qv*), but that variety shows occasional faint and irregular throat markings whereas 'Charles Rudd' never does. Both cultivars were entered in the 1962 trials, and these markings may have been seen as a defect, since 'Charles Rudd' took an Award of Merit and 'Countess of Dalkeith' did not. Many seed-raised plants resemble these two varieties.

'Cherry'
A graceful cultivar with red tubular flowers, good persistence and strong growth.

Typical Group 3A foliage – neat, unserrated and slightly bluish-green. Flowers tubular, 4.4 × 2.1cm (1¾ × ¾in), the tube itself only 7mm (¼in) wide. Upper lobes pointed, smaller than the lower which are quite rounded, the margins of all lobes minutely notched and hairy. Tube and lobes a uniform *rosine* (46C/D), throat white, marked with strong but well-defined parallel lines in magenta on the lower lobes, not coalescing at the mouth. The centre line of each lower lobe is faintly visible as a darker red line.

EKR John Kelly, 1989. Similar to both 'Cherry Ripe' (*qv*) and 'Windsor Red' (*qv*), but more vigorous and freer flowering than the former and slightly smaller in flower than the latter. Some 'Cherry Ripe', however, seems to be sold as 'Cherry'.

'Cherry Belle'
A recent release which appears to be closely related to 'Andenken an Friedrich Hahn' (*qv*) – in fact we have found no significant differences between the two, based on observations of plants grown under identical conditions.

EKR 1995, a source in Nottinghamshire.

'Cherry Ripe'
This cultivar presents itself with an airy delicacy few others can match, and owes part of its charm to the characteristic poise of the flowers. It is a delightful plant

needing good husbandry for long continuity of flowering. It is not overly persistent.

Typical Group 3A cultivar, erect habit up to 1m (3¼ft). Flowers 4.4 × 2.7cm (1¾ × 1in), both tubes and lobes uniformly *rosine* (46C). Mouth narrow, throat white, finely pencilled rosine or deeper. Upper lobes pointed, lower ones rounded with slightly but irregularly serrated edges. Short dense hairs on tube exterior impart a sheen in oblique sunlight. Flowers borne on open panicles and inclined downwards.

EKR Ron Sidwell, Evesham, Worcestershire 1955. Sometimes sold as 'Cherry' (*qv*).

'Chester'
Generally considered to be short for 'Chester Scarlet', although there is a school of thought which considers it as a separate variety through its having rather stronger throat markings. Based on the material which we have examined, it is open to some doubt whether this difference is sufficient to fall outside the normal range of variation present in 'Chester Scarlet'.

'Chester Scarlet' ♀
A majestic variety with large and elegant red flowers for those gardeners who like something really hot.

Group 3B, upright habit, up to 75cm (2½ft). Flowers 5 × 3.7cm (2 × 1½in), the tube quite narrow for the size of flower, and taller than wide – 1.1 × 1.4cm (¾ × ⅝in) at the mouth. Lower lobes larger than upper, and slightly more forward-pointing. Tube and lips mainly *carmine* (53C/D) but toning to *bright crimson* (63A) on the underside of the tube. Throat white with strong lines in a deeper carmine with even a few broken lines on the upper side. The lines of the lower lobes coalesce to form three- or four-sided smudges where the lobes meet, a useful guide to identification. Each lower lobe bears a coloured centre line to its outer margin edge.

EKR Barrs of Taplow, Berkshire 1922. Their description matches the form we have described, which seems to be the generally accepted version. Forbes, however, describe 'Chester Scarlet', which they listed only from 1945, as a medium-sized bedding variety. We have material from a national collection labelled 'Chester Scarlet' which fits the Forbes description fairly well, being very compact in habit and similar to 'Schoenholzeri' in flower. Moreover, the description of the 'Chester Scarlet' entered in the 1962 RHS trials is of a variety with medium-sized flowers. The possibility cannot be ruled out of two separate forms having been

introduced under the same name. See also 'Chester'.

'Chica'
A selection of *P. barbatus* which differs little from the species – see page 69.

'Claude Barr'
A form of *P. caespitosus* – see p 85.

'Cloud Barr'
A misnomer for 'Claude Barr'.

'Connie's Pink' ♀
One of earliest to flower of all European Hybrids. A very tall cultivar, offering a colour break from the normal reds of other members of its group.

Group 3A. Plants 1.2m (4ft) or more, with upright stems that are stiff and wind-resistant if plants are not overfed. Flowers 4 × 2.3cm (1⅝ × ⅞in), upper lobes narrower and more pointed than the lower. Edges of lobes slightly crinkled. Tube narrow, 8mm (¼in) wide, *bright rose* (54A) with underside slightly paler, lobes *cerise* (63A). Throat white with light pencilling in cerise, not extending above the midline of the two outer lower lobes, some coalescing at the mouth.

Raised by Ivor Dickings, Bedfield, Suffolk, before 1991, entered in the RHS trials of that year as a seedling of *P. isophyllus*, second parent unknown. Distributed commercially from 1993 onwards.

'Coral Sea'
A white and rose bicolour bred for large pot culture, of compact habit and with short panicles of close-packed flowers.

Group 3C. Flowers 4.3 × 3.5cm (1¾ × 1⅜in), with flared lobes to an open throat. The lobes show overlapping petals and ruffled edges. Lobes in a light *rose-crimson* (62A) with darker edges, the tube similar fading to white at its base. Throat off-white, unmarked. Sepals broad and pointed.

Raised by A.T Yates & Son, Congleton, Cheshire, from Group 2 and 3 pollen on 'Patio Pink' (*qv*). The colouring and lobe detail strongly suggest the influence of the large-flowered 'Apple Blossom' (*qv*). Released 1998.

'Cottage Garden Red'
A synonym of 'Windsor Red' (*qv*).

'Countess of Dalkeith'
A colourful symphony in purple and white, giving a strong garden effect which requires careful placing.

Group 3C. Flowers 4.2 × 4.4cm (1⅝ × 1¾in),

PLATE IX. Some of the darker varieties of Group 3.

PLATE IX

P. 'Blackbird'

P. 'Powis Castle'

P. 'Rich Ruby'

P. 'Port Wine'

P. 'Raven'

All flowers are shown at approximately ½ size

with large flared lobes (not all flowers are as 'over-square' as this in our experience). Tube dull purple. Throat white, usually faintly speckled in purple.

Raised by Forbes and introduced in 1923 as 'rich purple, pure white throat'. The description given above is based on that in the 1930 RHS trials report on material entered by Forbes themselves. Although the colour can differ according to incident light – we have observed changes from *bright purple* (72B) to *deep mauve* (77A) – the presence of the throat markings is less easily explained. The possibility cannot be ruled out that a reselection of the cultivar from seed occurred due to the original stock dying out. 'Countess of Dalkeith' was also entered in the 1962 RHS trials, but regrettably no description was preserved since it did not win an award. Forbes kept their description unchanged until their demise in 1968, nevertheless it would seem safer to regard forms with pure white throats as 'Charles Rudd' (*qv*). Old stock labelled 'Countess of Dalkeith' in our possession certainly has throat markings. Also found as 'Purpureus Albus' and 'Purple and White', although such names may not apply exclusively to this variety.

'Crystal'
A registered cross of *P. barrettiae* × *P. cardwellii* 'Albus' by Bruce Meyers, c. 1975.

'Dad's Pink'
A large-flowered cultivar with a pretty blend of rose and creamy-white.

Group 3C habit. Flowers 3.8 × 3.8cm (1½ × 1½in), shorter than usual for the group, but the large diameter tube, the wide mouth, and the flared equal lobes are typical. Lobes *bright rose* (54A) with *rosine* (46C) toning, and the occasional fleck of white, the colour suffusing onto the back of the tube, which is otherwise white. Throat creamy-white, the colour extending irregularly onto the lobes.

Introduced by Brian Hiley, Wallington, Surrey, before 1995, from stock of a wrongly named purchase of his father's, hence the name. 'Dad's Pink' is strongly reminiscent of 'Osprey' (*qv*) but the rose colour is noticeably less bright.

'Dazzler'
A vigorous and colourful old cultivar interesting for an unusual combination of features from two groups.

Bushy habit and medium-sized broad leaves, both typical features of Group 2B, but flowers tubular as in Group 3A. Flowers 4.8 × 3cm (1⅞ × 1¼in), tube 8mm (¼in) wide and 1.2cm (½in) tall. Lobes slightly twisted, the upper ones pointing forward and upward, the lower ones flared, all slightly pointed. The upper lobes overlap considerably. Tube and lobes uniformly *bright carmine* (53C), throat white, extending a little onto the lower lobes. Throat lightly and irregularly pencilled in crimson, the lines coalescing to give some smudging at the mouth. Pencilling may be totally absent, however, in some flowers.

Introduced by Forbes, 1931. Their customarily terse description broadly matches the above, but indicates rather heavier pencilling.

'Deep Velvet'
Reported to us as a cultivar of upright habit, with large velvety-red flowers and heavily pencilled throats. We have not seen it. Raised as a seedling of unknown parentage by Roger Springett, Hawera, New Zealand, and introduced in New Zealand in 1993.

'Devonshire Cream'
A tall-growing variety with flowers in a delicate shade of rose, not unlike those of 'Pennington Gem' (*qv*) in colour and markings, but with shorter and more abruptly expanded tubes.

Group 2B, but unusually tall for the group, reaching 1.2m (4ft) and more, the habit rather sparse and the flowers in well-spaced whorls. Flowers 3.7 × 3cm (1½ × 1¼in), the tube abruptly expanded giving a wide mouth, lobes rounded and slightly forward-pointing. Tube *rose* (54C), toning paler to underside, throat white with fine pencilling in a deeper shade of rose. Pencilling does not merge with colour on lobes, there being a clear white margin between.

EKR in this version Baker Straw, Perhill Nursery, Worcestershire, 1994. 'Welsh Dawn' appears to be the same variety. 'Heythrop Park' and 'Hower Park' are said to be similar. It is not unlike 'George Elrick' (*qv*), but is paler and has stronger pencilling. The name 'Devonshire Cream' has also been used for a slightly paler version of 'Hidcote Pink' with cream-coloured throat, very similar to 'Macpenny's Pink' (*qv*).

'Drinkstone'
A synonym for 'Drinkstone Red' (*qv*).

'Drinkstone Red'
A floriferous red cultivar typical of its group, and with many similarities to 'Schoenholzeri' including very good persistence. We are not convinced that we have

seen correctly named stocks, so some aspects of this entry are provisional.

Typical Group 2A with dense bushy habit to 80 cm (2¾ ft) Group 2A. Flowers 3.5 × 3.3cm (1⅜ × 1¼in), *scarlet vermilion* (45A), throat heavily pencilled *deep magenta* (72A), merging to form crescents at the base of each lower lobe.

A seedling from 'Andenken an Friedrich Hahn' (*qv*) selected by F. G. Barcock of Drinkstone, Suffolk, in 1956, and introduced by him as 'Drinkstone Red' in 1965.

'Drinkwater Red'

We are uncertain about the validity and origin of this name, but this hybrid is a distinct cultivar, easily assigned to its group. The major feature that separates it from other cultivars in the same group is its habit.

Group 2A. Habit extremely lax, even when very young. Many stems lie along the surface of the soil from an early age and then attempt to rise upwards. Unless growing vigorously it therefore does not develop the dense bushy habit characteristic of the group and we are unable to provide a typical height.

Compared to 'Schoenholzeri' (*qv*), the flowers are wider and the underside of the tube is more deeply curved; they are also a darker red, *rosine* (46C). The pencilling in the tube merges to form three crescents at the mouth, separated by white blotches. The upper lobes are unusual in that at least one of them has a tendency to be twisted relative to its base. Lower lobes bear a coloured central line almost to their outer edges. EKR *Plant Finder* 1993.

'Drinkwater'

A synonym for 'Drinkwater Red'.

'Eastgrove Wine'

A form of *P. heterophyllus* – see page 73.

'Edithae'

A cross of *P. rupicola* × *P. barrettiae* – see page 65.

'Eisberg'

An old cultivar of German origin, still thought to survive in continental Europe. Catalogued as a large-flowered pure white.

'Elfin Pink'

A hybridized form of *P. barbatus* – see page 69.

'English Tapestry'

A synonym of 'Stapleford Gem' (*qv*), encountered in both the UK and New Zealand.

'Erectus'

A form of *P. heterophyllus* – see page 73.

'Etna'

An addition to the long list of reds, 'Etna' has been bred principally for cultivation in large containers, being compact and erect with strong stems.

Habit normal for Group 3B, but leaves tend to be smaller and finer. Flowers 4.5 × 3.5cm (1¾ × 1⅜in), tube quite abruptly expanding near its base, lobes pointed. Tube and lobes coloured uniformly in nearly *bright scarlet* (45B/C), throat white with rather smudged markings in a darker red, particularly at the mouth. Flowers held in compact panicles, with a downwards pose.

Raised by A.T. Yates & Sons, Congleton, Cheshire, one of several crosses involving 'Patio Pink' (*qv*) treated with mixed pollen of large-flowered hybrids. In the flower it is a smaller version of 'King George V' (*qv*), and is only superior to that variety in its improved habit. Released in 1998.

'Evelyn' ♖

An ever-popular variety with small pink flowers on compact fine-leaved bushy plants. Sturdy and reliable, 'Evelyn' will appeal to any gardener requiring pastel shades for the front of the border.

The classic Group 1 cultivar. Habit erect, making a neat bushy plant with thin wiry stems to a height not usually greater than 70cm (2⅓ft). Flowers small, 2.6 × 1.6cm (1 × ⅝in). Upper surface of tube and upper lobes *dull rose* (51D), often with a light bluish tint. Tube pencilled *deep magenta* (72A). Lower lobes and front of upper lobes *carmine rose* (51C). All lobes generally of similar shape, lower ones widely separated and slightly reflexed. Underside of tube bears two longitudinal grooves.

EKR Slieve Donard, Ireland c.1934, probably raised there. Possibly the first of the modern Group 1 named varieties.

'Feuerzauber' (syn. 'Magic Fire')

Described as a brilliant brick-red self-coloured cultivar by its raisers, Wilhelm Pfitzer of Stuttgart, Germany, when they introduced it in 1938. It was represented as a great improvement on 'Southgate Gem', still considered one of the best hybrids in continental Europe at that time. The flowers were larger and the panicles were regarded as more elegant. Four years later they announced that they had developed a seed strain from it. Seed production is today continued by Samen Mauser, Winterthur, Switzerland. We are not aware that seed is marketed in the UK, and we have not seen it. It appears to be a Group 3B hybrid, but of moderate height, 60cm (2ft).

'Firebird'

The trade name for 'Schoenholzeri' (*qv*) in English-speaking countries.

'Flame'

A vigorous cultivar with good persistence. The bright red flowers are borne in profusion and give an outstanding display, even compared to the generally prolific reds within its group.

Typical Group 3B in most characters. Flowers 4.7 × 3.3cm (1⅞ × 1¼in), lobes pointing forwards, slightly crinkled edges, the lower ones larger than the upper. *Bright crimson* (63A) lobes, tube similar but lighter towards underside, which is white. Throat white, well-defined guidelines in *carmine-lake* (59B) on the lower lobes, the one in the centre of each lobe extending to its outer edge in a thin line. A shadowy band in carmine lake on the mouth distinguishes this variety from other reds of this group. EKR J.A.F. Ambery, Geddington, Northamptonshire, 1987.

'Flamingo'

A well-liked pink-with-white addition to its group, attractive for its characteristic markings.

Group 3C. Habit: an open clump up to 90cm (3ft). Flowers 4 × 4cm, (1⅝ × 1⅝in), tube exterior basically white, but partially suffused *bright rose* (54A). Lobes heavily reflexed, particularly the upper pair, bright rose, the white of the throat extending well beyond the mouth. Lower throat pencilled *rose carmine* (184C), deepening at the mouth, the centre one traversing each lower lobe almost to its outer edge. Although the tube is delicately coloured, the bulb at its base is shiny and strongly coloured *deep carmine* (60A), a useful identification character. Stiff green stems bear stiff short peduncles which display their flowers horizontally or slightly upwards and hold them away from the stem.

Raised by Ron Sidwell, Evesham, Worcestershire in the 1960s.

'Flathead Lake'

A cross of *P. barbatus* × possibly *P. glaber* – see page 69.

'Fujiyama'

A cultivar of compact, upright habit bred for large pot culture, but equally at home in open ground. The colour combination of mature flowers in pink against buds and young flowers in yellow is unusual and striking.

Group 2B habit and foliage but with flowers like a small 3C. Flowers 4.2 × 3.4cm (1¼ × 1¼in), the lobes flared and rounded, the tube moderately expanded to give an open throat. Lobes lighter than *cerise* (63A), and the tube even lighter. Throat a creamy-white, with strong but smudgy markings in a deeper rose. Buds and young flowers are coloured *bistre yellow* (153D), this colour only turning to creamy-white at the point of maturity. Sepals large, rounded and reddish in colour.

Raised by A. T. Yates & Son, Cheshire, as one of a series of crosses using 'Patio Pink' (*qv*) with mixed Group 2 and 3 pollen. 'Apple Blossom' (*qv*) (large-flowered) is the probable pollen parent, and the intermediate character of the cross is evident. Released in 1998.

'Gaff's Pink'

A pretty cultivar very close to 'Hidcote Pink' (*qv*), showing the same pink flower with strong throat markings. The differences are that its throat colour is a pale but distinct cream-yellow, and it is less robust.

EKR Church Hill Nursery, Kent, 1991, the origin thought to be a nursery in Herefordshire.

'Garden Red'

A synonym for 'Windsor Red' (*qv*).

'Garnet'

The trade name for 'Andenken an Friedrich Hahn' (*qv*) in English-speaking countries.

'Garnet Variegated'

A sport of 'Andenken an Friedrich Hahn' (*qv*) with variegated leaves, otherwise identical to that variety. All stock reported to us either died or reverted after a year or so to the normal form. We have encountered the same phenomenon with 'White Bedder' (*qv*). EKR Roger Norman (Worcestershire) c. 1993.

'George Elrick'

A delicately coloured variety in an attractive rose and white combination.

Group 2B, normal habit for the group. Flowers 3.8 × 3cm (1½ × 1¼in), lobes pointing slightly forward. Tube and lobes *bright rose* (54A) shading to white on the underside of the tube, lobes with a very thin white border to margins. Throat white, finely pencilled in magenta.

Introduced as a bedding variety by Forbes 1950, probably raised by them. It appeared in the 1962 RHS trials, the name apparently altered by an official to 'George Ulrich', a much earlier variety described by Forbes as 'fiery scarlet, white throat' and last offered by them in 1906. It was given a Highly Commended award, but clearly this was for 'George Elrick', not 'George Ulrich'.

'George Holmes'

A misspelling of 'George Home'.

'George Home'

A handsome old variety in a bright but refined shade of red, very free-flowering.

Group 3B, very strong, spreading plants. Flowers 4.5 × 3.5cm (1¾ × 1⅜in), narrow tubes – 1cm (⅜in) – and rounded lobes, forward-pointing. Tube *bright scarlet* (45C), lobes *scarlet* (47A), throat white and finely pencilled scarlet, the lines coalescing and blotching at the mouth and running into the coloured part of the lobes. A white patch appears in the angle between each pair of lobes.

Raised by Forbes, introduced 1901. Also found as 'Lord Home', 'George Hume' and 'George Holmes'. Some stock offered as 'George Home' appears to be 'Maurice Gibbs' (*qv*) misnamed.

'Gladiator'

We have not seen this cultivar, which occurs in Australia. It is reported as a large-flowered, white-throated red, similar in colour and form to 'Rubicundus', which is also grown there.

'Gloire des Quatre Rues'

A handsome purple and white variety similar to 'Charles Rudd' (*qv*). Raised by the Quatre Rues Nursery, near Nantes, France, before 1995.

'Heavenly Blue'

A form of *P. heterophyllus* – see page 73.

'Hewell Pink Bedder' ♔

A popular salmon-pink variety, one of the earliest hybrids still in existence to be offered by Forbes specifically as a bedding variety.

Group 2B but habit unusually upright, height 75cm (2½ft). Flowers 4.1 × 3cm (1⅝ × 1¼in), upper lobes forward-pointing, lower lobes flared. Tube and lobes *cerise* (63A), deepening a little at the base of the tube and at the edges of the lobes. Throat white, with pencilling in *deep carmine red* (53A) finely drawn, becoming denser at the mouth but separated from the main colour of the lobes. The centre lines of the lower lobes are pencilled almost to the margins.

Raised at Hewell Grange, Redditch, Warwickshire, introduced by Forbes 1914 as 'Pink Bedder', but listed under its present name a year later, although, strangely, Forbes entered it in the 1930 RHS trials under its original name. Variations of spelling abound – 'Hewell's',

'Ewell', 'Howell's' – and 'Bedder' is frequently omitted. 'Hewitt's Pink' is, however, a separate variety.

A plant offered as 'Newell Bedder' is known which is similar to 'Hewell Pink Bedder' but is in a deeper shade of cerise, added to which the plants sent to the 1991 RHS trial are reported as having a stronger colour than we have described. It was for some time offered as a seed strain, and if as a consequence recloning took place it may be that some variation is present between existing stocks.

'Hewitt's Pink'

With its strong but refined crimson-rose colour, this uncommon variety brings a glow to any border. Some attention to colour balance is necessary.

Group 2B for habit, but with 3B influence in the larger than usual flowers. Flowers 4.7 × 3.1cm (1⅞ × 1¼in). Tube *bright crimson* (63A), lobes *bright rose* (54A), the lower more-forward pointing than the upper. Throat open, white, with heavy markings in magenta, but restricted to the middle lower lobe and the inner halves of the two adjacent lobes. These markings coalesce at the mouth to form three blotches. A thin line bisects each lobe, extending fully to the outer margin. EKR Brian Hiley, Wallington, Surrey, 1991.

'Heythrop Park'

Reported as virtually identical to 'Devonshire Cream' (*qv*). EKR *Plant Finder*, 1991.

'Hidcote Pink' ♔

A tall, distinctive plant. One of the most popular of hybrid penstemons for its robust constitution, free-flowering nature and pretty pink flowers with striking markings. A cultivar grown in many countries.

Group 2B. Habit an erect clump with numerous flower stems to 1m (3¼ft) bearing palish green leaves. Flowers 3.5 × 2.2cm (1⅜ × ⅞in). Upper surface of tube *bright rose* (54A) fading to *carmine rose* (54C) with age, lower surface creamy white. Throat strongly pencilled *cerise* (63A). Upper and lower lobes bright rose with the white of the throat extending on to them, especially the upper ones.

EKR Bloom's of Bressingham, Norfolk, 1951. The variety is known to have been grown at the National Trust's famous Gloucestershire garden at Hidcote for many years, and is widely assumed to have been raised there, but we have been unable to confirm this. 'Gaff's Pink', 'Shell Pink', 'Species RLB' and 'MacPennys Pink' are very similar in being Group 2B pinks which

P. 'Hidcote Pink'.

have the same strong throat markings.

'Hidcote Purple'

A useful cultivar for any position where neatness is important, and suitable as a solitary specimen. The numerous flowers are compactly arranged and a cluster of them often forms at the apex of the inflorescence, providing a flat-topped appearance. A reliable cultivar with above-average persistence.

Group 2B. Habit an erect multi-stemmed clump with slightly dark foliage growing to a height of 80cm (2 ¾ft). Flowers slightly pendant, 3.4 × 2.5cm (1¼ × ⅞in). Upper surface of tube and reverse of upper lobes *deep mauve* (77A). From the front the upper lobes pale gradually from tips to mouth, the lower lobes are paler, *bright mauve* (77B). Lower lobes narrow, distinctly separate, often lying in one plane. Older flowers commonly develop a vitreous blue overtone on the upper surface of the tube appearing first at the calyx end.

EKR Brian Hiley, Wallington, Surrey, 1989. Not, according to general opinion, a Hidcote product, but we have been unable to confirm this. Other cultivars of generally similar appearance with which it can be confused are 'Purple Bedder' (*qv*) and 'Sour Grapes' (Type 2) (*qv*).

'Hidcote White'

A form very like 'White Bedder' (*qv*), but of even weaker persistence, and having a flower colour of poor substance. Gardeners need not mourn its loss to cultivation, which seems imminent.

EKR *Plant Finder* 1989. Not, according to general opinion, a Hidcote product, but we have been unable to confirm this. The name may also be used instead of 'White Bedder' (*qv*) by some nurseries.

'Hopleys Variegated'

The only European Hybrid with variegated leaves in which the variegation is reliably constant throughout the life of the plant. Gardeners are fundamentally split between those who hate it and those who find it a delightful change. For those tempted to cry 'Virus!' and head for the nearest bonfire with it, it needs to be said that the variegation is almost certainly genetic; moreover it does not appear to harm the plant, which is quite persistent, nor does it spread to neighbouring plants.

Group 2B but with a taller habit than normal for that group – up to 90cm (3ft). Leaves irregularly variegated in varying shades of yellow, requiring sun for full development. Flowers 3.7 × 0.2cm (1½ × ¾in), lower lobes more forward-pointing than upper. Tube *deep mauve* (77A) with a bluish blush at the base, and fading to white on the underside although some mauve streaks are also evident. Lobes deep mauve, throat white marked with broad streaks in the same shade.

Propagated by Hopleys Nursery, Hertfordshire, from a sport of 'Burgundy', introduced 1987. Other cultivars are known to sport variegation as young plants but the effect has always been found to disappear as the plant ages, nor have we heard of other examples where the flower is also of a different colour and character.

'Hower Park'

Very similar to 'Devonshire Cream' (*qv*) and identical in garden effect, but plants we have seen were slightly but distinctly lighter in overall colour compared to an example of that variety growing nearby. EKR *Plant Finder*, 1995.

'Husker Red'

A red-leaved clone of *P. digitalis* with pure white flowers – see page 93.

'Hyacinth-Flowered'

A seed strain offered by Burpee & Park Seed Co., from a development by the Bolger Seed Co. of Del Monte, California before 1982. An improved bedding strain originating in Colorado showing low growth, good colour range and constitution. A particularly good feature of the inflorescence is an absence of secundity, that is, the flowers radiate in all directions. Considered to be developed from *P. barbatus* but does not resemble that species in flower – see, for example, 'Kummel'.

'Ice Cream'

A misnomer for *P. hartwegii* 'Albus', of recent origin – see page 78.

'Jeannie'

A variety we have not seen, and our only information is that it has pale lilac-blue flowers. EKR Edinburgh Royal Botanic Gardens, 1986. The origin may be Devon.

'Jingle Bells'

A form of *P. barbatus* – see page 69.

'John Booth'

A good border variety, similar to 'Charles Rudd' (*qv*), but in a lighter shade of purple.

Typical 3C habit. Flowers 4.5 × 3.8cm (1¾ × 1½in), lobes flared, upper smaller than lower. Lobes *deep mauve* (78A), tube deep mauve toning to *mauve* (78C) at its base. Throat pure white, no markings.

Raised by John Booth, Worcestershire, before 1970 as a selected seedling from purchased seed. Named and introduced by Eastgrove Cottage Garden Nurseries, Worcestershire, in 1982.

'John Nash'

Although widely accepted as a separate variety to 'Alice Hindley' (*qv*) the differences would seem to lie only in it having a bushier and lower habit – not usually more than 75cm (2½ft). The flowers are certainly identical. Reputedly not very persistent, but this has not been our experience. EKR Margery Fish, East Lambrook, Somerset, before 1986.

'Johnsoniae'

A synonym of 'Flathead Lake' – see page 69.

'Joy'

On good authority, it appears that this name was erroneously applied to 'Chester Scarlet' (*qv*) by a helper of Ron Sidwell's, copying 'Joy' off the label when taking cuttings without realizing this referred to the donor of the plant! 'Joy' is widely used for what appears to be 'Chester Scarlet', and in the circumstances it must be regarded as a trade name only. But the name also appears on at least one other Group 3B red, thus confounding even further the problem of distinguishing the varieties in this very confused area. EKR *Plant Finder*, 1991.

'June'

Material in our possession from two independent sources appears identical to 'Pennington Gem' (*qv*). EKR *Plant Finder*, 1992.

'Jupiter'

A synonym in France for 'Andenken an Friedrich Hahn'.

'King George V'

An old variety that remains very popular for its enormous flowers in a bold display of royal scarlet.

Typical 3C habit. Flowers 4 × 4cm (1⅝ × 1⅝in), lobes flared, mouth wide. Tube and lobes *bright scarlet* (45B), throat white with short *deep carmine* (60A) lines, and some smudging, in the throat.

Raised by Forbes, introduced 1911 doubtless in celebration of the accession of George V to the throne the year before. One of the few penstemons named after royalty. The name is frequently shortened to 'King George'.

'Knight's Purple'

An unusual purple variety, notable for its tall habit and flowers of good substance, performing well at the back of the border.

Group 2B, but the habit is taller than normal – up to 1.2m (4ft) – and the flowers larger. We favour 2B, however, because the medium size of foliage and the bulbous shape of flower are typical. Flower 4.5 × 3cm (1¾ × 1¼in), tube expanded, lobes equal and forward pointing, the lower more so than the upper. Tube *deep mauve* (77A), lobes the same but darkening at the margin to *plum* (79B). Throat white, finely pencilled in mauve, the individual lines not coalescing. Sepals strongly coloured deep purple.

EKR Hunt's Court Nursery, Dursley, Gloucestershire,

Plate X (overleaf). A selection of medium-flowered cultivars from Group 2, with 'Hewitt's Pink' showing some features of Group 3. Note the narrow leaf of 'Garnet' (Group 2A) compared to the broad leaf of 'Knightwick' (Group 2B).

PLATE X

P. 'Russian River'

P. 'Burgundy'

P. 'Schoenholzeri' (syn. 'Firebird')

P. 'Andenken an Friedrich Hahn'
(syn. 'Garnet')

All flowers are shown at approximately ½ size

P. 'Knightwick'

P. 'Hewitt's Pink'

P. 'Sutton's Pink Bedder'

P. 'Pennington Gem'

c. 1991. Although the '2B purples' are a close family in appearance, 'Knight's Purple' does stand apart as an improvement in flower size; and in consistency of colour for those who do not like the vitreous blue/purple mixture common in other varieties of the group.

'Knightwick'

A new cultivar resembling 'Stapleford Gem' (*qv*), but showing distinct improvements in persistence and flowering performance.

A large member of Group 2B, making an erect, dense, multi-stemmed clump up to 1m (3¼ft). Flowers longer than broad, 3.3 × 2.2cm (1¼ × ⅞in), *deep mauve* (77A) paling to white on underside of tube. Lobes paler, the upper ones partly suffused white. Heavily pencilled throats without coalescence at the mouth, the midline of the lower lobes strongly pencilled to the margin, the upper lobes more lightly so. Edges of the lower lobes finely serrated.

Propagated by Perhill Nurseries, Great Witley, Worcestershire from a selected seedling, introduced 1993. 'Knightwick' lays claim to being among the most persistent of the European Hybrids, overwintering with us with scarcely a leaf discoloured. The flowers are overall darker than those of 'Stapleford Gem', but the presence of the pencilled midlines on the lobes is the best distinguishing feature of 'Knightwick'.

'Kummel'

A late summer-flowering variety with very large flowers in an unusual purple-red shade, not reliably persistent.

Group 3C. Compact habit, generally under 60cm (2ft). Flowers 4.2 × 3.2cm (1¼ × 1¼in), lobes rounded, and flared fully at right angles to the tube. Tube and lobes between *magenta* (59D) and *deep magenta* (72A), deepest on the lobe margins. Throat white with faint broken pencilling in the same colour.

Raised by Langthorns Plantery, Dunmow, Essex, c. 1991, a selected seedling from 'Hyacinth-Flowered Mixed'. Introduced 1993.

'Lavender Queen'

A form of either *P. calycosus* or *P. calycosus x P. digitalis* with light violet flowers. A registered variety from 1959.

'Le Phare'

A pretty cultivar, with long, graceful red flowers, the shade different from other reds of the group. The flowering season is long and persistence is quite good.

Habit compact for Group 3A. Flowers 4.9 × 3.1cm (2 × 1¼in), tube narrow, lobes small and pointed, the lower more rounded than the upper. Tubes and lobes *rosine* (46c) in early maturity, but the lobes rapidly shading to *cerise* (63A). Throat silvery white with a few short markings in the mouth, concentrated where the two outer lower lobes meet the centre lobe.

EKR Perhill Nurseries, Great Witley, Worcestershire, 1992. Origin presumably French. Frequently offered as 'Phare'.

'Lena Seeba'

A cross of *P. grandiflorus* with an unknown Peltanthera species. It is thought there may be a connection with, and resemblance to, the seed strain 'War Axe' – see page 82. Registered by Glen Viehmeyer, University of Nebraska, 1960.

'Lilac and Burgundy'

A bicolour, as the name suggests, with a strongly contrasting dark mouth against a lighter tube. It is not one of the most persistent cultivars, requiring a sheltered position if it is to thrive.

Group 3B habit, 3C flowers. Flowers 4.7 × 3.6cm (1⅞ × 1⅜in), narrow tube, large lobes, flared and rounded, equal in size, tending to fold back on themselves. Lobes and tube *mauve* (78C), but mottled and striped in paler mauve and white. Throat white, but strongly marked in *brown lake* to *crimson* (184A–187B), the mouth filled by two large triangles of colour extending well onto the lower lobes. Centre lines of all five lobes are coloured as far as the margins with a tendency to be edged in white.

EKR Clive and Kathy Gandley, Cullompton, Devon, c. 1990, but raiser unknown to us. The throat marking suggests 'Rich Ruby' (*qv*) in the parentage.

'Little Witley'

One of several cultivars of its group, with bulbous purple flowers. Free-flowering and persistent.

Group 2B. Flowers 3.8 × 3cm (1½ × 1¼in), tube expanded, lobes equal, the lower pointing forward more than the upper. Tube and lips slightly deeper than *bright purple* (72B), throat white with fine pencilling, not as strong as in other Group 2B purples. Inflorescences long, up to 45cm (18in).

Raised by Perhill Nurseries, Great Witley, Worcestershire, introduced 1993. Name sometimes abbreviated to 'Witley'.

'Lord Home'

A synonym for 'George Home' (*qv*).

'Lynette'

An attractive, small-flowered variety, with flowers in a glowing shade of purple-rose. A cultivar with proven persistence.

A typical Group 1 in every respect. Flowers 2.9 × 1.6cm (1¼ × ⅝in), tube abruptly expanding at base, mouth wide. Lobes equal, rounded, and flared or only slightly forward-pointing. Tube *deep magenta* (72A), paling to white on underside of tube, and to *magenta* (59D) on the lobes. Throat white with fine but clear deep magenta pencilling, the centre lines on the lobes continuing to their edges.

Raised c. 1975 by Paul Picton, Old Court Nurseries, Malvern, Worcestershire, from the cross 'Evelyn' × 'Andenken an Friedrich Hahn' (*qv*). Introduced 1980. Confusion with 'Threave Pink' (*qv*) is possible, but the flower shape is more bulbous and the colour deeper.

'MacPennys Pink'

A Group 2B cultivar similar in garden effect and appearance to the much better known 'Hidcote Pink' (*qv*), but with a provenance that is both distinct and unexpected. Comparing the two varieties is difficult since the flowers of both change considerably as they progress through and beyond maturity. On balance 'MacPennys Pink' is in a slightly lighter rose, and the throat markings are also a shade paler, nevertheless a good proportion of flowers of the two varieties taken at any one time are indistinguishable.

Raised by Douglas Bradwell Lowndes of MacPennys Nurseries, Christchurch, Dorset, in the 1960s. It arose as a sport of 'Appleblossom' (Type 2).

'Madame Golding'

Appears to be identical to 'Old Candy Pink' (*qv*). EKR Brian Hiley, Wallington (Surrey), 1990.

'Margery Fish'

One of the most persistent variants of *P. heterophyllus*, possibly hybridized with another species – see page 73.

'Mrs Golding'

A misnomer for 'Madame Golding' (*qv*).

'Maurice Gibbs' ♔

An old variety with flowers in an unusual and arresting shade of dark purple-red. A good enough grower, and free-flowering, but its persistence is low.

Group 3C. An erect plant forming open clumps which may reach 1m (3¼ft) on favourable sites. Large open-mouthed flowers 4 × 4cm (1⅝ × 1⅝in), boldly revealing their unmarked white interiors set against

tube and lobes in a dark shade of *bright magenta* (61B). Upper lobes very reflexed. Light amount of magenta mottling on the lower mouth. A midline streak crosses each lower lobe almost to its tip, with short subsidiary ones on either side.

Raised by the Hon. V. Gibbs, Aldenham House, Buckinghamshire, before 1930, receiving an Award of Merit in the RHS trials of that year. 'George Home' (*qv*), 'Lord Home' or 'George Holmes' in the same shade of purple red would appear to be 'Maurice Gibbs' misnamed.

'Merlin'

As reported to us, 'Merlin' is similar in flower to 'Raven' (*qv*), perhaps a shade lighter. Other differences are that it is very low-growing – under 60cm (2ft) – and the leaves are glossier, and more elliptical in shape compared to the narrow leaves of 'Raven'. EKR Beeches Nursery, Ashdon, Essex 1995.

'Mesa'

A registered cross from 1969 by Glen Viehmeyer, University of Nebraska, from 'Flathead Lake' and a species of Section Habroanthus. The smallish flowers are reddish-purple with deep purple guidelines. The habit is compact and the constitution robust.

'Mexicali Hybrids'

A series of seed strains developed in the 1980s by Bruce Meyers in Washington State, USA, the cross used being 'Mexicana' × 'Sensation', both hybrid mixtures themselves. The range of colours covers the full penstemon spectrum, and the strains are of two broad types – those of essentially *P. campanulatus* habit, relatively small-flowered, and those with bigger flowers and broader foliage where the European Hybrid influence (derived from the 'Sensation' parents) is evident.

'Mexicana Hybrids'

A seed strain developed in the 1970s by Bruce Meyers in Washington, USA, discussed on page 56.

'Midnight'

To date we have not encountered a plant of 'Midnight' that could be positively distinguished from 'Russian River' (*qv*). The name was in existence earlier than 'Russian River' however, but we have yet to find a reliable description. 'Midnight' is mentioned in the writings of Margery Fish in the 1950s as a misnomer for 'Stapleford Gem'.

'Mint Pink'

A pretty cultivar but probably almost pure *P. campanu-*

latus, nevertheless in a colour which is particularly clear and of good substance.

Group 1. Flowers 3 × 1.7cm (1¼ × ¾in), with expanded tube and wide mouth. Tube paler than *magenta* (59D), toning to white on the underside, throat white with pencilling in magenta, finely drawn but extending the whole length of the throat. Stamens protrude slightly through the mouth. EKR Michael and Hazel Brett, Maidstone, Kent, c.1994.

'Modesty'

A pretty hybrid of long standing in a good shade of rose, distinct from others in this colour range. Not as persistent as most members in its group.

Group 2B with a rather open habit, forming a loose clump to a height of 80cm (2¾ft). The flowers, 3.7 × 3.5cm (1½ × 1⅜in), are held horizontally in open panicles. Tube and rear of lobes *bright rose red* (45D), underside of tube and front of lobes paler. Throat white, the white extending a little beyond the mouth, lightly and irregularly pencilled in bright rose red.

Introduced by Forbes in 1931, listed by them continuously until 1968, their description matching ours fairly closely.

'Moerheim Gem'

Clear pink flowers with white interiors and similar to 'Southgate Gem' (*qv*), from which it is most probably derived. Raised by the Moerheim Nursery, Dedemsvaart, the Netherlands, and introduced by them in 1921.

'Mother of Pearl'

A cultivar which has much in common with 'Stapleford Gem' (*qv*) in terms of size, bearing and unusual colouring, but from which it is quite distinct in flower and foliage colour. Not liked by some, but adored by others.

Group 2B. A strong clump-forming plant producing many erect shoots to 90cm (3ft). Flowers 3 × 2.2cm (1¼ × ⅞in), creamy-white variably suffused lightish *mauve* (78C), with colour most persistent towards the rear of upper tube and the extremities of the lobes. Throat heavily pencilled in a deeper mauve, the lines branching into a network in the mouth and beyond. Each lower lobe marked along its midline to its outer edge.

Propagated in 1984 by Hopleys Nursery, Much Hadham, Hertfordshire, from a selected seedling of 'Sour Grapes' Type 1 (*qv*), introduced 1987. Older

stocks of a very similar character are also known. See also 'Astley'.

'Mrs Blakey'

A form of *P. heterophyllus* – see page 73.

'Mrs Miller'

A very late-flowering variety with large scarlet flowers, beautifully marked in the throat.

Group 3B, but tall and erect-growing for this group, up to 1.2m (4ft). Flowers 5 × 3.5cm (2 × 1⅜in), tube gradually expanding, lobes flared and rounded, the lower ones slightly pointing forward. Tube and lobes a uniform *bright scarlet* to *scarlet* (45C–47A), throat white, the white extending partly onto the lower lobes. Strongly but finely pencilled in deep red, three lines per lobe including, very faintly, the upper lobes. Lines branching at the mouth, and merging into the scarlet of the lobes, the centre lines of the lower lobes visible almost to their edges. Distinctive patches of colour occur in the angles where the lobes meet. Anther sacs often protrude beyond the mouth.

EKR Clive and Kathy Gandley, Cullompton, Devon, c.1994, raiser unknown to us.

'Mrs Morse'

A vigorous and showy red cultivar which makes an eye-catching display.

Group 3B. Habit open clump-forming, to a height of approximately 75cm (2½ft). Flowers slightly variable in size, to 4.5 × 3.3cm (1¾ × 1¼in) *deep rose red* (53B) throat heavily pencilled *carmine red* (46A). Upper lobes reflexed and overlapping, lower lobes forward pointing and separated and bluntly pointed, indistinctly showing a midline marking.

Introduced by Hopleys Nursery, Hertfordshire, in 1979, from a plant donated by a customer, Mrs Morse. Has similarities with Oaklea Red (*qv*) but distinguished by its broad, abruptly pointed sepals.

'Myddelton Gem'

Among the reddish-pink cultivars of medium height this old favourite still commands attention for its neat, fresh appearance and reliability.

Group 2B. Neat bushy habit, height 75cm (2½ft). Flowers longer than normal for the group, 4.5 × 3.3cm (1¾ × 1¼in), arranged in open panicles. Both tube and lobes *rosine* (46C), slightly paler on the front side of the lobes. At the junction of the upper lobes and the mouth a light bluish flush can sometimes be detected. Throat white, extending slightly onto lobes, a few faint

P. 'Oaklea Red'.

smudges may be present in the mouth. Upper, but not lower, lobes overlap consistently. Furthermost edges of lobes finely serrated.

Raised by Wallace & Co., Colchester, Essex, probably before 1905; Forbes listed it from 1911. Named after E. A. Bowles' house in Enfield, and mentioned by him as a favourite penstemon. The strange spelling of 'Myddelton' confounds most labellers and it is usually found as the more familiar 'Myddleton' or 'Middleton'. Similar to 'Southgate Gem' (*qv*), for which it can be mistaken.

'Myddelton Red'
Our information is that this form is indistinguishable from 'Myddelton Gem'.

'Newbury Gem'
The first of a type deliberately bred for bedding use at the end of the 19th century, and pivotal to the develop-

ment of several of the modern Group 2 hybrids – see page 25. The variety appears to have died out in the UK in the late 1980s, but has survived in Australia. Pending its expected reintroduction to cultivation in the UK, we quote the description which appeared in the RHS report on the 1914 trials:

'Slender, spreading, 50cm (20in); corolla 3.7cm (1½in) long, much longer than wide; throat compressed; shows all stages between fully developed staminode and a perfect stamen; carmine-scarlet, extending over the whole of the outside of the tube, passing on lower lip to heavy lines in the tube; lip segments pointed and slightly serrate. Dainty and very decorative.'

Raised by James Backhouse of York before 1900. 'Newbury Gem White' was also in existence in time for the 1914 RHS trials, and 'Newbury Gem Pink', 'Newbury Gem Scarlet', and 'Newbury Gem Cerise' were all to appear in the next ten years.

'Newell Pink'

A cultivar close to 'Hewell Pink Bedder', and discussed under that variety.

'Oaklea Red'

A Group 3B cultivar similar in colour and habit to 'Mrs Morse' (qv). Distinguished by flowers with taller than broad mouths, wavy and overlapping lobes, pencilling that terminates in three crescents and narrow, tapered, sepals. EKR Doddington Nurseries, Cambridgeshire, 1991. Variations of spelling include 'Oakley' and 'Oakleigh'.

'Old Candy Pink'

A very striking variety in a crimson shade which suffuses the whole flower. It flowers early, long, and freely. Provided care is taken in blending the powerful colour, it is a variety of great merit for the front of the herbaceous border.

Group 2B, with flowers 4×3.3cm (1⅝×1¼in), slightly large for the group. Tube expanded, throat wide, lobes rounded and flared, with crinkled edges. Tube and lips *bright crimson* (63A), shading to a slightly lighter colour on the tube underside, and where the colour suffuses onto the roof of the throat. Throat otherwise white with strong pencilling in a darker crimson, the lines coalescing in the mouth and merging into the crimson of the lower lobes. A distinct circular white patch appears at the junction of each pair of lobes.

Propagated by John Booth, Worcestershire, before 1970 from a selected seedling, introduced 1982 by Eastgrove Cottage Garden Nurseries, Little Witley, Worcestershire. 'Candy Pink' is a misnomer. 'Madame Golding' appears to be identical.

'Osprey' ♈

One of a number of cultivars that are white with some pink, but it is taller than most of them and therefore suited to planting further back in the border.

Group 3C. Habit a loose clump, height up to 1m (3¼ft). Close-packed inflorescence, with erect peduncles supporting up to seven flowers each, held tightly against the main stem. Flowers 4.2×4.2cm (1¼×1¼in). Upper lobes smaller than the lower ones and slightly reflexed, lower lobes slightly forward-pointing or at right angles to the tube. Ground colour of the tube creamy-white, lobes initially *rose-carmine* (184C) fading to *carmine-rose* (51C) at maturity, the colour by then suffusing onto the upper part of the tube, fading

progressively towards the calyx. Throat pure white, the white spreading beyond the mouth, and extended into three white lines partway across each lower lobe.

Raised by Ron Sidwell, Evesham, Worcestershire, in the 1960s.

'Papal Purple'

A valuable and distinct low-growing cultivar, useful for positioning near the edges and corners of paths. If kept judiciously trimmed in autumn its low mound of neat foliage is attractive in winter.

Group 1. Habit a low mound, occasionally to a height of 45cm (18in). Inflorescences form short panicles above fine bright foliage. Flowers 2.5 × 2cm (1 × ¾in), markedly bulbous, almost rectangular in side view. Exterior of tube *reddish violet* (83B), paling at the base, and to off-white beneath. Throat clearly pencilled *deep magenta* (72A), all lobes reddish violet.

Introduced 1981 by Paul Picton, Old Court Nurseries, Malvern, Worcestershire, from a seedling found in the garden of Valerie Finnis, Boughton House, Northamptonshire. 'Papal Purple' comes about 50 per cent true from seed, the remainder being of a lighter flower colour.

'Papal Purple' × 'Evelyn'

A cross without a name! This hybrid shows characteristics intermediate between its two parents and is as persistent and attractive as either of them.

Group 1, a little more upright in growth than either parent. Flowers 2.7 × 1.2cm (1⅛ × ½in), rectangular shape when viewed from the side (like 'Papal Purple'), small flared lobes. Tube and lobes *mauve* to *bright mauve* (78C–77B), white and mauve streaked on underside of tube. Throat white with some faint pencilling in bright mauve.

EKR Brian Hiley (Wallington) 1990.

'Park Garden'

Not seen by us. Reported to be similar to 'Thorn' but with larger flowers. EKR Perhill Nurseries, Great Witley, Worcestershire, 1992.

'Patio Coral'

A medium-flowered rose variety bred for large pot culture, with a partially drooping habit useful for covering the edge of the container.

The general appearance is typically Group 1 except for the larger than normal flower – 3.5 × 2.3cm (1⅜ × ⅞in). Lobes small and rounded, the lower ones pointing forward and down. Tube and lobes a uniform *bright rose*

(54A), throat white and unmarked. The flower buds are in a striking deep rose shade. With pedicels longer than the flowers the result is quite open and airy sprays.

Introduced by Royal Sluis, Over Peover, Cheshire, 1995, the result of a cross of 'Patio Pink' and selected large-flowered hybrids made by A. T. Yates & Son, Congleton, Cheshire.

'Patio Pearl'

An accidental misnomer for 'Patio Pink' (*qv*).

'Patio Pink'

A sport of 'Pink Endurance' notable for its upright habit, stiffer stems and outstanding flowering performance.

Group 1, habit stiffer otherwise typical for the group. Flowers 2.7 × 2.2cm (1⅛ × ⅞in), paler than *bright purple* (72B) above, very pale below, but slightly darker than 'Pink Endurance'; lower lobes *mauve* (78C), throat white, with pencilling.

Introduced by Royal Sluis, Over Peover, Cheshire, 1994. Due to a misunderstanding some nurseries sold this variety as 'Patio Pearl' during the 1996/7 seasons. Steps are being taken to eradicate this name.

'Patio Shell'

A pink-flowered form of stiffly upright habit bred for large pot culture.

Group 1, but with flowers slightly large for the group – 3.5 × 2.7cm (1⅜ × 1⅛in). Tube expands abruptly at base, lobes point forward and down, the lower ones noticeably longer than the upper. Lobes paler than *bright rose* (54A), tube suffused in the same colour, but paling to white at base and underside. Throat white, marked *deep magenta* (72A) in strong lines. Buds cream, tipped in magenta.

Introduced by Royal Sluis, Over Peover, Cheshire, 1995, raised by A. T. Yates & Son, Congleton, Cheshire, with mixed Group 2 and 3 pollen on 'Patio Pink'.

'Patio Wine'

A free-flowering variety bred for large pot culture, but can be equally as well used in open ground. The flower colour is the deepest of the 'Patio' series.

Group 1, but with flowers larger than normal. Stiff, upright habit, many-stemmed. Flower 3.7 × 2.6cm (1½ × 1in), a quite narrow tube with flared lobes. Petals even in size and rounded. Tube and lobes *magenta* (59D), throat white with heavy parallel markings in *deep magenta* (72A) on the lower lobes.

The markings partly coalesce at the mouth on each lobe, but not between lobes.

Raised by A. Yates & Son, Congleton, Cheshire, and introduced by Royal Sluis, Over Peover, Cheshire, in 1995. It is the result of using mixed Group 2 and 3 pollen on 'Patio Pink', the larger flower and deeper colour being explained by the incursion of, possibly, 'Oaklea Red' or 'Andenken an Friedrich Hahn'.

'Peace'

One of several very popular cultivars that are largely white with some pink.

Group 2B, but flowers longer than normal. Habit an open clump to a height of 60cm (2ft). Flowers 4.1 × 3cm (1⅝ × 1¼in), with lobes forward-pointing. Flowers essentially white, but lobes margined in *cerise* (63A), toning to a paler shade on the rest of the lips and at

P. 'Pennington Gem'.

times suffusing on to the back of the tube. Flower colour fades more rapidly and extensively than in similar cultivars, for example 'Apple Blossom' (Type 2).

It is tempting to equate this modern variety with one of the same name and description which Forbes listed only in the 1870s, but the complete gap in the record for over a century makes it highly unlikely they are connected – on which assumption the EKR is from Edinburgh Royal Botanic Gardens 1985.

'Pennington Gem' ♈
One of the best pink cultivars, taller than many in this colour, and with attractive foliage, reliable and of good persistence. Where winters are not too severe it can form a mound over 1m (3¼ft) in height and diameter.

Group 3B. Normally an erect clump-former, but older plants may spread with age and weight of flowers, the fallen stems self-layering readily. The distinctive rather greyish-green leaves are borne on numerous green stems, often lightly tinted reddish-brown, reaching 1.1m (3½ft). Flowers 4.1×3cm (1⅝×1¼in), tube and lobes *bright rose* (54A), the colour intensifying progressively towards the base of the tube and paling on the underside. A faint bluish wash can affect the colour of the rear of the upper ones. Tube interior white with a few faint magenta lines, some full length.

Introduced by Forbes in 1934.

'Pershore Carnival'
A vigorous new red cultivar of good promise.

Typical Group 3B to a height of 80cm (2¾ft). Flowers 4 × 3.2cm (1⅝ × 1¼in), bright glowing red with white throat lightly pencilled lilac and with noticeable blotches in mouth at the junctions between upper and lower lobes, and on either side of central lower lobe. All lower lobes are coloured along their midlines. Raised at Pershore College, Worcestershire, introduced 1998.

'Pershore Fanfare'
A stately new cultivar with lilac flowers.

Vigorous Group 2B plant reaching 90cm (3ft). Flowers 3.5 × 2.7cm (1⅜ × 1⅛in) deep lilac, paler on underside of tube. Throat white with flushes and pencilling in lilac. All lower lobes are coloured along their midlines. Raised at Pershore College, Worcestershire, and introduced 1998.

'Pershore Pink Necklace'
A new pink and white cultivar, attractive because the characteristic markings in the mouth, which resemble the shape of a necklace, are usually only found among

P. 'Pershore Pink Necklace'.

much darker-coloured members of its group.

Group 3C. A tall, loose, clump-forming plant up to 1 m (3¼ft). Flowers 3.5 × 3.7cm (1⅜ × 1½in), *bright rose* (54A) on the front of all lobes, generally lighter on their reverse sides, and suffusing the white tube irregularly towards its base, partly in streaks or lines. A transverse band of *rose-carmine* (184C) runs continuously across the bases of all three lower lobes. The rear edge of the band is not sharply defined and small specks of colour extend partway back into the throat. Each lower lobe has a bold midline in rose-carmine almost to its outer edge. Raised at Pershore College, Worcestershire, introduced 1995.

'Phare'
A shortened form of 'Le Phare' (*qv*).

'Phyllis'
A synonym for 'Evelyn' (*qv*).

'Pink Cloud' (or 'Pink Clouds')

Both the above names appear to be in use for a tall pink cultivar grown in both Australia and New Zealand. Reports indicate that it is either a synonym of 'Pennington Gem' (qv), or a cultivar extremely close to it with flowering stems in a stronger reddish-brown.

'Pink Dragon'

A *P. rupicola* hybrid raised by Jack Drake, Inshriach Alpine Nursery, Aviemore, Scotland, before 1983 – see page 65.

'Pink Elf'

A form of *P. barbatus* – see page 69.

'Pink Endurance'

An outstandingly floriferous and reliably persistent pink cultivar, ideally suited to a position at the border's edge because of its limited height.

Group 1. Habit, a low, dense, moderately lax bushy plant to 50cm (1¾ft) with an abundance of fine narrow leaves. Flowers 2.7 × 2.2cm (1⅛ × ⅞in), paler than *bright purple* (93B). Interior white with pencilling.

Introduced by Bloom's of Bressingham, Norfolk, in 1970, from a seedling brought in by a customer.

'Pink Profusion'

A pleasing free-flowering cultivar in an attractive purplish-rose showing elements of both Group 1 and 2 origin. Persistent enough, but sometimes slow to begin flowering.

Habit typical for Group 2B but leaves intermediate between it and Group 1 – narrow but coarse. Similarly the flowers show mixed character – Group 1 in shape, Group 2 in size. Flowers 3.5 × 2.1cm (1⅛ × ¼in), tube very bulbous, mouth wide, lobes equal and forward-pointing. Tube lighter than *bright purple* (72B) fading to white on underside, lobes mottled in the same colour and a shade lighter than *mauve* (78C). Throat white with a small number of fine and well-separated lines in crimson running almost the whole length of the throat. EKR Tim Ingram, Copton Ash Nurseries, Kent, 1994.

'Port Wine' ♀

A particularly good variety with large flowers in shades of claret and with pretty throat markings. Vigorous and persistent.

Typical habit of Group 3B. Flowers 5.3 × 4cm (2 × 1⅜in), lobes variably set, sometimes forward-pointing, sometimes more or less flared, the lower-middle smaller than the rest. Tube *deep claret* (187B/C), lobes similar but shading to *deep reddish purple* (71A). Throat white with fine parallel pencilling in deep claret, the centre line of each lower lobe being traced out as far as its margin. The pencilling becomes denser at the mouth with some smudging, but not forming blotches.

EKR P. J. Foley, Holden Clough Nursery, Clitheroe, Lancashire, who listed it from the late 1970s.

'Powis Castle'

A variety bearing strong similarities to 'Port Wine' (qv), and in any case having an identical garden effect. If there are differences it may be that the flowers of 'Powis Castle' are slightly longer and narrower, 5.5 × 3.5cm (2⅛ × 1⅜in); the colour tends to be more *deep reddish purple* (71A) than *deep claret* (187B/C) all over. EKR Perhill Nurseries, Great Witley, Worcestershire, 1992.

'Prairie Dawn'

A complex hybrid reminiscent of a pink form of *P. barbatus* – see page 69.

'Prairie Dusk'

A registered hybrid from a cross of 'Flathead Lake' × *P. strictus* – see page 71.

'Prairie Fire'

A 'Flathead Lake' type similar to *P. barbatus* – see page 69.

'Prairie Splendor'

A wide-spectrum seed strain intended as a general bedding mixture of bushy habit and small stature, with medium-sized flowers in a wide range of colours. Raiser Dale Lindgren, University of Nebraska, 1993, from a cross of *P. cobaea* x *P. triflorus*.

'Princess Rose'

A form of 'Flathead Lake' registered 1959 – see under *P. barbatus*, page 69. It is reported as a particularly sturdy form with rose flowers, but its survival to the present day is doubtful.

'Prinz Daniel'

A light yellow form of *P. barbatus* of recent German origin – see page 69.

'Priory Purple'

A very deep purple cultivar with the usual good habit and persistence of varieties of this colour. A sombre presence.

Typical Group 2B habit, making strong plants. Flowers 2.2 × 3.2cm (⅞ × ¼in), the 'over-square' dimensions due to the widely flared lower lobes. Upper lobes smaller and more pointed. Flowers are bicoloured at maturity, combining *deep mauve* (77A) on the lobes and upper tube with *violet* (90A) on the lower tube.

Throat virtually filled with *deep claret* (187C) lines, such that very little white shows through. Staminode short, but in a vivid white which stands out against the dark background. Pedicels longer than flowers, allowing the drooping flowers to make an open panicle.

EKR Hunt's Court Nursery, Dursley, Gloucestershire, 1991.

'Purdyi'

A trade name for *P. heterophyllus* ssp. *purdyi* – see page 74.

'Purple and White'

A description rather than a name that we have found attached to various large flowered cultivars, probably seed-raised, resembling such varieties as 'Charles Rudd' (*qv*), 'Countess of Dalkeith' (*qv*), and 'John Booth' (*qv*).

'Purple Bedder'

One of the large number of purples, a pretty enough subject, but with no outstanding features to recommend it above the others.

Typical 2B habit and foliage. Flowers 4 × 2.5cm (1⅝ × 1in), tube expanded, mouth wide, lobes bluntly pointed, and all pointing forward. Tube and lobes *deep mauve* (77A), the tube becoming *reddish violet* (83B) at the base. Throat white with several parallel lines in dark purple, not coalescing, the centre lines of each lobe extended to the margin.

Introduced by Forbes 1954 as a 'deep purple self', which hardly sounds the same plant, nevertheless it received an Award of Merit in the 1962 RHS trials under a description much closer to ours. It is remarkably similar to some forms claiming to be 'Sour Grapes' (*qv*). The name is often found misapplied to 'Rich Ruby' (*qv*).

'Purple Gem'

A prostrate alpine form, it is believed of *P. fruticosus*.

'Purple Passion'

An eye-catching addition to Group 2B. Habit, upright to 90cm (3ft). Grape-purple self-coloured flowers densely arranged in whorls on the flowering stems. The corolla tubes expand abruptly, and both upper and lower lobes are forward pointing. Introduced by Bay Bloom Nurseries, Tauranga, New Zealand in 1989.

'Purpureus Albus'

A synonym for 'Countess of Dalkeith' (*qv*), and possibly other large-flowered purple and whites.

'Rajah'

Material in our possession carrying this name bears a strong resemblance to 'Schoenholzeri' (*qv*), differing only in being of a lower growth and having perhaps slightly smaller flowers.

EKR Barr's, Taplow, Berkshire, 1934, under the description 'rich scarlet, white throat' which, while not contradictory, is hardly conclusive that our 'Rajah' is correctly named; moreover for a low-growing form of 'Schoenholzeri' to exist five years before that variety was introduced is difficult to explain. The accession list for Margery Fish's garden includes a 'Noel Rajah', but with no date or plant details.

'Raven' ♀

A very special Sidwell cultivar, in duskiest purple shades of great substance and beautifully marked. Less persistent than some, nevertheless highly recommended. Best in sunny isolation without competition.

Typical Group 3C. Flower 5 × 4.2cm (2 × 1¾in), regular flared lobes and wide throat. Tube *blackish purple* (79A), lips in slightly lighter purples (79B/C). Throat white with smudgy pencilling in red-purple, with coloured patches where the lower lobes join with one another, and where the upper and lower lobes meet.

Raised by Ron Sidwell, Evesham, not later than 1970. See also 'Merlin'.

'Razzle Dazzle'

A striking member of its group, much to be admired for its large, glowing, dark red flowers on attractive deep maroon stems; and for its persistence.

Group 2A, with bushy habit up to 90cm (3ft). Flowers held on looser panicles than normal for the group, on strongly coloured stems. Flowers up to 4.2 × 3.2cm (1¾ × 1¼in). Tube and rear of lobes *deep rose red* (53B), paling slightly towards *rosine* (46C) on front of lobes, this colour suffusing well up the throat. Throat indistinctly pencilled in a slightly darker colour, the separate lines having a tendency to coalesce at the mouth but seldom forming well-defined patches. Often the effect is virtually a self-colour. Lobes minutely serrated. Sepals brown.

EKR Perhill Nurseries, Great Witley, Worcestershire, 1995; the source of material, and the name, being an unidentified nursery in Devon. The same clone, or one virtually identical to it, has been available in Switzerland and the UK for some years under the incorrect name 'Schoenholzeri' (*qv*).

'Red Ace'

Not a common variety, but probably the largest-growing and most persistent of the large red-flowered cultivars and, happily, in a distinct shade which sets it apart.

Group 3B, making a large mound over 1m (3¼ft) across and about 90cm (3ft) high. Flowers 4.5 × 3.8 (1¾ × 1½in), lobes flared, almost suggesting Group 3C, but the tube remains trumpet-shaped. Tube and lobes a uniform *carmine-vermilion* (45A), throat white, finely marked in bright purple but mainly in the mouth and the front of the tube. The lines become suffused in the mouth, leaving well-defined white spots in the angles where the lobes meet. The centre lines of the lower lobes are scored and marked in purple but not always completely to the margin.

EKR Norwell Nurseries, Newark, Nottinghamshire, 1994.

'Red Emperor'
A strongly coloured red, of robust growth and with above-average persistence for its group.

Group 3B, erect habit up to 90cm (3ft). Flowers 5 × 4cm (2 × 1⅝in), all lobes slightly forward pointing, rounded. Tube and lobes a uniform *bright scarlet* (45B), throat white with well-marked pencilling in *carmine red* (46A), darkening but not coalescing in the mouth. Circular white patches evident in the angles between the lower lobes.

EKR 1987 Marwood Hill Gardens, Barnstaple, Devon.

'Red Knight'
A large-trumpeted red cultivar, strongly coloured but not garish. Good persistence.

Quite short habit for Group 3B, usually about 60cm (2ft). Flowers 4.7 × 3.5cm (1⅞ × 1⅜in), tube quite narrow, with a slight constriction behind the lobes. Lobes flared, pointed and minutely serrated, the upper ones smaller than the lower. Lobes and tube *scarlet* (47A) with some shading to *rosine* (46C), particularly on the lobes near the mouth. Throat white, few markings, but these are finely pencilled in magenta, notably a pair of fine but distinct lines running each side of the staminode. Small smudged areas occur in the angles between the lower lobes.

EKR *Plant Finder* 1991, but as 'Red Knight No. 2', suggesting some doubt as to the true form. We do not have an authoritative old description against which to test available material, but the pair of lines each side of the staminode do appear to be a good distinguishing feature.

'Red Sea'
A fine red variety bred for large pot culture with strong habit and good flowering performance.

P. 'Razzle Dazzle'.

Habit of Group 2B, but the flowers, which are held in loose panicles, are larger and of a shape resembling 3C. Flowers 3.9 × 3cm (1⅝ × 1¼in), wide at the mouth, all lobes pointing slightly forward, the upper ones pointed, the lower ones rounded. Lobes *bright rose red* (45D), the tube a paler shade of the same colour, throat a pink-toned white marked irregularly with a few lines in *magenta* (59D). Flowers noticeably translucent. Sepals brown and pointed.

Raised by A. T. Yates & Son, Congleton, Cheshire, from Group 2 & 3 pollen on 'Patio Pink' (*qv*), the pollen parent possibly 'King George V' (*qv*). Released in 1998.

'Red Star'
A form of *P. digitalis* – see page 95.

'Rich Purple'
A tall, strong-growing plant with showy purple flowers, in effect like a larger form of 'Burgundy' in both habit and flower.

Flower shape and leaves Group 2B, but flowers are larger and the plant reaches 1.5m (5ft) in height.

Flowers 4.2 × 2.8cm (1¼ × 1⅛in), the tube well expanded, the lobes equal, bluntly pointed, and forward-pointing. Tube and lobes a uniform *bright purple* (72B) except for some light streaks on the underside of the tube. Throat white, showing many well-defined bright purple lines running its full length, confined to the floor of the throat, and not coalescing in the mouth. Small blotches appear in the angles between the lower lobes. Staminode white, long, prominent, and decorative, with more hair than usual in the hybrids.

Raised by Cottage Garden Plants in Sussex, UK, c.1994.

'Rich Ruby'

A delightful cultivar with attractive dark upright stems to complement its richly coloured trumpets. The large flowers are so closely packed as to form continuous vertical bands of colour.

Normal Group 3B habit. Flowers 4.3 × 4cm (1¼ × 1½in), tube and lobes *crimson* (181B), paler on reverse of lower lobes. A bluish tone may be present at the junctions between mouth and upper lobes. Throat very heavily pencilled, most strongly on lower surface, the lines coalescing at the mouth to form a diamond-shaped patch of *brown purple* (183A) spreading on to the base of each lobe. A thin streak of the same colour follows the midline of the lower lobes, almost to their outer edges. EKR *Plant Finder* 1988.

'Ridgeway Red'

An uncommon cultivar in a very attractive rose colour.

Normal 3B habit, flowers 5 × 4cm (2 × 1⅝in), lobes rounded, roughly equal in size, the lower lobes forward-pointing, the upper ones less so. There is overlapping of the lobes, particularly of the centre lower lobe. Tube *bright rose* (54A) shading lighter to the base and sides, and darker onto the lobes. Throat white, finely and incompletely pencilled bright rose, with the central line on each lower lobe extending to the margin. Unjoined patches of colour mark the mouth on the lower lobes, and there are blobs of colour in the angles between upper and lower lip.

EKR 1993 Pershore College, Worcestershire, brought in by Vera Memberson, a voluntary worker at the Specialist Plant Unit. The throat markings resemble those of 'Flamingo', but the two varieties differ in colour and shape of flower.

'Roehrslev'

A form of *P. heterophyllus* from Denmark – see page 73.

'Ron Sidwell'

The gardener is not short of choice for white-throated pink-flowered penstemons, but this cultivar adds distinction to the category by dint of its attractive foliage and dainty flowers in a colour of particularly fine substance.

Group 2B. Habit bushy, height 70–80cm (2¼– 2 ¾ ft). Young foliage shiny mid-green on upper surface, matt below. Flowers 3.8 × 3cm (1½ × 1¼in), with lower lobes flattened and lined up side by side. Flowers held horizontally in loose panicles, the lower ones well away from the flower stem on exceptionally long peduncles up to 10cm (4in). Flower colour *cerise* (63A), paler on underside of tube, throat white, occasionally with a few faint magenta flecks, the white colour extending slightly beyond the mouth. Tufts of hair in the mouth are colourless but prominent.

This cultivar was in Ron Sidwell's collection at Evesham, Worcestershire, in the 1950s, under a name that has now been proved incorrect. Grown by David continuously since that period, and named in 1998 in commemoration of a great penstemon-lover. 'Suttons Pink Bedder' is similar but the flowers are paler and less uniformly coloured.

'Rose Elf'

A form of 'Flathead Lake' – see page 69.

'Rosy Blush'

A relatively new variety in an interesting combination of purplish-rose and creamy-white which fully justifies its name.

Group 3C with flowers at the small end of the range – 4 × 3.2cm (1⅝ × 1¼in) – otherwise typical. Tube abruptly expanded to a wide mouth, lobes rounded and flared. Tube *bright rose* (54A) toning to creamy white on the underside, throat open, creamy white.

Grown from seed and raised, it is thought, by George Stapleton, Gloucestershire, before 1991. Hunt's Court Nursery, Dursley, Gloucestershire, listed it from that year. It was chosen in 1996 as a Heritage Plant by the National Council for the Conservation of Plants and Gardens with the name changed to 'Rose Blush', using Hunt's Court material. Unfortunately, some material circulating under this name has a *mauve* (77A) colouring, which appears to be in error.

P. 'Red Ace'.

'Rose Queen'
An old hybrid form suggested to be *P. calycosus* × *P. digitalis*, registered 1959, but no longer commercially offered.

'Roy Davidson'
A variety of *P. procerus* – see page 89.

'Royal White'
A synonym for 'White Bedder' (*qv*).

'Rubicundus' ♀
For some the ultimate 'parks and gardens' penstemon with the largest scarlet and white flowers yet achieved, for others an object of wonder at what can be done by careful breeding. Not reliably persistent.

Group 3C, quite low habit. Flowers up to 5.8 × 4.6cm (2¼ × 1¾in), but can be as short as 4.5cm (1¾in). Lobes equal, rounded and flared. Wide-mouthed – up to 2cm (¾in). Tube and lobes *scarlet* (45A), throat silvery-white flecked with a few faint dashes of scarlet.

Said to have emanated from Lyme Park, Cheshire, 1906 but our EKR is 1908 as a seedling from 'Beckett's Strain'; Edwin Beckett was head gardener at Aldenham House, Elstree, Buckinghamshire, at that time. This seed strain had received an Award of Merit in 1906, and apparently several forms were then selected for cloning as named varieties. Originally named 'Rubicunda'. Curiously, Forbes never listed it, possibly to protect their own raisings of similar forms. The species *P. rubicundus* is quite unrelated.

'Ruby'
Considerable uncertainty surrounds the present position, since this name has been used in four contexts to our knowledge:
Type 1 For a prostrate form of *P. newberryi* from c. 1962.
Type 2 As a synonym of 'Schoenholzeri' (*qv*), possibly due to the entry of 'Schoenholzeri' in the 1962 RHS trials being misidentified as 'Ruby'. This conclusion is based on colour comparisons made between the 1962 and 1991 trials, which both used standard reference systems to record colours.
Type 3 For a large-flowered cultivar of Group 3B in crimson with markings in the throat, and which some believe to be the correct name for 'Ruby Field' (*qv*). Bloom's of Bressingham in 1965 listed a 'Ruby' simply described as 'deep crimson' which was quickly withdrawn but could be the same variety.
Type 4 For a Forbes introduction of 1928, withdrawn

1939, described as 'purplish violet, throat pencilled and margined chocolate' which equates only roughly with the previous form, and would require excessive imagination to suppose it is the same variety.

'Ruby Field'
This cultivar presents almost as many problems as 'Ruby', the name being applied in three different ways to our knowledge:
Type 1 As a misnomer for 'Rich Ruby' (*qv*) which can be quickly dismissed. The throat markings of 'Rich Ruby' are unique and unmistakable.
Type 2 To a Group 3B variety bearing some resemblance to 'Port Wine', but distinct. Flower 5 × 3.7cm (2 × 1½in), tube quite narrow, lobes wide with flat tips, only slightly forward-pointing. Tube *crimson* (187B) with some flushing in *deep mauve* (77A), the lobes in crimson. Throat white with fine crimson markings, somewhat broken and irregular, stronger in the mouth but not coalescing or smudging. The origin of this version is unknown, and there is a school of thought that holds the name 'Ruby Field' to be a labelling error, and that this cultivar is correctly named 'Ruby' (*qv*).
Type 3. To a Group 3C form very similar to 'Countess of Dalkeith' (*qv*), having slightly redder colouring – *deep magenta* (72A) – on the lobes, but the same white throat with faint markings. EKR Homebase Garden Departments, 1995, under a label describing 'Ruby Field' as a 'popular old variety'.

'Russian River'
One of the darkest-flowered of all European Hybrids. Its dusky-purple flowers are closely set on upright stems bearing very dark green foliage, making it a striking plant.

Group 2B, habit strong multi-stemmed upright clumps to a height of 70cm (2¼ft). Flowers 3 × 2.4cm (1⅛ × ⅞in), upper tube and rear of lobes *deep reddish violet* (83A) to *deep reddish purple* (71A), lower tube and roof of throat paler, flushed violet, front of lobes *deep mauve* (77A). Lobes may have one or two notches, creating an irregular edge. Lower lobes frequently twisted, the upper ones pointed. Throat white but very heavily pencilled in *plum* (79B), coalescing into blotches in the mouth. Conspicuous tufts of long white hairs line the mouth.

Name given by Alan Robinson, RHS Gardens, Surrey c. 1983, to a plant found in cultivation in California. See also 'Midnight'.

'Saskatoon Hybrids'

See 'Scharf Hybrids'.

'Scarlet Queen'

The approved trade name for 'Scharlachkoenigin' (*qv*) used in English-speaking countries.

'Scharlachkoenigin'

This popular large-flowered red and white seed strain represents one of the very small number of Group 3C seed strains of uniform type and colour available today – most strains are in mixed colours. Two types of plant can occur in roughly equal numbers, a version with marked throat flowering earlier than one with plain white throat. Persistence is superior to many other large-flowered and large-leaved cultivars.

A Group 3C plant, reaching a height of 80cm (2¾ ft) and generally typical of its group, but with less symmetrical flowers, the upper lobes being narrower than the lower ones. Flowers 3.2 × 3.5cm (1¼ × 1½in), the upper surface of the tube darker than *scarlet* (47A), lower surface scarlet with a triangular zone in white. All lobes scarlet. Throat densely white. Flowers held close to the stem on erect peduncles, slightly pendant, and with 3–4 slightly larger flowers clustered at the tip. The form with light pencilling is slightly darker on the lobes.

EKR Ernst Benary, Munden, Germany, 1932, subsequently also using the translated name 'Scarlet Queen' for its English catalogues. Benary have no record of being the actual raisers but they were stated as such when the plant was entered for trial by the RHS in 1958, it receiving an Award of Merit (as 'Scarlet Queen').

'Scharf Hybrids'

A seed strain derived from crosses of 'Prairie Fire' × *P. cardinalis*. The result is a persistent strain of small plants around 35cm (15in) in height with densely packed flowers in a range of colours from deep purple through red to pink. The individual flowers are reminiscent of *P. glaber* in shape.

Raised by Alan Scharf, Saskatoon (Canada) before 1972. 'Saskatoon Hybrids' are a selection from 'Scharf Hybrids' from the same source, also with very good persistence.

'Schoenholzeri' ♔

The variety commonly known as 'Firebird' in English-speaking countries, but usually by its original name elsewhere. It is one of the most popular of all hybrid penstemons for its spectacular and long-lasting flowering season with flowers in a glowing shade of red. It was bred for persistence, and shows its breeding.

Group 2A. It has a slightly lax but dense, bushy habit, reaching 90cm (3ft). Flowers slightly variable in size, up to 3.3 × 3.2cm (1¼ × 1¼in), tube *bright carmine* (53C), lobes more *rosine* (46C), the lower ones strongly reflexed. Throat heavily streaked *deep magenta* (72A), merging to form crescents at the base of each lower lobe, which are pencilled partway along their midlines and finely serrated. The roof of the mouth is lightly suffused with *mauve* (77c).

Raised by Paul Schoenholzer, Riehen, Switzerland, introduced 1939 – see page 26 for detailed provenance. The variety is sometimes found misnamed 'Ruby' (*qv* and see below), also 'Paul Schoenholzer'.

A second less common hybrid has also attracted the name of 'Schoenholzeri' – a superb variety which is larger in flower and, often, almost a self in *deep rose red* (53B) without any hint of 'blueing' of the colour. It is still available in Switzerland as well as the UK, so it is possible that both varieties stem from the same cross. However, an article in the magazine *Schweizer Garten* of March 1939, announcing the original introduction of 'Schoenholzeri', described it as being cinnabar-purple-red with dark purple-red throat. This leaves little doubt that the better-known variety is correctly named 'Schoenholzeri'. A complication is that the second variety does seem to have appeared in the 1962 RHS trials as 'Schoenholzeri', since the plant was described as having an unmarked pink throat, while a plant entered as 'Ruby' had a description which matches the true 'Schoenholzeri' – hence, we suppose, the misnomer mentioned earlier. None of this alters the fact that the second variety remains without a valid name, although the variety 'Razzle Dazzle' (*qv*) resembles it so closely in every respect that we suspect that someone has already filled that gap.

'Schooley's Yellow'

A form of *P. barbatus* – see page 69.

'Sensation Hybrids'

An American seed strain giving a wide range of large-flowered hybrids which flower in their first year from an early sowing. Not persistent under American conditions without winter protection. Group 3C. Important in the breeding of the 'Mexicali Hybrids' (*qv*).

EKR Park Seed Co, USA, 1951. An improved form,

P. 'Sour Grapes' (Type 1) well matching the 'metallic blue and mauve' of the earliest known description of this variety.

'Sensation Hybrid Rainbow', with even larger flowers and wider colour range, appeared in 1959.

'Shell Pink'

A variety very similar to 'Hidcote Pink' (*qv*), with the same heavy throat markings. Possibly not quite so tall, but can still attain nearly 90cm (3ft). EKR Perhill Nurseries, Great Witley, Worcestershire, 1994.

'Sherbourne Blue'

A pretty variety in the 'Stapleford Gem' (*qv*) mould, with a robust spreading habit.

A Group 2B cultivar, making broad mounds, over 1m (3¼ ft) across and 60cm (2ft) high. Flower 3.8 × 2.4cm (1¼ × 1in), tube flattened, mouth wide. Lobes forward pointing, the lower longer than the upper. Tube *reddish lilac* (79D) paling to white on the underside and to *lavender* (94D), or lighter, on the lobes. Throat white with fine red-purple lines, with some joining up at the mouth but not smudging.

EKR Perhill Nurseries, Great Witley, Worcestershire, 1994, the material from Burford, Oxfordshire.

'Sissinghurst Pink'

A synonym for 'Evelyn' (*qv*).

'Six Hills Hybrid'

A *P. rupicola* hybrid with an uncertain pollen parent – see page 65.

'Skyline Mix'

A shorter than normal European Hybrid seed strain in mixed colours, some with purple markings in the throat, height 45cm (18in). Popular in several parts of the world. Developed by the Pan-American Seed Co.

'Snoqualamie'

A natural hybrid of *P. rupicola* × *P. fruticosus* with deep grey-green leaves.

'Snowstorm'

A synonym for 'White Bedder' (*qv*).

'Snowflake'

A synonym for 'White Bedder' (*qv*).

'Sour Grapes'

The true nature of this cultivar is one of the most hotly debated issues among penstemon enthusiasts. There are two distinct varieties in Group 2B laying claim to the name, while some enthusiasts reject both of these, claiming that a third variety, which has not apparently been seen for some years, is the true one.

Type 1 Low-growing habit, up to 60cm (2ft), quite compact. Flowers 3.7 × 2.4cm (1⅜ × 1in), tubes expanded and slightly flattened, lobes pointing well forward, angular but not pointed, with frilled edges. Tube darker than *cobalt* (98C), or in some flowers dull *violet blue* (97B) with fine purple lines. Lobes paler than *mauve* (77C). Throat white, with fine but strongly defined markings in maroon, deepening but not coalescing in the mouth, the markings confined to the bottom lobe and the lower halves of the two outer lobes.

We believe that this form was introduced, but probably not raised, by Nellie Britten of Washfield Nursery, Devon (later Kent) in the late 1930s, and was originally described as 'metallic blue and mauve'. It is also known that the plants were of low habit. Although a direct link is unproven, several examples of stock of long provenance are known under the label of 'Sour Grapes' which fit the description. These differ slightly from one another, but all bear a strong resemblance in flower to 'Stapleford Gem' (*qv*). 'Stapleford Gem' is, however, quite tall-growing, with flowers more lilac than blue in shade. It was introduced in 1930 by Forbes, so one possibility is that this 'Sour Grapes' was a dwarf selection from 'Stapleford Gem', or came from a seedling thereof, with more compact habit and improved flowering performance – 'Stapleford Gem' can be shy to flower.

Type 2 Spreading habit, usually under 75cm (30in) high. Flowers 3.8 × 2.6cm (1½ × 1in), tube abruptly expanded, lower lobes pointing well forward and rounded, the upper ones smaller and only slightly forward pointing. Tube bright *reddish violet* (86B) at the base toning to *deep mauve* (77A) at the lobes, the lobes themselves *deep mauve* toning lighter (77A–78A). Throat white, markings as in Type 1 in deep mauve. Flowers in the first flush are bunched at the apex of the stem, but later flowering is normal.

This form is apparently based on a plant given to Margery Fish of East Lambrook Manor, Somerset, in the 1950s and much prized by her for the tendency of the first flushes of flowers to be massed at the top of the stems like a bunch of grapes – an effect heightened by their being green in bud, maturing through a strong purple/dark violet bicolour, until at late maturity the purple colour is dominant. The plant came to her under the name *P. gordoni* (syn. *P. diffusus* 'Sour Grapes'). Since *P. gordoni* is now *P. glaber*, and *P. diffusus* is *P. serrulatus*, and the two have never at any time been remotely considered synonymous, perhaps not too much reliance should be placed in the labelling, nevertheless the bunching of the flowers into a terminal crown is a feature of very few species – one of which is *P. serrulatus*. It is an intriguing possibility.

Type 3 As reported in an article in *Gardens Illustrated* of October 1996, the main distinguishing features of this form are that the flowers have tubes waisted behind the lips and green markings in the throat. We have found no earlier report in the literature which mentions such a type, and can only comment that, while green colouring is often found in young penstemon flowers, it is not present at the mature stage, except for the green anther sacs of *P. murrayanus* (see page 81). Nevertheless, recalling those restless genes we discussed in Chapter I, it has to be conceded that, with penstemons, practically anything can happen.

It is for readers to draw their own conclusions: ours are that, first, there are too many independent citings of stock of long provenance of both Types 1 and 2 for a simple labelling error to have spread so wide, implying that both independently received the name 'Sour Grapes' by intent; second, that the rules of precedence are difficult to apply in this case because the date of one naming is unknown; third, that even if those rules were invoked, it would be as inappropriate to label a rejected Type 1 'Stapleford Gem' as it would be to label an rejected Type 2, say, 'Hidcote Purple'. Perhaps a slight renaming to 'Washfield Sour Grapes' and 'Lambrook Sour Grapes' is the easiest way out of the dilemma, changing the rules to permit this if necessary.

'Southcombe Pink'
This rather uncommon cultivar is one of the best for colour in the pink-cerise range, and its flowers are of a particularly fine shape.

Group 2B habit, spreading, the outer flowering stems tending to flop if not supported. The flower measures 3.9×3.3cm (1⅝×1¼in) overall, rather large for 2B, moreover the flared and even-sized lobes suggest some 3C influence. Tube uniform *cerise* (63A), with a small white band on the underside. Lobes cerise, slightly pointed and noticeably wavy-edged. Throat white with light pencilling in a darker cerise, the centre line extending to the point of each lower lobe, and the white partly extending onto both upper and lower lobes. The white staminode protrudes slightly from the mouth.

EKR Pershore College, Worcestershire, 1994. A variety of similar description was raised at Southcombe Gardens, Devon, in the mid-1970s, but no definite provenance has been established.

'Southgate Gem'
A bright reddish-pink cultivar that has attracted attention throughout its long history as a graceful and profusely flowering plant.

Group 2B. Forms an open multi-stemmed clump to a height of 75cm (2½ft) with flowers borne on open panicles, slightly pendant. Flowers 4×3.4cm (1⅝×1¼in) or longer, *bright rose red* (45D), paling on underside of tube, white throat colour extending well onto lower lobes, throat sparsely lined *bright crimson* (63A), but only for half the length. Lower lobes blunt, streaked to halfway along their midlines.

Raised by J. Bradshaw of Southgate, London, a cross between 'Newbury Gem' (*qv*) and *P. hartwegii*, before 1910. This cultivar has the unusual record of being submitted three times to RHS trials, in 1914, 1930 and

1991, and the descriptions from these trials are not identical. One comment from the 1914 trial was that the throat was wider than tall, and that the throat was heavily pencilled. A year later, a picture and description appeared in the catalogue of the Moerheim Nursery, Dedemsvaart, Holland, which suggest a lightly marked throat, and not flattened. In 1930 the colour was stated to be pillarbox red and in 1991 it was described as 52A, virtually identical to 45D, but neither approaching pillarbox red. The 1914 trial was colour-coded on an old system which suggested a colour near *rosine* (46C), which is intermediate between 45D and 'pillarbox red'. Seed strains of 'Southgate Gem' have appeared from time to time in the UK and in continental Europe. One submitted to trial in 1930 as 'Southcote Gem' was commended for uniformity but one as 'Southgate Gem' yielded variable stock. It is possible, therefore, that some variation has been introduced by recloning from seed strains, perhaps from an early date.

'Souvenir d'Adrien Regnier'

A medium-height cultivar with attractive deep pink flowers having beautifully marked throats.

A Group 3B plant in habit and general characteristics. Flowers 3.5 × 3cm (1⅜ × 1¼in) *deep pink* (48A), paling towards base and underside of tube. Upper lobes slightly reflexed, lower ones spreading, all lightly serrated. Throat white, spreading onto base of lobes lightly pencilled. The lines in the throat partly coalesce in two smudges opposite the junctions between the central lower lobe and its two neighbours.

EKR France in the 1940s, the original stock imported from California.

'Souvenir d'André Torres'

A vibrant bright red cultivar, yet in no sense garish. Can be regarded as a smaller-flowered version of 'Chester Scarlet' (*qv*) although the shade of red is slightly different. Of good habit, and notably persistent.

Group 3B, forming a large bush. Flowers 4.4 × 3.4cm (1¾ × 1¼in), lower lobes more forward-pointing than upper, and more rounded. Tube and lobes uniformly brighter than *rosine* (46C), throat white with slightly protruding anthers. Throat finely pencilled carmine most of its length, the colour coalescing into a triangular patch at the angle at the junctions of the lower lobes.

EKR 1985 Eastgrove Garden Nursery, Worcestershire, the origin presumably French.

'Species RLB'

A cultivar of the 'Hidcote Pink' type, but with unusual features which clearly differentiate it from that variety. It is persistent.

Group 2B, of very compact habit, under 60cm (2ft). Flowers 3.5 × 2cm (1⅜ × ¾in), tube narrow, lobes pointed well forward, the upper ones small and rounded, the lower larger and pointed. Tube and lobes a mixture of *bright rose* (54A) and cream, giving a mottled effect. Throat cream, heavily pencilled in *carmine* (185B), the lines merging at the mouth and continuing in a band on each lower lobe almost to its margin.

Propagated from a chance seedling by Roger Bennett, Northumberland c. 1980, introduced by Langthorns Plantery, Dunmow, Essex, 1985.

'Stapleford Gem'

A distinctive cultivar popular with many gardeners for its display of two-tone flowers, arranged in whorls on stiff stems bearing dark, dense foliage.

Group 2B. A tall, strong, clump-forming plant with numerous erect shoots to 1 m (3¼ft). Flowers 3 × 2.2cm (1¼ × ⅞in), *bright lilac* (86D) variably suffused blue. The extent and degree of blue suffusion may depend on growing conditions and season. Underside of tube white. Front of upper lobes whitish suffused mauve, lower ones darker, but may be mottled white. Lower lobes usually angled forwards. Leaves dark green, and tightly packed on the stems giving the plants a characteristic appearance, especially when they are growing rapidly in spring.

Raised by Mr Graham, Stapleford Park, Melton Mowbray, Leicestershire, before 1930, introduced by Forbes 1930. See also 'Sour Grapes', 'Sherbourne Blue' and 'Knightwick'.

'Susan'

A pale pink and white cultivar grown in Australia and New Zealand, but not seen by us. The reports we have received are not totally consistent. It has been described as a spontaneous seedling similar to 'Thorn' (*qv*) found in Australia, and as a synonym for 'Osprey' (*qv*). We are forced to leave our Australasian readers to reach their own conclusions.

'Sutton's Large Flowered'

A seed strain with a very long history, offered in British catalogues. The plants have the characters which place them in Group 3C. The colour range is very wide and includes self-colours, bicolours, marked and unmarked

P. 'Stapleford Gem'.

white throats and a variety of patterning. The strain acquired its present name at the end of the 19th century, and is still available today. Introduced by Suttons Seeds, Reading, Berkshire.

'Sutton's Pink Bedder'

A long-established pink cultivar with medium-sized flowers, a bushy habit and moderate persistence.

Group 2B, making a compact bushy plant with shiny green foliage to a height of 80cm (2¾ ft). Flowers 3.5 × 3cm (1⅜ × 1¼in), tube *carmine rose* (51C) paling towards the upper lobes, and white underneath. Throat unmarked white, the white extending on to all lobes. All lobes paler than carmine rose, the rear of the upper pair speckled.

Introduced as a seed strain in 1933 by Suttons Seeds, Reading, Berkshire, but now available only in clonal form. Similar in habit and flower size to 'Ron Sidwell'

(*qv*) but in a lighter and less uniform shade of rose.

'Swan Lake'

A synonym for 'White Bedder' (*qv*) found in New Zealand and Australia.

'Taoensis'

An eye-catching plant with elegant long-tubed rose-red flowers cascading from a shrubby structure which can reach 2m (6½ft). It is of good persistence given a sheltered position, and is best against a wall.

Group 3A habit, a branched shrub, somewhat floppy, leaves typically bluish and blunt at their ends. Flower up to 4.8 × 2.2cm (1¾ × ⅞in), but often smaller. Tube narrow, taller than wide, 0.7 × 1cm (¼ × ⅜in), lobes pointed with minutely serrated edges, all forward-pointing, the upper ones longer and much narrower than the lower. Tube *bright rose red* (45D), paling to *rose* (54C) on the underside, lobes *bright rose* (54A). Throat creamy white with heavy lines in *carmine* (185B) running the length of the tube, smudging but not coalescing in the mouth. Anthers pale yellow before opening, filling the tall narrow mouth which is also toned pale yellow.

EKR *Plant Finder* 1987, later under the misnomer *P. linarioides glabrescens taosensis*. Obviously close to *P. isophyllus*, but the yellowish mouth and smaller flowers distinguish it from that species.

'The Juggler'

An impressive new cultivar giving a fine display of mauve and white flowers.

Group 2B, an erect clump-former to 1.1m (3½ ft). Foliage a distinctive light grey-green, reminiscent of 'Pennington Gem' (*qv*), borne on strong, erect stems. Flowers 3.3 × 2.7cm (1¼ × 1in), tube and rear of upper lobes between *bright mauve* (77B) and *deep mauve* (77A), fading to white on underside except for a few mauve streaks. Throat white with magenta pencilling, commonly localized to the rear of the lower central lobe. Face colour of all lobes bright mauve, suffused by white extending from the throat. Upper lobes strongly overlap, the lower lobes are extremely reflexed, and all lobes show distinct, if fine, serrations along their edges. Flowers borne in tight whorls on erect stems, well-separated by long internodes.

Found in 1994 by Mrs Hazel Evans, Aston-by-Great Budworth, Cheshire, as a chance seedling with

Plate XI (overleaf). A selection of Group 3B and 3C varieties.

PLATE XI

P. 'Joy'

P. 'Maurice Gibbs'

P. 'Flamingo'

P. 'Ruby Field' (Type 3)

All flowers are shown at approximately ½ size

P. 'Souvenir d'Andre Torres'

P. 'Flame'

P. 'Pershore Pink Necklace'

P. 'Barbara Barker'

'Stapleford Gem' (*qv*) a probable parent. Introduced in 1998 by Proculture Plants, Badsey, Worcestershire.

'Thorn'

It has proved difficult to locate authenticated material because this plant is frequently confused with the large-flowered form of 'Appleblossom' (*qv*), 'Beech Park' (*qv*) and 'Peace' (*qv*), all cultivars with generally similar pink and white colouring. We believe that 'Thorn' is taller, to 80cm (2⅗ft), has narrower leaves and tubes, and is more resistant to fading. Perhaps the main point of distinction is that the flowers retain a noticeable cream or light yellow tint on the lobes even when fully mature. EKR *Treasurers of Tenbury*, Herefordshire, 1987.

'Threave Pink'

Similar to 'Evelyn' (*qv*) but in a deeper red-purple shade, as pretty but possibly not quite as persistent.

Typical Group 1 cultivar of compact habit. Flowers 3 × 1.4cm (1¼ × ⅝in), tube angled at the base and moderately expanded. Small flared lobes, rounded. Tube and lobes *magenta* (59D), lightening to white on underside of tube. Throat white, lightly but clearly striped in *deep magenta* (72A) for most of throat length, the lines not coalescing. Hairy staminode, like a toothbrush, projects beyond mouth.

Possibly originated at Threave Gardens, Scotland, but named after rather than by Threave. EKR *Plant Finder* 1987. A distinct variety, closest to 'Lynette' (*qv*) in colour but smaller in flower, and not so dark.

'Torbay Gem'

We believe this to be a misnomer for 'Torquay Gem' (*qv*).

'Torquay Gem'

A handsome and elegant subject with tubular deep red flowers. It is not vigorous – it is persistent enough but slow to recover from a hard winter.

Group 3A flowers, but definitely 2A foliage – long, narrow, and light green. Shrubby character but usually only some 60cm (2ft) high. Flower 4.8 × 2.1cm (1⅞ × ¾in), narrow tube, lobes pointed, the upper ones narrower and smaller than the lower, all forward-pointing. Tube and lips a uniform *deep rose red* (53B). Throat white, marked in carmine with strong parallel lines for its whole length, not coalescing in the mouth, but small patches of colour mark the angles of the lower lobes.

EKR *Plant Finder* 1988, but the earlier entries were probably 'Windsor Red' (*qv*). The flower colour and foliage distinguish 'Torquay Gem' from other 3A

subjects, the foliage being particularly interesting in suggesting a 2A parent in its genealogy.

'True Blue'

A form of *P. heterophyllus* – see page 73.

'Vesuvius'

A cultivar bred for large pot culture with flowers of a particularly deep mauve colour.

Group 2B, but with narrower leaves than usual for the group. Flowers 3.6 × 2.9cm (1½ × 1⅛in), the tubes in *deep mauve* (77A), even darker on the lobes. Lobes rounded and forward-pointing. Throat white with markings in very deep mauve. The pedicels are longer than the flowers, giving an open appearance to the inflorescence.

Raised by A. T. Yates & Son, Congleton, Cheshire, from their trials with mixed hybrid pollen on 'Patio Pink' (*qv*) as seed parent. The probable pollen parent is one they received as 'Sour Grapes Purple'. Released in 1998.

'Violet Beauty'

A form of 'Flathead Lake' – see page 69.

'Violet Queen'

A hybridized form of *P. barbatus* – see page 69.

'Walker Ridge'

A form of *P. heterophyllus* – see page 73.

'War Axe'

A selected seed strain of *P. grandiflorus* in a wide range of colours, possibly hybridized – see page 82.

'Welsh Dawn'

From comparisons made at Pershore College, this cultivar appears identical to 'Devonshire Cream' (*qv*). 'Welsh Dawn' is the name given in 1996 to a plant entered into the 1991 RHS trials, and identified in the trials report as Tall Pink Unnamed: it lacked a cultivar name since it had been submitted in error as 'Pennington Gem'. The possibility of there being a common origin for 'Devonshire Cream' and 'Welsh Dawn' cannot be ruled out. On the strict rules of nomenclature 'Devonshire Cream' takes precedence.

'White Bedder' ♔

The most commonly grown white cultivar, which appears under a variety of names. Totally white in terms of garden effect, but slight colour tints can often be seen at close quarters. It has low persistence.

Group 2B. Bushy habit to 70cm (2¼ft). Buds and immature flowers greenish-cream; open flowers white, but a pink suffusion, palest in newly open flowers, somewhat darker and more obvious in older flowers, is often present toward the lobe margins. This feature may not be present at all times or in all flowers. Flower size 3.5 × 3cm (1⅜ × 1¼in). Throats unmarked. All stem structures bright green.

Introduced by Forbes in 1912 apparently as a clone, but in 1930 it received an Award of Merit as a seed strain, indicating good uniformity. Various nurserymen have attempted to segregate named clones based on whether the flowers are completely white throughout, or are pink in bud but white at maturity, or develop a pink suffusion on the lobes, or a thin pink rim to the lobes. The RHS in the 1991 trials judged these variations to be more random than constant, and having seen all these forms on a single panicle we are inclined to agree. Synonyms include 'Burford White', 'Hidcote White', 'Snowflake', 'Snowstorm', 'Swan Lake' and 'Bisham Seedling' (qv), although this last name also relates to a distinct cultivar.

'Whitethroat'

We have found this name used independently for two separate cultivars:

Type 1 A white-throated dark pink cultivar that is suitable for a position where strong upright growth is needed.

Group 2B, forming erect multi-stemmed dense clumps to 90cm (3ft), leaves on vegetative shoots characteristically shiny green. Flowers broader than long, 3.4 × 4cm (1¼ × 1½in), *cerise* (63A), paler on upper lobes, throat pure white, the white extending slightly onto the lower lobes, but halfway across the upper ones. Lower lobes slightly wavy with fine serrations on some edges. Raised by Ron Sidwell, Evesham, Worcestershire, in the 1960s.

Type 2 A purple cultivar with white throat similar to 'Charles Rudd' (qv), with pendant flowers, which has been in circulation since at least 1989. We suspect this is a seedling which has taken its 'nursery identification' into the market place. A form labelled 'Purple, white throat' of similar character is also known. See also 'Purple and White' and 'Purpureus Albus'. This colour combination is frequently encountered in seed-raised stock.

'Willy's Purple'

A cultivar found in an old garden in Scone, Australia. Not seen by us, but reported as the most vigorous cultivar grown in Australia, similar in character to 'Purple Passion' (qv) but much taller.

'Windsor Red'

A strong-growing cultivar with tubular red flowers borne in great profusion over a long season.

Group 3A, bushy with narrow-leaved foliage. Flowers borne on open panicles to a height of 70cm (2¼ft). Narrow, 0.8–1cm (⅜in) wide tubes, with an overall flower length and breadth of 4.5 × 2.8cm (1¾ × 1⅛in) uniformly coloured *deep rose red* (53B). Throat white with fine but strong magenta pencilling. Lower lobes widely separated and often reflexed, upper ones erect, pointed and overlapping. All lobes with serrated edges. EKR M. Wickenden, Crawley Down, West Sussex, 1987. Synonyms: 'Cottage Garden Red', 'Garden Red'.

'Zuriblau'

A form of *P. heterophyllus* – see page 73.

APPENDIX I
SPECIES CHECKLIST

Below is a checklist of all species and their main features. All information relates to typical plants and habitats, and there are many exceptions. Subspecies, varieties and forma are omitted if these are not of gardening significance. If a name you are looking for does not appear in this list, check Appendix II in case it is a synonym.

Group means lowest available classification within the genus for the species, and may be subgenus, section or subsection.
Habitat is covered here in very general terms – see Appendix IV for more information on unusual habitats.
Height is taken as 'maximum typical'; most plants are shorter, a few may be taller. Height includes inflorescence – the vegetative base of

herbaceous and mat forms is 2.5–15cm (1–6in) according to species.
Flower size given is for overall length from base of sepals to tip of lobes. Small = less than 1.3cm (½in); medium = 1.3–2.5cm (½–1in); large = 2.5–3.8cm (1–1⅛ in); very large = more than 3.8cm (1½in).
Flower colour Only the commonest colour is shown: see Appendix III for unusual colourings.

SPECIES	GROUP	HABITAT	HABIT	HEIGHT	FLOWER SIZE AND COLOUR		NOTES
abietinus	Caespitosi	dry upland	mat	15cm (6in)	small	blue	
absarokensis	Habroanthus	screes	herbaceous	15cm (6in)	medium	blue	
acaulis	Caespitosi	dry upland	tufted	2.5cm (1in)	medium	blue	
acuminatus	Anularius	dryland	herbaceous	45cm (18in)	medium	blue	
alamosensis	Centranthifolii	rocky	herbaceous	75cm (2½ft)	medium	red	protected
albertinus	Humiles	alpine	mat	20cm (8in)	medium	blue	
albidus	Aurator	plains	herbaceous	45cm (18in)	large	white	
albomarginatus	Arenarii	desert	herbaceous	20cm (8in)	small	pink	rare
alluviorum	Penstemon	open wooded	herbaceous	1.2m (4ft)	medium	white	
alpinus	Habroanthus	dry upland	herbaceous	75cm (2½ft)	large	blue	
ambiguus	Ambigui	dryland	shrub	60cm (2ft)	medium	pink	
ammophilus	Habroanthus	dunes	tufted	15cm (6in)	medium	purple	
amphorellae	Perfoliati	dryland	herbaceous	40cm (16in)	large	pale blue	
angelicus	Peltanthera	dryland	herbaceous	1.6 m (5¼ft)	medium	scarlet	
anguineus	Humiles	open wooded	herbaceous	75cm (2½ft)	small	violet	
angustifolius	Anularius	plains	herbaceous	45cm (18in)	medium	blue	
arenarius	Arenarii	dunes	herbaceous	25cm (10in)	medium	pink	
arenicola	Anularius	dryland	herbaceous	15cm (6in)	small	blue	
aridus	Humiles	screes	herbaceous	20cm (8in)	medium	violet	
arkansanus	Penstemon	moist soils	herbaceous	45cm (18in)	medium	white	
attenuatus	Proceri						
ssp. *attenuatus*		open wooded	herbaceous	60cm (2ft)	medium	violet	
ssp. *militaris*		open wooded	herbaceous	30cm (12in)	medium	deep blue	
atwoodii	Aurator	dryland	herbaceous	25cm (10in)	small	violet	
auriberbis	Aurator	dryland	herbaceous	20cm (8in)	medium	lilac	
australis	Penstemon	alluvial	herbaceous	90cm (3ft)	medium	purple	
azureus	Saccanthera	open wooded	subshrub	50cm (20in)	large	azure	
baccharifolius	Baccharifolii	dry cliffs	shrub	20cm (8in)	large	red	uncommon
barbatus	Elmigera						
f. *flaviflorus*		dryland	mat	1.2m (4ft)	large	yellow	
other sorts.		dryland	mat	1.2m (4ft)	large	red	
barnebyi	Aurator	dryland	herbaceous	20cm (8in)	small	violet	
barrettiae	Dasanthera	rocky	shrub	40cm (16in)	v. large	purple	uncommon
bicolor	Peltanthera	dryland	herbaceous	1m (3¼ft)	medium	pink	rare
bolanius	Campanulati	dry upland	herbaceous	70cm (2⅓ft)	medium	purple	Mexican

Species	Group	Habitat	Habit	Height	Flower size and colour		Notes
bracteatus	Anularius	dry alpine	herbaceous	15cm (6in)	medium	violet	localized
breviculus	Aurator	open wooded	herbaceous	25cm (10in)	medium	dark blue	uncommon
brevisepalus	Penstemon	mixed	herbaceous	90cm (3ft)	medium	lavender	localized
buckleyi	Anularius	plains	herbaceous	75cm (2¹/₂ft)	medium	lavender	
caesius	Saccanthera	dryland	mat	45cm (18in)	medium	purple-blue	
caespitosus	Caespitosi	dry upland	mat	5cm (2in)	medium	light blue	
calcareus	Aurator	dry cliffs	herbaceous	7.5cm (3in)	small	red	localized
californicus	Linarioides	open wooded	spreading	15cm (6in)	medium	purple-blue	rare
calycosus	Penstemon	open wooded	herbaceous	75cm (2¹/₂ft)	large	purple	
campanulatus	Campanulati	mixed	herbaceous	75cm (2¹/₂ft)	large	violet	Mexican
canescens	Penstemon	open wooded	herbaceous	60 cm (2ft)	medium	lavender	
cardinalis	Elmigera	dryland	herbaceous	60 cm (2ft)	large	red	
cardwellii	Dasanthera	alpine	shrub	25cm (10in)	v. large	purple	
carnosus	Anularius	dryland	herbaceous	35cm (14in)	medium	lavender	
caryi	Habroanthus	dry upland	mat	20cm (8in)	medium	deep blue	
centranthifolius	Centranthifolii	dryland	herbaceous	1.2m (4ft)	medium	scarlet	
cerrosensis	Centranthifolii	dryland	herbaceous	45cm (18in)	medium	scarlet	rare
cinicola	Proceri	dryland	herbaceous	30cm (12in)	small	violet	
cleburnii	Aurator	desert	herbaceous	20cm (8in)	large	purple	
clevelandii	Peltanthera	dryland	herbaceous	60cm (2ft)	large	crimson	
clutei	Peltanthera	dryland	herbaceous	1m (3¹/₄ft)	large	pink	
cobaea	Aurator						
ssp. *cobaea*		plains	herbaceous	30cm (12in)	v. large	white	
ssp. *purpureus*		cliffs	herbaceous	30cm (12in)	v. large	purple	
comarrhenus	Habroanthus	dryland	herbaceous	60cm (2ft)	large	pale blue	
compactus	Habroanthus	dryland	herbaceous	25cm (10in)	medium	blue	endangered
concinnus	Aurator	dryland	herbaceous	60cm (2ft)	medium	purple	
confertus	Proceri	open wooded	mat	50cm (20in)	medium	yellow	
confusus	Centranthifolii	dryland	herbaceous	25cm (10in)	large	purple	
coriaceus	Perfoliati	dryland	subshrub	1m (3¹/₄ft)	large	red	Mexican
crandallii	Caespitosi	alpine	shrub	10cm (4in)	medium	blue	
cusickii	Saccanthera	dryland	herbaceous	45cm (18in)	medium	lavender	
cyananthus	Habroanthus	dry upland	herbaceous	60cm (2ft)	large	deep blue	
cyaneus	Habroanthus	dryland	herbaceous	60cm (2ft)	large	blue	
cyanocaulis	Habroanthus	dryland	herbaceous	35cm (14in)	medium	violet	
cyathophorus	Anularius	dryland	herbaceous	45cm (18in)	medium	many	see App. III
dasyphyllus	Dentanthera	dryland	herbaceous	40cm (16in)	medium	blue	protected
davidsonii	Dasanthera						
ssp. *davidsonii*		alpine	mat	15cm (6in)	large	violet	
var. *praeteritus*		alpine	mat	15cm (6in)	v. large	violet	
deamii	Penstemon	plains	herbaceous	75cm (2¹/₂ft)	medium	white	
deaveri	Habroanthus	dry upland	herbaceous	60cm (2ft)	medium	mauve	
debilis	Habroanthus	dry upland	mat	unknown	medium	white	rare
degeneri	Humiles	open wooded	herbaceous	40cm (16in)	medium	blue	rare
deustus	Deusti	dryland	herbaceous	60cm (2ft)	medium	white	
digitalis	Penstemon	mixed	herbaceous	100cm (40in)	large	white	
diphyllus	Serrulati	dryland	shrubby	60cm (2ft)	small	lavender	
discolor	Linarioides	dryland	mat	20cm (8in)	small	pale lilac	rare
dissectus	Dissecti	sandy	herbaceous	45cm (18in)	large	purple	uncommon
distans	Aurator	open wooded	herbaceous	60cm (2ft)	medium	violet	
dolius	Aurator	dryland	herbaceous	60cm (2ft)	medium	violet	
duchesnensis	Aurator	dryland	herbaceous	60cm (2ft)	medium	violet	
eatonii	Elmigera	dryland	herbaceous	75cm (2¹/₂ft)	large	scarlet	
elegantulus	Humiles	alpine	herbaceous	30cm (12in)	medium	violet	

Species	Group	Habitat	Habit	Height	Flower size and colour		Notes
ellipticus	Dasanthera	scree	mat	15cm (6in)	v. large	lavender	
eriantherus	Aurator	plains	herbaceous	60cm (2ft)	large	purple	
euglaucus	Proceri	dryland	mat	50cm (20in)	small	violet	
eximeus	Peltanthera	dryland	herbaceous	1.5m (5ft)	medium	white	Mexican
fasciculatus	Fasciculi	alpine	mat	50cm (20in)	large	red	Mexican
fendleri	Anularius	plains	herbaceous	60cm (2ft)	medium	violet	
filiformis	Saccanthera	dryland	subshrub	50cm (20in)	medium	blue-purple	
filisepalis	Fasciculi	alpine	herbaceous	60cm (2ft)	large	red	Mexican, rare
flavescens	Proceri	alpine	herbaceous	40cm (16in)	medium	yellow	
floribundus	Saccanthera	dry upland	subshrub	20cm (8in)	large	violet	rare
floridus	Peltanthera	desert	herbaceous	1.2m (4ft)	large	pink	
flowersii	Anularius	badlands	herbaceous	30cm (12in)	medium	pink	
franklinii	Aurator	dryland	herbaceous	25cm (10in)	medium	lavender	
fremontii	Habroanthus	dryland	herbaceous	25cm (10in)	medium	blue-purple	
fructiformis	Peltanthera	dryland	shrub	60cm (2ft)	medium	white	
fruticosus	Dasanthera						
ssp. *fruticosus*		alpine	shrub	40cm (16in)	v. large	violet	
ssp. *scouleri*		alpine	shrub	40cm (16in)	v. large	violet	
ssp. *serratus*		alpine	shrub	20cm (8in)	large	violet	
gairdneri	Gairdneriani	dryland	mat	40cm (16in)	medium	lavender	
gentianoides	Fasciculi	high woodland	herbaceous	1m (3¼ft)	large	purple	Mexican
gentryi	Campanulati	dryland	herbaceous	60cm (2ft)	large	lavender	Mexican
gibbensii	Habroanthus	dryland	herbaceous	20cm (8in)	large	blue	
glaber	Habroanthus	plains	herbaceous	60cm (2ft)	large	blue	
glandulosus	Serrulati	dryland	herbaceous	1m (3¼ft)	v. large	lavender	
glaucinus	Proceri	open wooded	herbaceous	35cm (14in)	medium	blue-purple	endangered
globosus	Proceri	alpine	herbaceous	60cm (2ft)	medium	blue	
goodrichii	Aurator	badlands	herbaceous	35cm (14in)	small	lavender	
gormanii	Aurator	dryland	herbaceous	30cm (12in)	medium	lavender	
gracilentus	Saccanthera	open wooded	subshrub	45cm (18in)	medium	purple	
gracilis	Penstemon	plains	herbaceous	75cm (2½ft)	medium	pale lilac	
grahamii	Aurator	dryland	herbaceous	15cm (6in)	large	lavender	
grandiflorus	Anularius	plains	herbaceous	1.2m (4ft)	v. large	lavender	see App. III
grinnellii	Peltanthera	dryland	shrub	60cm (2ft)	medium	white	
guadalupensis	Aurator	dryland	herbaceous	35cm (14in)	medium	white	
hallii	Habroanthus	alpine	herbaceous	20cm (8in)	medium	violet	
harbourii	Harbouriani	alpine	mat	15cm (6in)	medium	lavender	
harringtonii	Anularius	dry upland	herbaceous	75cm (2½ft)	medium	lavender	
hartwegii	Fasciculi	high woodland	subshrub	1m (3¼ft)	v. large	red	Mexican
havardii	Havardiani	rocky	herbaceous	1.8m (6ft)	large	scarlet	
haydenii	Anularius	dunes	herbaceous	1.2m (4ft)	v. large	lavender	protected
henricksonii	Elmigera	high forest	herbaceous	60cm (2ft)	large	red-purple	Mexican
heterodoxus	Proceri	alpine	shrub	15cm (6in)	small	violet	
heterophyllus	Saccanthera	alpine	subshrub	60cm (2ft)	large	blue	also purple
hidalgensis	Perfoliati	open forest	herbaceous	2m (6½ft)	v. large	purple	Mexican
hintonii	Campanulati	open forest	herbaceous	unknown	large	violet	Mexican, rare
hirsutus	Penstemon						
var. *hirsutus*		lowland	herbaceous	60cm (2ft)	large	purple	
'Minimus'		lowland	herbaceous	30cm (12in)	large	purple	
'Pygmaeus'		lowland	herbaceous	10cm (4in)	large	purple	
humilis	Humiles	dryland	herbaceous	60cm (2ft)	medium	violet	
idahoensis	Habroanthus	alpine	herbaceous	20cm (8in)	medium	violet	
imberbis	Elmigera	dryland	herbaceous	60cm (2ft)	large	red	Mexican
immanifestus	Anularius	desert	herbaceous	75cm (2½ft)	medium	lavender	

Species	Group	Habitat	Habit	Height	Flower size and colour		Notes
incertus	Peltanthera	dryland	shrub	80cm (2²/₃ft)	large	blue	
inflatus	Humiles	open wooded	herbaceous	60cm (2ft)	medium	blue	
isophyllus	Fasciculi	open wooded	herbaceous	1m (3¹/₄ft)	v. large	red	Mexican
jamesii	Aurator	plains	herbaceous	50cm (20in)	large	lavender	
janishiae	Aurator	dryland	herbaceous	20cm (8in)	large	purple	
kingii	Saccanthera	dryland	herbaceous	25cm (10in)	medium	purple	rare
kunthii	Campanulati	mixed	herbaceous	75cm (2¹/₂ft)	large	red	Mexican
labrosus	Elmigera	open wooded	herbaceous	70cm (2¹/₃ft)	large	scarlet	
laetus	Saccanthera						
ssp. *laetus*		open wooded	subshrub	80cm (2²/₃ft)	large	lavender	
ssp. *roezlii*		open wooded	subshrub	80cm (2²/₃ft)	medium	lavender	
laevigatus	Penstemon	mixed	herbaceous	75cm (2¹/₂ft)	medium	purple	
laevis	Habroanthus	dryland	herbaceous	1m (3¹/₄ft)	large	blue	
lanceolatus	Dentanthera	open wooded	herbaceous	55cm (22in)	large	scarlet	
laricifolius	Ericopsis						
ssp. *laricifolius*		plains	herbaceous	20cm (8in)	medium	purple	
ssp. *exilifolius*		plains	herbaceous	20cm (8in)	medium	white	
laxiflorus	Penstemon	mixed	herbaceous	75cm (2¹/₂ft)	medium	white	
laxus	Proceri	dryland	herbaceous	70cm (2¹/₃ft)	small	blue	
leiophyllus	Habroanthus	dry upland	herbaceous	60cm (2ft)	medium	violet	
lemhiensis	Habroanthus	open wooded	herbaceous	70cm (2¹/₃ft)	large	blue	
lentus	Anularius	dryland	herbaceous	50cm (20in)	medium	blue	uncommon
leonardii	Saccanthera	dryland	subshrub	40cm (16in)	medium	deep blue	
leonensis	Fasciculi	high forest	herbaceous	50cm (20in)	large	purple	Mexican
linarioides	Linarioides	alpine	subshrub/mat	50cm (20in)	medium	lavender	habit variable
longiflorus	Habroanthus	dry upland	herbaceous	60cm (2ft)	large	deep blue	
lyallii	Dasanthera	alpine	shrubby	75 cm (2¹/₂ft)	v. large	lavender	
marcusii	Aurator	desert	herbaceous	25cm (10in)	small	violet	
mensarum	Habroanthus	alpine	herbaceous	75cm (2¹/₂ft)	medium	blue	
miniatus	Fasciculi	alpine	herbaceous	1.2m (4ft)	large	red	Mexican
miser	Aurator	dryland	herbaceous	40cm (16in)	medium	violet	
moffattii	Aurator	dryland	herbaceous	30cm (12in)	medium	blue	
mohinoranus	Fasciculi	open wooded	herbaceous	1m (3¹/₄ft)	v. large	red	Mexican, rare
monoensis	Aurator	dryland	herbaceous	30cm (12in)	medium	rose	
montanus	Dasanthera	alpine	shrub	30cm (12in)	large	lavender	
moriahensis	Habroanthus	open wooded	herbaceous	50cm (20in)	large	blue	
moronensis	Perfoliati	open forest	shrub	50cm (20in)	large	violet	Mexican
multiflorus	Multiflori	open wooded	herbaceous	60cm (2ft)	medium	white	
murrayanus	Havardiani	open wooded	herbaceous	1.8m (6ft)	v. large	red	
nanus	Aurator	dryland	herbaceous	15cm (6in)	small	violet	rare
navajoa	Habroanthus	open wooded	herbaceous	45cm (18in)	medium	blue	
neomexicanus	Habroanthus	open wooded	herbaceous	70cm (28in)	large	purple	
neotericus	Saccanthera	open wooded	subshrub	60cm (2ft)	large	blue	
newberryi	Dasanthera						
ssp. *berryi*		alpine	shrub	30cm (12in)	large	pink	
ssp. *newberryi*		alpine	shrub	30cm (12in)	large	red	
ssp. *sonomensis*		alpine	shrub	30cm (12in)	large	purple	
nitidus	Anularius	plains	herbaceous	30cm (12in)	medium	blue	
nudiflorus	Habroanthus	dryland	herbaceous	60cm (2ft)	medium	lavender	
occiduus	Fasciculi	alpine	herbaceous	60cm (2ft)	large	violet	Mexican, rare
oklahomensis	Penstemon	mixed	herbaceous	60cm (2ft)	large	white	
oliganthus	Humiles	open wooded	herbaceous	45cm (18in)	medium	blue & white	
ophiantus	Aurator	plains	herbaceous	50cm (20in)	medium	lavender	
osterhoutii	Anularius	dryland	herbaceous	80cm (2²/₃ft)	medium	mauve	

SPECIES	GROUP	HABITAT	HABIT	HEIGHT	FLOWER SIZE AND COLOUR		NOTES
ovatus	Humiles	open wooded	herbaceous	1m (3¹/₄ft)	medium	blue	
pachyphyllus	Anularius	dryland	herbaceous	30cm (12in)	medium	blue	
pahutensis	Habroanthus	open wooded	herbaceous	35cm (14in)	medium	lavender	
pallidus	Penstemon	mixed	herbaceous	90cm (3ft)	medium	white	
palmeri	Peltanthera	dryland	herbaceous	1.8m (6ft)	large	white	fragrant
papillatus	Saccanthera	open wooded	herbaceous	40cm (16in)	medium	violet	
parryi	Centranthifolii	desert	herbaceous	1.2m (4ft)	medium	rose	
parviflorus	Aurator	dryland	herbaceous	30cm (12in)	small	purple	rare
parvulus	Saccanthera	alpine	subshrub	35cm (14in)	medium	azure	
parvus	Habroanthus	dryland	herbaceous	20cm (8in)	medium	deep blue	
patens	Centranthifolii	dry upland	subshrub	60cm (2ft)	medium	purple	
payettensis	Habroanthus	dryland	herbaceous	70cm (2¹/₄ft)	medium	blue	
paysoniorum	Habroanthus	dryland	herbaceous	25cm (10in)	medium	violet	
peckii	Proceri	open wooded	mat	50cm (20in)	medium	lavender	
penlandii	Habroanthus	dryland	herbaceous	25cm (10in)	small	violet	
pennellianus	Habroanthus	dry upland	herbaceous	60cm (2ft)	large	blue	
perfoliatus	Perfoliati	high forest	herbaceous	1m (3¹/₄ft)	v. large	purple	Mexican, rare
perpulcher	Habroanthus	dryland	herbaceous	90cm (3ft)	medium	blue	
personatus	Cryptostemon	dryland	herbaceous	55cm (22in)	medium	deep purple	
petiolatus	Petiolati	dryland	herbaceous	20cm (8in)	medium	violet	rare
pinifolius	Fasciculi	dry upland	mat	15cm (6in)	v. large	red	
pinorum	Aurator	dryland	herbaceous	20cm (8in)	small	violet	rare
plagapineus	Fasciculi	high forest	subshrub	1m (3¹/₄ft)	v. large	red	Mexican
platyphyllus	Saccanthera	dry upland	subshrub	60cm (2ft)	medium	lavender	fragrant
potosinus	Campanulati	open forest	subshrub	1m (3¹/₄ft)	large	purple	Mexican
pratensis	Proceri	damp meadow	herbaceous	50cm (20in)	small	white	
pringlei	Aurator	. . .	. . .	. . .	. . .	no information – status doubtful	
procerus	Proceri						
ssp. *brachyanthus*		alpine	mat	35cm (14in)	small	violet	colours vary
ssp. *formosus*		alpine	mat	15cm (6in)	small	violet	colours vary
ssp. *procerus*		alpine	mat	45cm (18in)	small	violet	colours vary
ssp. *tolmiei*		alpine	mat	15cm (6in)	small	blue	colours vary
pruinosus	Humiles	dryland	herbaceous	40cm (16in)	small	deep blue	
pseudoparvus	Humiles	alpine	herbaceous	30cm (12in)	medium	mauve	
pseudoputus	Habroanthus	dryland	herbaceous	40cm (16in)	medium	mauve	rare
pseudo-spectabilis	Peltanthera	desert	herbaceous	1m (3¹/₄ft)	large	rose	
pudicus	Saccanthera	high forest	sub shrub	45cm (18in)	large	blue	
pumilus	Aurator	dryland	prostrate	15cm (6in)	medium	purple	
punctatus	Aurator	plains	unknown	unknown	small	violet	Mexican, rare
purpusii	Saccanthera	alpine	shrub	20 cm (8in)	large	violet	
radicosus	Humiles	dryland	herbaceous	40cm (16in)	medium	mauve	
ramaleyi	Caespitosi	alpine	subshrub	30cm (12in)	large	blue	
ramosus	Dentanthera	dryland	herbaceous	55cm (22in)	large	scarlet	
rattanii	Humiles	open wooded	herbaceous	1.2m (40in)	large	purple	
retrorsus	Caespitosi	dry upland	mat	20cm (8in)	medium	violet	
richardsonii	Serrulati	dryland	subshrub	80cm (2²/₅ft)	medium	lavender	
rostriflorus	Emersus	dryland	subshrub	75cm (2¹/₂ft)	medium	scarlet	
rotundifolius	Havardiani	dryland	subshrub	30cm (12in)	large	scarlet	
rubicundus	Peltanthera	dryland	herbaceous	1.2m (4ft)	large	rose	
rupicola	Dasanthera	alpine	mat	10cm (4in)	large	rose	
rydbergii	Proceri	moist upland	herbaceous	70cm (2¹/₄ft)	medium	blue	
saltarius	Perfoliati	open wooded	herbaceous	35cm (14in)	large	violet	
saxosorum	Habroanthus	dry upland	herbaceous	80cm (2²/₅ft)	medium	deep blue	

SPECIES	GROUP	HABITAT	HABIT	HEIGHT	FLOWER SIZE AND COLOUR		NOTES
scapoides	Saccanthera	dryland	subshrub	40cm (16in)	large	lilac	
scariosus	Habroanthus	mixed dry	herbaceous	50cm (20in)	large	blue	
schaffneri	Campanulati	mixed	shrub	75cm (2½ft)	large	red	Mexican
secundiflorus	Anularius	mixed	herbaceous	50cm (20in)	large	lavender	
seorsus	Gairdneriani	dryland	mat	40cm (16in)	medium	purple	
sepalulus	Saccanthera	scree	subshrub	80cm (2⅔ft)	medium	lavender	
serrulatus	Serrulati	moist ground	subshrub	70cm (2¼ft)	medium	purple	
shastensis	Proceri	moist upland	herbaceous	50cm (20in)	small	mauve	
smallii	Penstemon	lowland	herbaceous	60cm (2ft)	large	purple	
spatulatus	Proceri	alpine	mat	25cm (10in)	small	violet	rare
speciosus	Habroanthus	dryland	herbaceous	90cm (3ft)	large	blue	
spectabilis	Peltanthera	desert	herbaceous	1.2m (4ft)	large	blue	
stenophyllus	Dentanthera	dryland	herbaceous	90cm (3ft)	large	violet	
stephensii	Peltanthera	desert	herbaceous	1m (3¼ft)	medium	rose	
strictiformis	Habroanthus	open wooded	herbaceous	60cm (2ft)	large	blue	
strictus	Habroanthus	dry upland	mat	80cm (2⅔ft)	large	deep blue	
subglaber	Habroanthus	mixed	herbaceous	70cm (2¼ft)	large	blue	
subserratus	Humiles	open wooded	herbaceous	75cm (2½ft)	medium	blue	
subulatus	Centranthifolii	dryland	herbaceous	70cm (2¼ft)	medium	scarlet	
sudans	Deusti	dryland	herbaceous	70cm (2⅓ft)	medium	cream	
superbus	Centranthifolii	mixed dry	herbaceous	1.2m (4ft)	medium	scarlet	
tenuiflorus	Penstemon	lowland	herbaceous	60cm (2ft)	large	white	
tenuifolius	Perfoliati	alpine	shrub	35cm (14in)	large	lavender	
tenuis	Penstemon	lowland	herbaceous	60cm (2ft)	medium	mauve	
tepicensis	Campanulati	alpine	herbaceous	40cm (16in)	large	lavender	Mexican, rare
teucrioides	Caespitosi	dryland	mat	10cm (4in)	medium	blue	
thompsonii	Caespitosi	dry wooded	shrub	4cm (1½in)	small	violet	
thurberi	Ambigui	dryland	shrub	60cm (2ft)	medium	lavender	
tidestromii	Habroanthus	open wooded	herbaceous	60cm (2ft)	medium	blue	
tracyi	Deusti	dry upland	subshrub	12cm (5in)	small	pink	rare
triflorus	Aurator	plains	herbaceous	60cm (2ft)	large	red	
triphyllus	Serrulati	dryland	subshrub	75cm (2½ft)	small	lavender	
tubaeflorus	Tubaeflori	alluvial	herbaceous	90cm (3ft)	medium	white	
uintahensis	Habroanthus	dry upland	herbaceous	15cm (6in)	medium	blue	
utahensis	Centranthifolii	dryland	herbaceous	60cm (2ft)	large	red	
venustus	Serrulati	alpine	subshrub	75cm (2½ft)	large	purple	
virens	Humiles	open wooded	herbaceous	30cm (12in)	medium	violet	
virgatus	Habroanthus						
ssp. *virgatus*		dry upland	herbaceous	80cm (2⅔ft)	medium	violet	
var. *putus*		dry upland	herbaceous	50cm (20in)	medium	white	
vizcainensis	Peltanthera	dryland	herbaceous	2.4m (8ft)	medium	rose	Mexican
vulcanellus	Perfoliati	alpine	subshrub	30cm (12in)	medium	lavender	Mexican
wardii	Habroanthus	open wooded	herbaceous	30cm (12in)	large	light blue	
washingtonensis	Proceri	damp ground	herbaceous	25cm (10in)	small	deep blue	
watsonii	Proceri	dry upland	herbaceous	60cm (2ft)	small	deep blue	
whippleanus	Humiles	alpine	herbaceous	60cm (2ft)	medium	wide range	
wilcoxii	Humiles	open wooded	herbaceous	90cm (3ft)	medium	blue	
wisconsinensis	Penstemon	plains	herbaceous	75cm (2½ft)	medium	pale lilac	
wislizeni	Elmigera	dryland	mat	60cm (2ft)	large	scarlet	Mexican
wrightii	Centranthifolii	mixed	herbaceous	90cm (3ft)	medium	red	

APPENDIX II
PENSTEMON SPECIES –
COMMON SYNONYMS AND MISNOMERS

This is a selection of synonyms still found in common use or commonly attached to important species in the past, intergeneric transfers, and some frequently encountered misnomers. The persistence of some old names is remarkable. The date in the 'Name Used' column is the date the obsolete name was first published, and that in the 'Correct Name' column the date when the obsolescence was technically established by a contrary publication. In most cases the correct name predates the synonym, and was preferred throughout by most, but not all, sources.

Name Used	Correct Name
Acuminati (1906)	Anularius (1951)
alluviorum deamii (1963)	P. deamii (1987)
angustifolia (HBK 1817)	P. kunthii (1963)
angustifolia (Steud. 1821)	P. angustifolius (1920)
antirrhinoides (1846)	Keckiella antirrhinoides (1967)
– microphyllus (1857)	Keckiella antirrhinoides microphyllus (1951) (NB. not P. davidsonii menziesii 'Microphyllus')
apetiticus (1959)	P. miniatus (1967)
arkansanus pubescens (1922)	P. pallidus (1935)
attenuatus varians (1912)	P. rydbergii (1984)
arizonicus, a species (1899)	P. whippleanus (1945)
atropurpurea (1828)	P. kunthii (1963)
atropurpureus (1930s)	P. campanulatus (1963)
barbatus	
– albus	P. barbatus 'Albus'
– coccineus (Hort.1839)	P. barbatus 'Coccineus'
– hybridus (Hort. 1890s.)	Hort. form (= 'Praecox'?)
– labrosus (1876)	P. labrosus (1959)
– praecox (Hort.)	P. barbatus 'Praecox'
– praecox nana (Hort.)	P. barbatus 'Praecox Nanus'
– wislizeni (1862)	P. wislizeni (1959)
brachyanthus (1941)	P. procerus brachyanthus (1957)
brandegei (1900)	P. alpinus brandegei (1954)
brandegeei or brandegii	brandegei
breviflorus (1837)	Keckiella breviflora (1967)
bridgesii (1868)	P. rostriflorus (1984)
– rostriflorus (1903)	P. rostriflorus (1984)
caeruleus (1818)	P. angustifolius (1935)
caeruleus Hort. (1867)	P. hartwegii (1904)
campanulatus	
– angustiflora (1894)	P. kunthii (1946)
– angustifolium (1842)	P. kunthii (1946)
– pulchellus (1894)	P. campanulatus (1946)

Name Used	Correct Name
– roseus (1894)	P. campanulatus (1946) (= P. camp. 'Roseus'?) (= P. kunthii?)
Chelone	
– albida (1825)	P. albidus (1920)
– alpina (1827)	P. alpinus (1920)
– angustifolia (HBK 1817)	P. kunthii (1946)
– angustifolia (Steud.1820)	P. angustifolius (1920)
– atropurpurea (1828)	P. campanulatus (1800)
– barbata (1794)	P. barbatus (c.1876)
– bradburii (1820)	P. grandiflorus (1920)
– campanulata (1791)	P. campanulatus (1800)
– centranthifolia (1835)	P. centranthifolius (1835)
– caerulea (1825)	P. angustifolius (1920)
– cristata (1825)	P. eriantherus (1920)
– digitalis (1825)	P. digitalis (1935)
– erianthera (1820)	P.eriantherus (1920)
– gracilis (1818)	P. gracilis (1920)
– grandiflora (1825)	P. grandiflorus (1920)
– hirsuta (1753)	P. hirsutus (1935)
– imberbis (1817)	P. imberbis (1959)
– nemorosa (1828)	P. nemorosa, then Notochelone nemorosa (1966)
– pentstemon (1753)	P. laevigatus (1935)
– gentianoides (1817)	P. gentianoides (1962)
Chionophila jamesii (1846)	valid, not P. jamesii (1846)
cinarescens (1906)	P. laetus roezlii (1951)
cinereus (1913)	P. humilis (1959)
coccineus (Engelm.1848)	P. wislizeni (1959)
coccineus (Hoffmgg.1842)	P. hartwegii (1904)
coeruleus (Nutt.1818)	P. angustifolius (1920)
coeruleus (Torr. 1856?)	P. barbatus (1904)
confertus	
– aberrans (1895)	P. procerus aberrans (1920)
– attenuatus (1908)	P. attenuatus (1951)
– globosus (1900)	P. globosus (1951)
– modestus (1925)	P. procerus modestus (1957)
– ochroleucus (1839)	P. confertus (1957)

Name Used	Correct Name
– procerus (1893)	P. procerus (1920)
– rigidus (1925)	P. heterodoxus (1945)
– violaceus (1839)	P. procerus (1920)
cordifolius (1835)	Keckiella cordifolia (1967)
corymbosus (1846)	Keckiella corymbosa (1967)
crassifolius (ex Benth.)	P. hirsutus (1904)
crassifolius (many, 1838+)	P. fruticosus (1920)
cristata (1825)	P. eriantherus (1920)
cristatus (1818)	P. eriantherus (1920)
cyananthus brandegei (1874)	P. alpinus brandegei (1954)
diffusus (1828)	serrulatus (1951)
diffusus albiflorus (1929)	P. serrulatus (1959) (= P. serrulatus 'Albus'?)
digitalis	
– albidus (1839)	P. digitalis (1935)
– attenuatus (1839)	P. attenutaus (1945)
– glaucus (1839)	P. gracilis (1945)
– gracilis (1839)	P.gracilis (1920)
– laevigatus (1839)	P. laevigatus (?)
– multiflorus (1860)	P. multiflorus (1913)
douglasii (1838)	P. fruticosus (1951)
edithae/edithiae	P. 'Edithae' (P. rupicola × P. barrettiae)
elegans (1838)	P. campanulatus (1904)
ellipticus (Greene 1906)	P. rydbergii (1959)
erianthera (1813)	P. glaber (1920)
formosus (1904)	P. procerus formosus (1957)
francisci-pennellii (1965)	P. leiophyllus francisci-pennelli (1984)
fremontii parryi (1871)	P. watsonii (1920)
frutescens (1811)	Pennellianthus frutescens (1970)
fruticosus cardwellii (1906)	P. cardwellii (1959)
gentianoides (Lindl. 1838)	P. hartwegii (1962)
– coccineus (Hort. 1839)	P. hartwegii (1962)
glaber (Pursh. 1814)	valid, but see next
glaber (Gray 1878)	P. speciosus (1984)
– alpinus (1862)	P. alpinus (1920)
– cyananthus (1862)	P. cyananthus (1920)
– fremontii (1908)	P. fremontii (1920)
– occidentalis (1862)	P. speciosus (1951)
– speciosus (1875)	P. speciosus (1984)
– utahensis (S.Wats.1871)	P. subglaber (c.1906)
– utahensis (Jeps. 1925)	P. speciosus (1959)
– wardii (1908)	P. wardii (1920)
Glabri (1920)	Habroanthus (1951)
glaucus (1829)	P. gracilis (1925)
gloxinioides	invalid
gordoni (1813)	P. glaber (1920)
– splendens (Hort. c.1895)	P. glaber (c.1934)
Graciles (1920)	Penstemon (1979), a section.

Name Used	Correct Name
hallii arizonicus (1878)	P. deaveri (1967)
hartwegii albus	P. hartwegii 'Albus'
harvardii	havardii
heterophyllus	
– azureus (1925)	P. azureus (1959)
– latifolius (1871)	P. platyphyllus (1920)
hirsutus	
– minimus (1966)	P. hirsutus 'Minimus'
– pygmaeus (1963)	P. hirsutus 'Pygmaeus'
hybridus (Voss 1896)	Hort. form of P. hartwegii
– gloxinioides (1899)	invalid
– grandiflorus (1883)	invalid
idahoensis	valid species, not P. montanus idahoensis
jaffrayanus/jeffreyanus (1858)	P. azureus (1951)
jamesii (1846)	valid species, not Chionophila jamesii (1846)
laevigatus	
– calycosus (1941)	P. calycosus
– canescens (1890)	P. canescens (1935)
– digitalis (1878)	P. digitalis (pre-1935)
latifolius (Hoffmng 1824)	P. hirsutus (1904) (cf. P. heterophyllus latifolius)
leiostemon	
– ambiguus (1906)	P. ambiguus (1920)
– purpureus (1832)	P. ambiguus (1920)
– thurberi (1906)	P. thurberi (1959)
lemmonii	Keckiella lemmonii (1967)
linarioides	
– californicus (1924)	P. californicus (1937)
– taosensis (1937)	P. crandallii glabrescens taosensis (1960) (NB not P. 'Taoensis')
lobbii (1862)	Keckiella antirrhinoides (1951)
mackayanus (1838)	P. hirsutus (1904)
menziesii (1838)	P. davidsonii (1957)
– crassifolius (1838)	P. fruticosus (1920)
– davidsonii (1906)	P. davidsonii (1957)
– douglasii (1862)	P. fruticosus (1951)
– lewisii (1862)	P. fruticosus (1951)
– lyallii (1862)	P. lyallii (1959)
– newberryi (1878)	P. newberryi (1951)
– robinsonii (1872)	P. newberryi (1951)
– scouleri (1857)	P. fruticosus scouleri (1959)
– thompsonii (1951)	P. davidsonii (1959) (see also thompsoniae)
minor (1940)	P. anguineus (1945)
modestus (1906)	P. procerus (1957)

Name Used	Correct Name
montanus idahoensis	valid, not P. idahoensis
mucronatus (1979)	P. pachyphyllus mucronatus (1987)
nelsonae (1935)	P. attenuatus (1951)
nemorosus (1839)	Nothochelone nemorosa (1966)
newberryi rupicola (1900)	P. rupicola (1951)
nuttallii (1828)	P. digitalis (1935)
olgae	P. 'Olgae' (1956), sp. unknown
ovatus pinetorum (1901)	P. wilcoxii (1951)
pallidus arkansanus (1963)	P. arkansanus (c.1970)
palmeri grinnellii (1922)	P. grinnellii (1937)
palustris (1941)	P. attenuatus palustris (1951)
pauciflorus (Buckley1861)	Phlox pilosa (1960)
pauciflorus (Greene 1881)	P. lanceolatus (1959)
Pentastemon (1802)	Penstemon (1935), a genus
Pentstemon (1802)	Penstemon (1935), a genus
procerus geniculatus (1921)	P. heterodoxus (1945)
procumbens (1901)	a) P. suffrutescens (1920)
	b) P. caespitosus suffruticosus (1937)
	c) P. crandallii (1937)
puberulentus (Jeps. 1925)	Keckiella corymbosa (1967)
puberulentus (Rydb. 1917)	P. gairdneri oreganus (1959)
puberulus (Gray 1859)	P. barbatus torreyi (1984)
puberulus (Jones 1908)	P. humilis (1945)
puberulus (W&S 1909)	P. whippleanus (1945)
puberulus (Penn. 1941)	P. cinicola (1959)
pubescens (1789)	P. hirsutus (1935)
– angustifolius (1789)	?P. laevigatus (1935)
– gracilis (1862)	P. gracilis (1892)
– latifolius (1789)	P. hirsutus (1935)
– multiflorus (1846)	P. multiflorus (1913)
pulchellus (Lindl. 1828)	P. campanulatus (1963)
pulchellus (Greene 1898)	P. procerus formosus (1957)
puniceus (1859)	P. superbus (1960)
– parryi (1859)	P. parryi (1037)

Name Used	Correct Name
– lilja (1843)	P. hartwegii (1904)
putus (1937)	P. virgatus putus (1967)
regalis (1934)	P. cardinalis regalis (1960)
roseus (G. Don 1839)	P. campanulatus (1904) (not P. bicolor roseus (1939))
rothrockii (1878)	Keckiella rothrockii (1967)
rubicundus	valid, not P. 'Rubicundus'
schoenholzeri (1939)	P. 'Schoenholzeri'
scouleri (1829)	P. fruticosus scouleri (1951)
serpyllifolius Hort.	P. davidsonii menziesii 'Serpyllifolius' (1960)
serratus	P. fruticosus serratus (1951)
sonomensis (1891)	P. newberryi sonomensis (1959)
Spectabiles (1920)	Peltanthera (1979)
spectabilis (Gray 1856)	valid, but see next entry
spectabilis (W&S 1915)	P. pseudospectabilis connatifolius (1942)
'Taoensis'	a hybrid, not P. crandallii glabrescens taosensis
ternatus (1859)	Keckiella ternatus (1967)
thompsoniae	a valid species, but see next
thompsonii	see menziesii thompsonii
tolmiei (1838)	P. procerus tolmiei (1957)
– brachyanthus (1945)	P. procerus brachyanthus (1957)
– formosus (1945)	P. procerus formosus (1957)
– modestus (1906)	P. procerus modestus (1957)
torreyi (1846)	P. barbatus torreyi (1939)
tusharensis (1979)	P. caespitosus suffruticosus (1987)
tweedyi (1890)	Chionophila tweedyi (1900)
unilateralis (1906)	P. virgatus asa-grayi (1967)
virgatus arizonicus (1939)	P. deaveri (1967)
wislizenii	wislizeni
yampaensis	P. acaulis yampaensis (1987)

APPENDIX III
PENSTEMONS WITH
UNUSUAL-COLOURED FLOWERS

In these lists the colour shown appears either exclusively, or in a good percentage of plants, unless otherwise indicated. Most purple or blue species will occasionally produce some white or pink forms. White flowers often have coloured guidelines in the throat and/or some tinting in pale pink or purple. European Hybrids are not included.

White (or nearly so)
P. albidus
P. alluviorum
P. arenarius
P. arkansanus
P. barbatus 'Albus'
P. cardwellii 'Albus'
P. c. 'John Bacher'
P. clutei 'Albiflorus'
P. cobaea
P. davidsonii 'Albus'
P. deamii
P. debilis
P. deustus
P. digitalis
P. d. 'Husker Red'
P. discolor
P. fructiformis
P. fructicosus 'Albus'
P. fruticosus scouleri 'Albus'
P. gormanii
P. grandiflorus 'Albus'
P. g. 'Prairie Snow'
P. guadalupensis
P. hartwegii 'Albus'
P. hirsutus 'Albiflorus'
P. h. 'Pygmaeus Albus'
P. laevigatus
P. laricifolius exilifolius
P. laxiflorus
P. lentus albiflorus
P. multiflorus
P. oklahomensis
P. pallidus
P. pratensis
P. rupicola 'Albus'
P. serrulatus 'Albus'
P. sudans
P. tenuiflorus
P. tubaeflorus

Pink/Rose
P. albo-marginatus
P. ambiguus
P. angustifolius var. dulcis
P. barbatus 'Elfin Pink'
P. barbatus 'Pink Elf'
P. barbatus 'Roseus'
P. bicolor
P. calcareus
P. calycosus 'Rose Queen'
P. cardwellii 'Carolyn'
P. c. 'Roseus'
P. clutei
P. cobaea
P. × 'Crystal'
P. floridus
P. flowersii
P. × 'Gina'
P. glaber 'Roseus'
P. gormanii
P. laricifolius laricifolius
P. laxiflorus P. pallidus
P. palmeri
P. p. 'Cedar'
P. × parishii 'Pilitas Pink'
P. parryi
P. petiolatus
P. 'Pink Dragon'
P. 'Pink Dust'
P. 'Prairie Dawn'
P. 'Princess Rose'
P. rubicundus
P. rupicola 'Diamond Lake'
P. stephensii
P. subserratus 'Neve'
P. thurberi
P. tracyi
P. triflorus triflorus
P. palmeri

Yellow
P. attenuatus attenuatus
  (syn. P. nelsonae)
P. barbatus flaviformis
P. barbatus 'Schooley's Yellow'
P. bicolor (rarely)
P. confertus
P. c. 'Case's Yellow'
P. c. 'Kittitas'
P. × 'Dusty'
P. flavescens
P. × 'Goldie'
P. pinifolius 'Mersea Yellow'
P. rostriflorus (rarely)

Variable in Colour with Good
Percentage in Colours Shown

P. angustifolius (pink, white)
P. cyathophorus (pink, white)
P. grandiflorus (pink, rose)
P. kunthii (deep pink)

In the text, where strict accuracy is necessary in colour description, the name of the colour, quoted in italics, is from the **Stanley Gibbons Stamp Colour Key** which is available by mail order (including overseas) from: Stanley Gibbons Publications Ltd, Parkside, Christchurch Rd, Ringwood, Hampshire BH24 3SH, UK.

APPENDIX IV
PENSTEMONS WITH
UNUSUAL HABITAT TOLERANCE

The classic penstemon habitat is dry, with open drainage and full sun, and soils which are neutral to alkaline. The lists below note some species which tolerate other conditions, and a few which prefer them.

Accept Acid Soils
P. attenuatus
P. barrettiae
P. cinicola
P. clutei
P. dissectus
P. euglaucus
P. flavescens
P. gentianoides
P. harbourii
P. mohinoranus
P. multiflorus
P. neotericus
P. purpusii*
P. rupicola
P. virens
P. vulcanellus
P. whippleanus

* prefers acid soil but neutral also suitable

The usual medium for the above species is volcanic or granitic

Grow on Clay Soils
P. albidus
P. angustifolius
P. arkansanus
P. attenatus
P. azureus
P. breviculus
P. caespitosus
P. comarrhenus
P. confusus
P. dolius

P. eriantherus
P. flowersii
P. goodrichii
P. moffattii
P. multiflorus
P. thompsoniae
P. wardii

Waterlogging not tolerated. Soil should be opened up with added gravel or sand

Prefer Moist Conditions
P. alluviorum
P. arkansanus
P. attenatus palustris
P. globosus
P. heterodoxus
P. ovatus
P. pratensis
P. rydbergii
P. serrulatus
P. tenuis
P. tubaeflorus

Tolerate Moist Conditions
P. albidus
P. attenatus
P. azureus
P. calycosus
P. canescens
P. confertus
P. cyananthus
P. digitalis
P. heterophyllus
P. laevigatus
P. neomexicanus

P. pinifolius
P. procerus
P. smallii
P. subglaber
P. washingtonensis

Shade Tolerant
P. abietinus (1)
P. alluviorum (2)
P. anguineus (1)
P. arkansanus (2)
P. attenuatus (1)
P. caesius (1)
P. caespitosus (1)
P. californicus (1)
P. calycosus (2)
P. canescens (1)
P. cardwellii (1)
P. comarrhenus (2)
P. degeneri (1)
P. digitalis (1)
P. dissectus (3)
P. euglaucus
P. hartwegii (1)
P. henricksonii (2)
P. humilis breviculus (1)
P. inflatus (1)
P. kingii (1)
P. labrosus (2)
P. laevigatus (1)
P. leonensis (1)
P. linarioides (1)
P. montanus (2)
P. moriahensis (1)
P. multiflorus (1)
P. newberryi (1)
P. oliganthus (3)

P. ovatus (1)
P. pahutensis (1)
P. pallidus (1)
P. payettensis (1)
P. peckii (1)
P. procerus (1)
P. rattanii (1)
P. saltarius (1)
P. scaiosus (1)
P. serrulatus (2)
P. smallii (2)
P. stephensii (1)
P. strictiformis (1)
P. strictus (2)
P. subserratus (1)
P. tenuis (2)
P. thompsoniae (2)
P. tidestromii (1)
P. virens (1)
P. virgatus (1)
P. wardii (1)
P. washingtonensis (1)
P. whippleanus (1)
P. wilcoxii (1)
P. wrightii (1)

(1) = habitat includes open woodland.
(2) = likes dappled or part-day shade.
(3) = likes moderate shade.

In general, need for shade increases with temperature, and amount of flower decreases as shade increases.

APPENDIX V
WHERE TO SEE AND WHERE
TO BUY PENSTEMONS

WHERE TO BUY SEED OF SPECIES

Several plant societies operate for their members seed exchange or supply schemes in which penstemons are included. The seed is usually but not always of garden origin. Also wholesale seed companies in several parts of the world supply seed of a limited range of species for packaging by retail seed houses in individual countries. Correct nomenclature can be a problem with both these sources of supply.

The safest way to obtain correctly identified species is from seed supplied by wild seed collectors, most of whom record the date of collection, locality and soil conditions in their catalogues. Ethical practices are followed. The following collectors specialize in *Penstemon*, most of them offering a mail-order service.

Alplains, 32315 Pine Crest Court, Kiowa, CO80117, USA
Jim & Jenny Archibald, 'Bryn Collen', Ffostrasol, Llandysul, Dyfed SA44 5SB Wales, UK
Northplan/Mountain Seed, PO Box 910, Moscow, ID 83843, USA
Northwest Native Seed, 4441 S. Meridian St. +363, Puyallup, WA 98373, USA
Plants of the Southwest, Rt. 6 Box 11A, Santa Fé, NM87501, USA
Rocky Mountain Rare Plants, 1706 Deerpath Rd., Franktown, CO 80116–9462, USA
Rogue House Seed, 250 Maple St., Central Point, OR 97502, USA
Southwestern Native Seeds, Box 50503, Tucson, AZ 85703, USA
Western Native Seed, PO Box 1463, Salida, CO 81201, USA

WHERE TO BUY SEED STRAINS (GARDEN FORMS AND HYBRIDS)

The commercial production of seed strains is carried out by a number of major seed firms in USA, Europe and elsewhere. The retail seed houses that package this seed for sale may use different names for the same product. The following publications list the kinds available, including species, and a wide range of suppliers:

The Seed Search (first edition 1997), compiled and published by Karen Platt, 37 Melbourne Rd, Sheffield S10 1NR, UK. Lists many suppliers, mainly with UK addresses, but many of these will be prepared to export. Future editions may be more international.

Source List of Plants and Seeds, edited by R. Isaacson and published by Andersen Horticultural Library, University of Minnesota, USA. Contains a list of species and cultivars available commercially in the USA, and the nurseries supplying them.

WHERE TO BUY PLANTS
USA and Canada

Certain nurseries specialize in selling penstemon plants, both species and named varieties. For the most part these originate from wild-collected seed:

A High Country Garden, 2909 Rufina St, Santa Fé, NM 87505–2929, USA
Alplains, 32315 Pine Crest Court, Kiowa, CO 80117, USA
Bear Mountain Alpines, PO Box 2407, Evergreen, CO 80439–2407, USA
Heronswood Nursery Ltd, 7530 NE 288th St., Kingston, WA98346, USA (mail order nursery – no seed)
Joy Creek Nursery, 20300 NW Watson Rd., Scappoose, OR 97056, USA
Laporte Avenue Nursery, 1950 Laporte Ave., Fort Collins, CO, USA 80521, USA
Mt Tahoma Nursery, 28111 112th Ave., Graham, WA 98338, USA
Pacific Rim Native Plants, 44305 Old Orchard Rd, Sardis, BC V2R 1A9, Canada
Plants of the Southwest, Rt 6 Box 11A, Santa Fé, NM 87501, USA
Siskiyou Rare Plant Nursery, 2825 Cummings Rd., Medford, OR 97501, USA

Western Europe as a whole

The German publisher Eugen Ulmer, Wollgrasweg 41, 7000 Stuttgart 70, periodically issues a Europe-wide plant directory under the title *P.P.P. Index*.

Although not responsible for the genus *Penstemon*, the German-based international registration authority for hardy plants, the ISU, hold an informal list of species and cultivars reported to exist in members' nurseries. Information may be available by contacting: Internationale Stauden-Union, Mur-Strausse 22, 85356 Freising.

British Isles

Most nurseries and garden centres offer the commoner varieties of European Hybrid, but care needs to be taken even here since naming can sometimes be erroneous. For the more unusual varieties the nurseries mentioned in Chapter 9 are for the most part penstemon specialists holding a wider than usual range of stock. Other nurseries will be found in the *Plant Finder*, published annually by the Royal Horticultural Society and available in book or CD-Rom forms.

France

A limited range of hybrid cultivars is offered by an increasing number of nurseries. Information on the cultivars available and their suppliers can be found in a directory of plants and nurseries published periodically by the Société Nationale d'Horticulture de France (SNHF, 84 Rue de Grenelle, 75007, Paris) under the title *25,000 Plantes*.

The Netherlands

The commoner hybrid cultivars and plants of the more persistent seed strains, mainly derived from *P. barbatus*, are widely offered in garden centres. Leading nurseries offer a wider range of cultivars suitable for the Dutch climate. The full range available is listed in *Plantenvinder voor de Lage Landed*, published annually by Terra (postbus 188, 7200 AD Zutphen).

Germany

In Germany species outnumber the limited range of European hybrids on offer. Information on the sources of both is listed in *Pflanzen – Einkaufsfuehrer*, published periodically by Eugen Ulmer, Wollgrasweg 41, 7000 Stuttgart 70.

Australasia

We are unaware of any plant directories for Australasia equivalent to those available in the USA and Europe for advice on local sources of penstemons. We therefore supply the following list of nurseries known to us as specialists in penstemons, though we regret that it may be incomplete:

Lambley Nursery, Burnside, Lesters Rd, Ascot, Victoria 3364, Australia

Bay Bloom Nurseries, PO Box 502, Tauranga, New Zealand

Eden Cottage Perennials, 51 Eden St, Island Bay, Wellington, New Zealand

Mara Nurseries, Allen Rd, RD12, Hawera, New Zealand

WHERE TO SEE PENSTEMONS

USA

The best place to see penstemons in the USA is in the wild. As the largest North American genus, penstemons are widely distributed, but are rarely very common. Road verges and cuts are the most promising places to find them provided the grass is fairly sparse. State and local floras offer good guides on what species occur in particular localities. National and state parks almost always have a range of species; information is available in the visitor centres. Information found in National Parks is also available from the American Penstemon Society (see Appendix VII).

NB The collection of plants, and even seed, from the wild is often forbidden in the case of state and federal endangered species, and the penalties are severe. Would-be collectors should make themselves thoroughly familiar with the local situation.

Many botanic gardens in USA display ranges of penstemon species native to their localities, and of cultivars which perform well locally. Chicago and Santa Ana Botanic Gardens show a wider-than-usual range of the large-flowered European Hybrids as well as species, while the alpine collection at Denver Botanic Gardens is particularly extensive. A new collection is currently under development at the Santa Fé Botanic Gardens.

British Isles

There is a significant number of collections of European Hybrids. Several are privately maintained by penstemon enthusiasts and offer limited or no public access, others by horticultural establishments are open to the public on a regular basis. Several have national collection status under the aegis of the National Council for the Preservation of Plants and Gardens. Details of location and access to these collections, which change from time to time, can be obtained from NCCPG, The Pines, Wisley, Woking, Surrey GU23 6QP.

Gardens regularly open to the public where displays or collections of European Hybrids are a feature include:

Berkshire – The Savill Gardens, Windsor

County Down – Rowallane Garden, Saintfield, Ballynahinch, N. Ireland

Dorset – College of the Countryside, Kingston Maurward, Dorchester

Gloucestershire – Hunts Court Garden, North Dibley, Dursley

Surrey – RHS Garden, Wisley, Woking

Wigtownshire – Logan Botanic Garden, Port Logan, Stranraer, Scotland

Worcestershire – Eastgrove Cottage Garden, Sankyns Green, Nr Shrawley, Little Witley; Old Court Nurseries, Colwall, Nr. Malvern; Pershore and Hindlip College, Avonbank, Pershore

Yorkshire – Harlow Carr Gardens, Harrogate

APPENDIX VI
PENSTEMONS KNOWN AS NAMES ONLY

We are aware of the following names having been applied to penstemon cultivars but are unable to offer any information about them:

'Bridget's White' (UK, EKR *Plant Finder* 1991)
'Craigieburn Chenille' (UK, EKR *Plant Finder* 1995)
'Craigieburn Taffeta' (UK, EKR Plant Finder 1995)
'Delaware' (UK, EKR *Plant Finder* 1995)
'Diane' (UK, EKR *Plant Finder* 1994)
'Dragontail'
'Early Dawn' (Belgium)
'Fanny's Blush' (EKR 1996 Special Plants, Cold Ashton, Wiltshire)
'Gletscher' (Germany, in *Plant Finder* 1994 as 'Gletsjer')
'Hugues' (the Netherlands)
'Knoll Surprise' (UK)
'Mountain Wine' (UK, EKR RHS Wisley Garden Centre, 1990)
'Mrs Greenwood' (UK)
'Oeschberg' (Germany)
'Old Silk' (UK)
'Pat' (UK)
'Peacock' (UK)
'Pink Blush' (UK)

'Pink Ice' (EKR Hillview Hardy Plants, Worfield, Shropshire)
'Prairie Pride' (EKR Penstemons by Colour, Hanwell, London, 1997. Not a North Platte introduction under this name)
'Primrose Thomas' (EKR *Plant Finder* 1993)
'Purple Dragon'
'Purple Lace'
'Raspberry Ripple' (EKR Little Rhyndhaston Nurseries, Pembrokeshire 1996)
'Red Coat' (New Zealand)
'Red Ensign' (Australia)
'Robin Hood'
'Rosa Belton' (New Zealand)
'Roundhay' (UK, EKR *Feeber's Hardy Plants*)
'Strawberry Ice' (South Africa)
'Threave White' (UK, EKR *Plant Finder*, 1991)
'Whigley' (France)
'Whippet' (France)

APPENDIX VII
PENSTEMON ORGANIZATIONS

The American Penstemon Society

The American Penstemon Society is the only society dedicated specifically to the advancement of knowledge about penstemons, their introduction into cultivation, and the development of new and improved cultivars. The Bulletin of the APS is published in January and July, and is available to members only. Other publications may be purchased through the society. Access to the library and the slide collection is also available.

Membership is currently $10.00 a year for US and Canada. Overseas membership is $15.00 payable in US funds, which includes 15 free selections from the seed exchange. US life membership is $200.00. The secretary is:

Ann Bartlett, 1569 South Holland Court, Lakewood, CO80232, USA (e-mail abart111@aol.com)

International Registration for the Genus *Penstemon*

Forms for the registration of new penstemon selections are obtainable from:

Prof. D.T. Lindgren, University of Nebraska, West Central Research Centre, Route 4, Box 46A, North Platte, NE 69101, USA (e-mail WCRC013@UNLVM.UNL.EDU)

Penstemon Website

A website was installed in 1996 at:
http://www.biosci.ohiostate.edu/~awolfe/Penstemon/Penstemon.htm

APPENDIX VIII
PENSTEMON RELATIONSHIPS

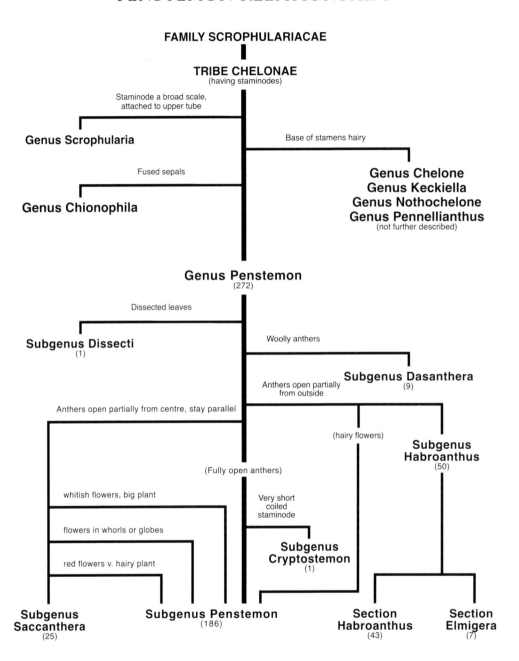

FAMILY SCROPHULARIACAE

TRIBE CHELONAE
(having staminodes)

Staminode a broad scale,
attached to upper tube

Genus Scrophularia

Base of stamens hairy

Fused sepals

Genus Chionophila

Genus Chelone
Genus Keckiella
Genus Nothochelone
Genus Pennellianthus
(not further described)

Genus Penstemon
(272)

Dissected leaves

Subgenus Dissecti
(1)

Woolly anthers

Anthers open partially
from outside

Subgenus Dasanthera
(9)

Anthers open partially from centre, stay parallel

(hairy flowers)

Subgenus Habroanthus
(50)

(Fully open anthers)

whitish flowers, big plant

Very short
coiled
staminode

flowers in whorls or globes

Subgenus Cryptostemon
(1)

red flowers v. hairy plant

Subgenus Saccanthera
(25)

Subgenus Penstemon
(186)

Section Habroanthus
(43)

Section Elmigera
(7)

Fig. 10 Structure of the Chelonae Tribe with identification features. To use the diagram to identify a plant's genus or subgenus, follow the central line until a branch has a description which fits the plant's group. Note that all four species in Subgenus Penstemon lose their way and have to be directed back to their proper home. Some authorities regard the Subgenus Habroanthus as a Section in Subgenus Penstemon.

GENUS   SUBGENUS   SECTION   SUBSECTION

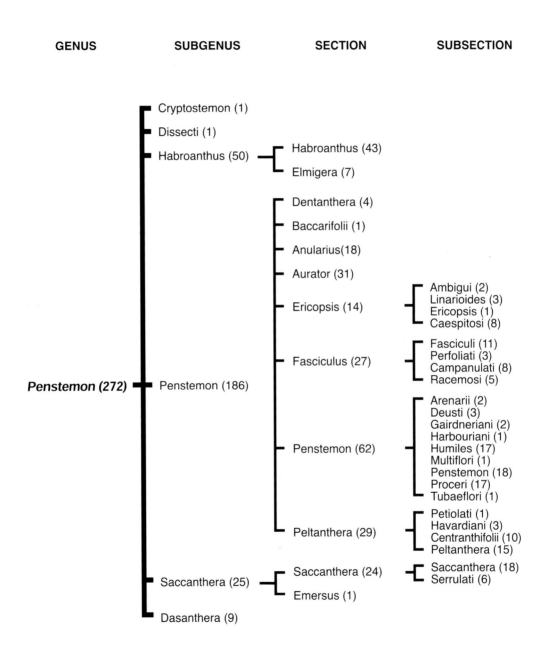

Fig. 11 Grouping of species within the genus Penstemon (after Dale Lindgren). (The number of species in each grouping is shown in brackets.)

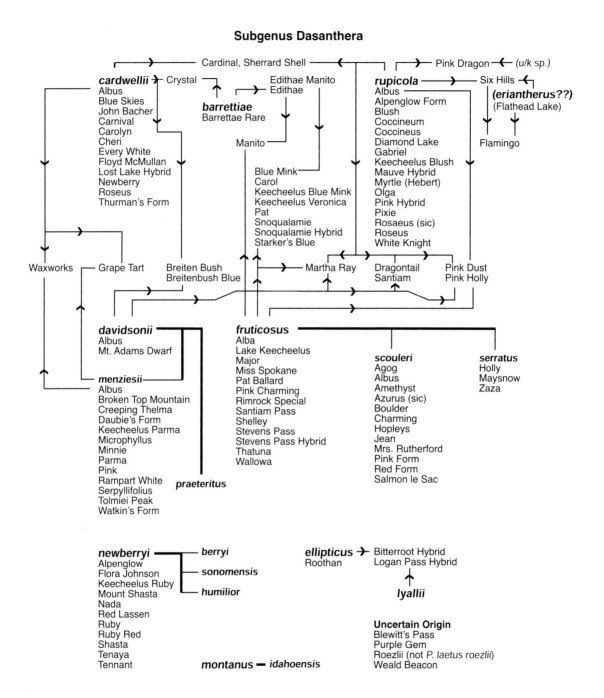

Fig. 12 A diagram of all known species, and named varieties and hybrids in the Subgenus Dasanthera. Bold type indicates botanical forms with variants in italics. Ordinary type indicates named varieties, without distinction between wild and garden forms. Known or probable crosses are shown by dotted lines linking the parents, while 'pure', or nearly so, species variants are listed under the relevant species. Some synonymy is possible.

INDEX

Italic page numbers refer to picture captions

ACKNOWLEDGEMENTS

So many people have helped us with our enquiries that it would require a book in itself to mention them all. First and foremost we thank our wives, Anke Way and Doreen James, for their practical support and very considerable involvement in the preparation of this book; and then the past and present members of the American Penstemon Society whose painstaking records of the past 50 years have been indispensable to us, and have guided us throughout. If we single out for special mention Professor Dale Lindgren of the University of Nebraska, and the Lodewicks, Kenneth and Robin, the other members of the APS will fully understand the justification for so doing.

Our sincere thanks also to Thompson & Morgan (England) for unlimited access to their records, and for having that sense of history which allows them not to throw much away; to the Royal Horticultural Society and the Linnean Society of London for access to their records, and to the RHS again for assistance with the chapter on pests and diseases; to Pam Shaw and Diane Stacey of the National Collection at Pershore College for their help on many 'penstemonial' matters; to Rose Clay and Elizabeth Strangman for help with the vexed 'Sour Grapes' question, and Gary Dunlop who threw valuable light on the Irish scene; to David Glenn for his energetic help from Australia; to Thomas A. Brown of Petaluma, California for his advice on early horticulture in that state; to Monique Chevry, whose research into the early years of hybridization in France has proved invaluable to us; to Klaus Pfitzer in Germany for open access to the records of his great-grandfather's firm, also to Adelheid Schmidt for translation and other assistance; to Wim Snoeijer in the Netherlands for much obscure bibliographical material; to Roger Springett and Phillipa Park in New Zealand for their energetic and enthusiastic supply of information in a race against time; to Barbara Knox-Shaw for leading us by the hand through unknown territory in South Africa; and finally in Switzerland to Paul Schoenholzer and Nicole Newmark for great assistance in tracing the 'Swiss connection'.

Finally, our thanks to the many correspondents several of whose names appear in the text who took the trouble to respond to our queries, many of them busy nurserymen with little time to spare from their professional duties.